AFRICAN ETHNOGRAPHIC STUDIES
OF THE 20TH CENTURY

Volume 66

ECONOMICS IN PRIMITIVE
COMMUNITIES

ECONOMICS IN PRIMITIVE COMMUNITIES

RICHARD THURNWALD

Routledge
Taylor & Francis Group

LONDON AND NEW YORK

First published in 1932 by Oxford University Press for the International African Institute.

This edition first published in 2018
by Routledge
2 Park Square, Milton Park, Abingdon, Oxon OX14 4RN

and by Routledge
711 Third Avenue, New York, NY 10017

Routledge is an imprint of the Taylor & Francis Group, an informa business

British Library Cataloguing in Publication Data
A catalogue record for this book is available from the British Library

ISBN: 978-0-8153-8713-8 (Set)
ISBN: 978-0-429-48813-9 (Set) (ebk)
ISBN: 978-1-138-59868-3 (Volume 66) (hbk)
ISBN: 978-1-138-59873-7 (Volume 66) (pbk)
ISBN: 978-0-429-48617-3 (Volume 66) (ebk)

Publisher's Note
The publisher has gone to great lengths to ensure the quality of this reprint but points out that some imperfections in the original copies may be apparent.

Disclaimer
The publisher has made every effort to trace copyright holders and would welcome correspondence from those they have been unable to trace.

ECONOMICS
IN PRIMITIVE
COMMUNITIES

By

RICHARD THURNWALD

Published for the
INTERNATIONAL INSTITUTE OF
AFRICAN LANGUAGES AND CULTURES
by HUMPHREY MILFORD
OXFORD UNIVERSITY PRESS
1932

OXFORD UNIVERSITY PRESS
AMEN HOUSE, E.C. 4
LONDON EDINBURGH GLASGOW
LEIPZIG NEW YORK TORONTO
MELBOURNE CAPETOWN BOMBAY
CALCUTTA MADRAS SHANGHAI
HUMPHREY MILFORD
PUBLISHER TO THE
UNIVERSITY

CONTENTS

CONTENTS

NOTES ON TERMS EMPLOYED

The ethno-sociological terms in current use are not always apt or accurate. Their vagueness may lead to misunderstanding. A word of explanation is necessary with regard to some such terms employed in this book.

Evolution, development, develop, &c., should be regarded as words expressing a change or consecutive changes in certain directions, not as terms of an evolutionary theory.

Borrowing. A term sometimes applied to the acquisition of technical skill, the use of implements, ideas, devices for treating the sick, dealing with supernatural ideas, social institutions, &c., is often misleading in its use. In most of these cases there is no question of a subsequent return. For the purpose of ethnological inquiries the only meaning considered is that of 'taking over'. Therefore the term *borrowing* has been as far as possible avoided in the text.

Clan, sept, tribe, and *family,* are words of more direct bearing on the subject of this book. They are somewhat indiscriminately used in anthropological literature. American writers have introduced an additional term, *gens,* to designate a patrilineal clan. Its acceptance by English and German authors would help to enrich the terminology required. In this volume, however, the term has not been used.

Clan. Primitive life is based on clan life. The clan generally forms the supreme unit economically and politically. It represents a more stabilized aggregation of families. Among hunting and collecting tribes these aggregations are seldom permanent. Under the influence of stratification the clan changes. It is resolved partly into more or less independent manors, partly into castes and guilds.

The term *clan* by no means always connotes the same idea. Its meaning changes with the conditions of life. The clan is an association of close relatives, originally residing on the same spot and observing their own traditions. These traditions often survive even the changes brought about by divisions and migrations. The new settlements may unite on certain occasions for the performance of a common ritual, or the fractions of clans—the *septs*—who have taken up their abode together may unite against a hostile attack. A new clan may of course originate from the breaking up of the old one. Then the links with the latter fall into oblivion.

The greatest danger which threatens a clan is its *stratification* by a foreign tribe belonging to another cultural zone, e.g. pastoral people may force on the agriculturists an unfair exchange of their respective produce. Once stratification has been established the clan institution changes and begins to dissolve (see Part III, Chap. I). As a consequence, the patriarchal family becomes paramount. The caste consists of an aggregation of families within a stratified society. Ancient clan relations may partially survive as ceremonial or marriage units. If these are obliterated generally strict observances subsist in the form of traditions.

Sept. If a clan with fixed traditions splits, these splits are termed septs. By the time a sept becomes a clan it loses its relations to the mother clan. Several septs may unite.

Tribe. A tribe is generally European inference from a number of clans having similar language, institutions, and implements. In fact it is rarely a conscious unit, still less a political body. The term 'tribe' is loosely used for a number of clans not expressly named but enjoying similar institutions.

A *tribe* means a simple group, speaking a common language, using similar weapons, implements, and contrivances. It is primarily a cultural unit, its political organization, if there is any, being of secondary importance. Economically the clans and settlements of the tribe usually exchange their goods. They are in *commercium* and often also in *connubium* with each other. The phrase *tribal life* generally refers to life in clans, septs, or associations of clans. The term *detribalization* refers to the breaking-up of the traditional clan organization and should rather be termed declanization.

Family. The expression *family* in this book is used in the sense of a group consisting of a man, his wife (or wives), and his dependent children, own or adopted. This definition seems simple; the reality, however, is far from being so. Among predatory tribes of hunters and collectors the family is usually part of a clan, but has some characteristic traits. It consists of persons of differing age and sex, acting in co-operation for economic purposes and mutual help, whereas a clan is mainly led by men and has chiefly political, religious, and social aims.

Patriarchal families are different from those within the clan-bond. This is a *familia* (extended family, *Grossfamilie*, *famille globale*), in the ancient Roman sense of the word. It may include the married children, grand-children, and great-grandchildren, and associates a number of serfs, often holding tenants in dependence. It is distinct from the clan or sept in that it always resides on the same spot under a partiarchal head. An exception is the polygamous family, in which a man has not only several wives in different huts but also in different villages, paying them visits in rotation.

The distinction between *clan* and *family* is important and difficult. Both terms pertain to a group of relatives. But the clan is essentially something lasting, the family comes to an end when the parents die and the children marry. In more primitive conditions the clan is of superior importance to the family, economically as well as socially, for the clan is the representative of political power.

State. A term employed for any aggregation of clans, castes, &c., under a dominant family, sept, or clan.

Settlement. A village settlement can consist of one or more clans or septs, of castes and guilds. As to terms for the various settlements: the houses of a sept may be called a *hamlet*; a *village* may be inhabited by several septs living together; the habitation of a *familia* with serfs and slaves may be termed a *manor*. For a political aggregation of families settled in one place the term *community* is applied.

Ethnic is used in reference to racial (physical), social, and spiritual traditions together, rather than to those of habits and customs only.

Society may be called:

(*a*) *Homogeneous*, if it is without institutional group-distinctions of birth or wealth (an individual in a homogeneous society may, however, acquire personal prestige).

(*b*) *Stratified*, if it is composed of two or more ethnical bodies having a definite traditional position in relation to one another. That is to say, the one considers the others as superior or inferior, and these valuations are accepted by each. Ethnical origins may be blurred by blending, by the growing importance of wealth, and by the rise of persons born in a lower stratum while those of higher origin may correspondingly decline. This leads to *social stratification*. Conforming institutions correspond to these conditions.

(*c*) *Graded*, if it has an elaborate system of rank as between persons, families, and septs within the same stratum, whose relative positions are determined by combined consideration of birth and wealth and expressed by corresponding traditions and institutions.

Finally, two implements have to be described: the *digging-stick* and the *hoe*. The *digging-stick* is a pointed wooden tool, varying in length from 3 feet to 4 feet six inches (seldom more), similar to a Dutch hoe but without the metal tip. It is almost exclusively used by women, for planting out seedlings. The *hoe* is a tool composed originally of two sticks fastened together, like the *mer* of ancient Egypt. One stick is used as a handle to push the other into the soil. The second stick has a pointed end and may be tipped with a sharpened stone or piece of metal. It is mostly used by women, but also (as for instance in W. Africa) by men, to prepare the ground before the cereals are sown.

Particulars as to questions of family, kinship, political and social organization, law, &c., may be found in volumes II, III, and IV of the author's recently published five-volume work *Die menschliche Gesellschaft*.

INTRODUCTION

§ 1. Fallacy of 'the three stages'. § 2. Of what does economics consist?
§ 3. Variety of economic phenomena. § 4. Certain characteristic features
of primitive thought.

§ **1.** In discussions on the economics of primitive society the
problem of food-supply has until recently been the only one taken
into account. Furthermore, thought in the last century was domi-
ated by the theories of Darwin and Spencer, which tended to conceive cultural development along one line only. Consequently, we
find economics treated from the same point of view, and this led to
the theory of 'the three stages', by which all primitive economic
development was traced through evolution from hunting to pastoral
life and thence to agriculture. This has lasted until the present day.

The most effectual criticism of this theory was that of Edward
Hahn, who insisted on the following points:

(1) Methods of tilling the soil must be distinguished according
to whether the hoe and the digging-stick are used, or the ox-drawn
plough. Therefore he differentiates between hoe- and plough-culti-
vation, the latter implying the use of animals to drag the implement.

(2) Hoe-cultivation must in no case be considered as an evolutionary step in pastoral development. It is rather directly connected with the women's custom of collecting fruits and roots.

(3) He laid stress on the special part played by women in providing such a regular daily supply.

(4) He suggested a religious motive for the use of oxen with the
plough, as also for the invention of the wheel and the cart.

§ **2.** It is unquestionable that the provision of food is of greater
importance and demands a larger percentage of energy in the
economic field among primitive communities than in our own. But
the science of economics is not confined to the providing of food.
Of what then does it consist? The devouring of newly killed beasts
and the eating of freshly picked fruits and roots, pulled from the
soil, certainly cannot be called economics. More than this is
implied in the term. If there ever was a time when man, or his
ancestor, lived from moment to moment on what he killed or
caught, it was a time without economics. Economics is concerned
not merely with the direction of the instincts, with the plans and
calculations of the individual: it is a social affair, dealing with

different men as parts of a piece of interlocking machinery. The economics of the community practically consist of the economics of individual households. For example, among agricultural people, relatives and neighbours help one another and can be certain of equal assistance in their turn (a manifestation of the underlying principle of labour freely given for payment in kind). Hunting parties are also organized along the same lines. The members do not merely march together in a crowd, but give each other mutual support in the various operations of driving the game, beating the bush or setting it on fire, making pitfalls and ambuscades. The traditional hunting-grounds, the cultivated soil, and, among pastoral people, the pasture lands are similarly defended by mutual agreement and co-operation. Finally, commercial relations also are based on this principle, as we shall see later on. In primitive life the connexion between single households and the economics of the community is very close. Owing, however, to prejudice and to failure in adapting our thought to primitive conditions, false impressions have been given, and, consequently, the meaning of the evolutionary evidence has been distorted.

§ 3. The above classification of food-procuring methods is not, however, commensurate with the great variety of economic phenomena. Take, for instance, the South Sea people. From New Guinea to the Caroline and Mary Islands, from Timor to beyond Samoa, Hawaii, and Easter Island, the men are hunters, trappers, and fishers, while the women till the soil, with assistance from the men in clearing the bush. Over the whole of this vast area, the economic material is the same, but the organization of it is different. The Micronesian and Polynesian peoples have another political arrangement. There is a stratified population with a ruling aristocracy and a sacred king. The chiefs of the aristocratic clans, and especially the kings as the representatives of the first clan, receive the revenue, redistributing it later in the form of largesse among the population. Naturally they always keep something back for themselves and the maintenance of their slaves. In this way an exchange of economic goods from various districts is effected. This form of economics is quite distinct from that prevalent in Papua and Melanesia, where every small community is self-sufficing and almost independent of the rule even of a headman. Further, economics is not only concerned with methods of obtaining food, but also with the development of handicrafts, which have reached a relatively high level among, for example, the Micronesians and Polynesians, while the Papuans and Melanesians are, in general, somewhat backward in this respect. In addition to this, the special spheres of activity of men and women ought to be considered.

§ 4. If we want to understand economics of primitive peoples we must also bring our minds back to the way in which primitive man thinks, and especially must we understand his interpretation of manual work and of every natural process as the manifestation of some magic power. In more complicated economic undertakings, as well as in the more involved technical processes, he tries to ensure success by certain ritual acts, as, for instance, the observing of omens and portents or the consulting of oracles.

A characteristic feature of primitive economics is the absence of any desire to make profits either from production or exchange. If money exists at all, its function is quite different from that fulfilled by it in our civilization. It never ceases to be concrete material, and it never becomes an entirely abstract representation of value. Consequently economic transactions refer more to the quality and kind of the real articles than to abstract values. The ambition of individuals, therefore, is not directed towards the acquisition of wealth, but is more interested in the kind of the work. In spite of their having no definite idea of economic profits, difficulties sometimes arise in barter because relative values are not always clearly apprehended. There is always perplexity when the existing rate of exchange has to be adapted to meet a new situation. With the *Kula* exchange, for instance, the gifts must be presented with due ceremonies, but without haggling. Nevertheless, owing to the common human failings of vanity, selfishness, and envy, complaints and disputes may arise, sometimes issuing in an actual fight. Generous gifts, however, are unquestionably received with gratitude, although such prodigality has generally to be returned with corresponding lavishness.

In addition to these purely personal considerations, the situation in graded societies is further affected by the relative rank of the people concerned in the transactions. For example, a king or a chief or a member of an aristocratic clan is often bound to give a higher compensation than a commoner.

The whole theoretical system, however, may be completely altered by certain personal factors, if these happen to suit the exigencies of the moment. The importance of such alterations must not be under-estimated in the lives of the natives, since they are the germs of change in customs and institutions. We are accustomed to overlook them because we usually deal with only one recent phase of native existence.

In each primitive society all aspects of life are harmonized into a complete whole. This is undoubtedly the consequence of a long adaptation of mental and institutional life to technical conditions. However adventurous the fate of the migratory tribes in Africa, Oceania, or Asia, &c., may have been, all their fights and wanderings brought relatively few acquisitions in new knowledge, abilities, and technical skill. They moved—spiritually and socially—therefore more in a circle than on a progressive line, and petrified mentally to some extent. They always fell back upon the same ways of procuring and caring for their livelihood. This indicates the enormous momentum of their traditional economics.

Progress needs contact and intermingling of ideas, institutions, and men as inciting factors. But regularly, after a period of impregnation, a combination and consolidation is required in order to establish a harmonized and balanced system of new mental habits, usages, and social institutions. Progress is a rhythm of human life, not a mechanical line, and it passes through stages of impregnation, of consolidation, and of dissolution. Those tribes could not progress who stuck to their old customs and lived an isolated peripheral life, but those who adventured upon new ideas and searched for an impact of cultures in an association of peoples. The most inspiring examples are the many forms of contact between herdsmen and agriculturists—whereas the hunters, trappers, and collectors fled and retired to the peripheral regions of the centres of human cultural life, such as forests, deserts, and ice regions, and remained as isolated relics of man's past.

PART I
CONDITIONS OF PRIMITIVE ECONOMICS

I

GENERAL CONSIDERATIONS
THE PROBLEMS OF PROGRESS AND DEVELOPMENT

§ 1. The material to be dealt with. § 2. Diverse attitudes towards economic questions. § 3. Variety of economic types. § 4. The question of development. § 5. An illustration from the hunter stage. § 6. Rate of development governed by character of social body. § 7. Illustrations: blood feud, slavery, origin of kingship. § 8. Secret societies; the *suque*. § 9. Economic importance of political processes.

§ **1.** In order to obtain a general survey of the subject, it may be advisable to make a rough classification of the material to be dealt with. As things are among primitive peoples, the obtaining of food is undoubtedly of chief importance, so that we may be justified in allowing it to dominate our arrangement. It should not, however, induce us to lose sight of other important facts. Among these, the factors of climate, configuration, flora, and fauna should be taken into account. The manner of life, nomadic or settled, the relative extent of settlements, and differentiation (temples, courts, and forts) must also be taken into consideration, since they are themselves the outcome of political and social conditions. Economics are determined by two main factors: first, by the interplay of geographical and social conditions, such as the proportion of land to population and the distribution of the latter; secondly, by the number and position of the different groups of which the society is made up, and their influence on one another. Starting from these points, we may deduce certain types of economic life, though these will inevitably be imperfect and cannot be expected adequately to represent the whole of the facts presented by history and ethnological research.

In building up these types we shall chiefly use ethnographical material, always remembering that we have to do with the results of a long period of development, the history of which is for the most part unknown to us. We have for the present purpose treated the facts which form our data as if they stood by themselves, without roots in the past.

§ **2.** On the other hand, these types also imply diverse attitudes towards economic questions, that is to say, attitudes different from our own and differing among themselves. These are accounted for by alien scales of value and by points of view depending on particular conditions of life. In economic research this point has often been overlooked under the dominance of an abstract *homo oeconomicus*. I think we have to construct several *homines oeconomicos*, each representing the economic tendency of one type, or even of one stratum within it.

§ 3. In elaborating the details of these types a special point is made of the division of labour between the sexes. The attitude of the sexes towards the main occupations about to be studied varies at the outset on account of physical conditions. This has led to a complete systematization of the distinct functions of men and women. It has also been extended to handicrafts and even to the use of certain tools and implements. Consequently, some institutions in primitive life have come to be associated with one sex exclusively, and the balance of influence varies. For instance, in a community of field-workers, where the women provide the regular food by means of the digging-stick, descent is mainly matrilineal. On the other hand, a pastoral community, where the main resources are drawn from the herds kept by the men, and where the women's importance in supplying food is only secondary, is chiefly correlated with patrilineal descent. This has all to be taken into consideration in building up economic types.

The development of any one of the many types to be discussed is not necessarily dependent on the preceding one. For instance, an agricultural mode of life does not originate in cattle-keeping or vice versa. Each single type, moreover, contains many variants. The hunters and trappers of big game, for instance, lead an entirely different life from the fishermen of the rivers, who are also to be considered as trappers. Among the tillers of the soil, again, a distinction must be made between those who plant cuttings (for instance from yams and taro) with the help of the digging-stick, and those who sow cereals, loosening the soil beforehand by means of the hoe, or who plant trees, a work chiefly carried out by the men. Pastoral life similarly varies according to the kind of animal kept, for the breeders must adapt their habits to the requirements of the beast they tend. This means that the lives of reindeer-herdsmen, shepherds, goatherds, cattlemen, and camel-drivers, &c., although classed as pastoral, are in detail far apart. Each type, therefore, includes many sub-divisions.

In addition to this, more advanced communities often comprise several sections, each devoted to obtaining food in its own peculiar way. These sometimes are further assigned to the men and the women respectively. In South Africa, for instance, the former are cattle-breeders and hunters, while the latter till the soil. This specialization of function is generally the outcome of a mixture of race, which has taken place sometime in the past history of the people. Very often a society appears to be homogeneous, but investigation afterwards shows that in fact it is compounded of the special traditions of several ethnic bodies. In the course of time the dividing lines between distinct cultures have gradually become effaced, so that now the observer is presented with one harmonious whole. On this account it is practically impossible for any scheme of types to keep pace with the reality. Nevertheless, we need such types to bring the enormous mass of facts into some measure of order.

§ 4. These considerations strengthen the conviction that it is impossible to bring any given type into a genetic relation with the preceding one. Connexions between some of the types, however, can be traced within certain limits, and these are extremely important in relation to the question of development. Tilling of the soil, for instance, probably had a twofold origin. On the one hand, it may have arisen from the use of the digging-stick to extract roots from the ground, which would suggest the possibility of putting others in. On the other hand, it may have been furthered by the discovery that stray seeds and rubbish left at an old camping-place would grow, and might furnish a supply of food in the future.

The probable development of cattle-keeping from hunting may be deduced from the consideration of the following facts. Among the Indians of the North-American plains we know that whole communities used to follow one particular herd of buffaloes, with which they thought themselves connected in a mystic way. At certain times they used to hold a ceremonial hunt. It may be suggested that this ritual strengthened the sense of connexion between the community and its herd. This means that the life of a community became bound up not only with one species of animal, but even with one particular herd. One special group of men regularly followed one special group of beasts. In this way the men gradually became dependent on the herd and its movements, and thus their nomadic life was to some extent influenced by the beasts. On the other hand, they gradually gained some measure of control over the movements of the herd, and from directing came ultimately to tend them. This tending is expressed in primitive ways of thinking by ceremony and ritual. From the economic point of view such hunters gained an advantage over others in that they could always obtain ample provision from their herds. The size of the community thus corresponded with that of the herd. In this way the bonds within the community were strengthened, since the herd was considered as a possession, and its increase meant greater prosperity and security for every one. Such conditions we still find among present-day herdsmen. These facts may provide the basis for a hypothesis concerning the original development from hunting to cattle-keeping.

Such transitions, however, cannot have been easy. Probably they were promoted by special conditions which we to-day can hardly imagine. The difficulties involved in them can be conjectured from what we know of people who are at the present day still in the hunting stage. There is, for instance, the case of the Bergdama of South-west Africa. Many of them had been serfs of the Herero (cattle-breeders), who used them as watchmen for their cows. When they returned to their own tribe they were sometimes allowed to take some cows with them, but the possession of these never induced the Bergdama to keep them for their milk or to let them breed. Instead they very soon slaughtered them for food. Thus, even in spite of their close neighbourhood and intimate connexion with cattle-keepers, whose customs and methods of treating the beasts they had learnt, they could not be persuaded to keep cattle, although the natural conditions of their country would have been as favourable for the purpose as those of the Herero country.

Difficulties of this kind involved in a transition period have been known to occur even among people in a higher stage of development. The Berber tribes (Tuaregs) of the Sahara, for instance, and the East-African cattle-breeders all faithfully adhere to their traditional mode of life and cannot adapt themselves to agricultural conditions if they do not mix with women agriculturists.

§ 5. It follows from this that these changes must have been brought about by special conditions, and the tracing of these conditions to their source would seem to be the most important part of our task. The hunting stage of society, for example, has had two parallel developments. On the one hand, the activity of

the men has led to cattle-keeping, while, on the other, the work of
the women in collecting food has developed into agriculture.
Definite progress is shown by a comparison of the pastoral with
the hunter's life, and of the respective activities called out by
agriculture and by food-gathering. The change from the one to
the other has resulted in the acquisition of new facilities in
obtaining food, which implies an accumulation of skill and knowledge amounting to an increase in the communal resources. Such
an accumulation of skill is especially clear when we consider the
development from pastoral life and from the digging-stick and
the hoe to cultivation by means of the ox-drawn plough. This
means that the digging-stick has been improved into a hoe by
the addition of a piece of sharpened stone and a handle. From
this, again, after the introduction of draught cattle, was evolved
the plough. In so far as the economic type is concerned with these
technical stages they are in a progressive relation to one another.
We have, therefore, two branches of progress from the hunter
stage. The one, roughly speaking, leads from the hunting activity
of the men to pastoral life, the other, from the collecting activity
of the women to the tilling of the soil. Plough cultivation, where
they meet, represents the fusion of these two main branches.
The use of cattle in drawing the plough implies the taming of
a draught animal, and also a certain symbiosis (living together)
between herdsmen and tillers of the soil. (See Diagrams at
the close of text.)

§ 6. Looking back, we may be surprised, from our modern point
of view, to find that progress in these primitive technical stages was
so slow, and may be at a loss to conjecture the cause of this tardiness.
If we remember how difficult it is for any given people to change
their mode of life (as may be seen in the case of the Bergdama, the
Berber, and various East-African tribes), we can better conceive the
obstacles which lie in the way of progress, however slight, and
realize that modifications had necessarily to be few and far between.
Innovations were made with great difficulty, and were mostly due
to new influences both within and without the community. It
was one of the chief defects of the older theories that they took no
account of complications arising from contact with foreign communities, which differed according to whether these belonged to the
same ethnical group or had an entirely strange set of traditions. In
primitive life, communities are somewhat isolated, and on this

account contact between one and the other is comparatively rare and slow. When it occurs, the mutual effect upon the parties concerned is not unlimited, but a restricted selection of technical means, ideas, and customs takes place. This is determined by the traditions, the institutions, and the character of the people chiefly affected. The elements so taken over are not, however, preserved in their original state, but undergo certain transformations, being, so to speak, digested and assimilated. Among peoples of the Sudan, for instance, the throwing-stick was merely a weapon, whereas among certain Bantu tribes it acquired religious meaning. The boomerang, again, among the Australians is used in fighting, while in the New Hebrides and the Solomon Islands, I observed it being used in ceremonial dancing. In this connexion it has not yet been pointed out that very often an implement used in one tribe cannot be manufactured locally, but must be bought from another.

In considering the effect of one tribe upon another, we must be careful to ascertain the precise forms of contact between tribes which are known to occur. These are undoubtedly of various kinds, and by their nature affect the process of selection. No doubt one of the most important methods of influence, especially among lower tribes, is the taking or exchanging of women. Thus (as I observed in the island of Popoko, near Kieta in Bougainville, Solomon Islands, South Seas), the Alu men founded a colony on Popoko, and got their women from the mountains in the interior (Koromida) of Bougainville. These women spoke a different language and belonged to a different culture from the men. Their children first spoke the mothers' language, but later, the young boys especially, acquired their fathers' words also. Thus a new language sprang up. The women's implements and tools were mostly those of the mountain people, while the men continued to use those of the Alu. Most probably in South Africa, where the women till the soil while the man tend the cattle, their traditions have come from two different ethnical roots, but, owing to the lapse of time, we naturally cannot say to-day that they represent two races, for in the meantime they have intermarried and again become more or less homogeneous.

All these points show that technical progress, the transfer of ideas, customs, or implements, cannot be considered as if each existed in a state of isolation. They are brought about, not by individuals, but by human beings living in a community. Therefore, such transferences are part of a complete system of ideas and institutions, and if they are taken over by another people they enter a new system of communal life, which also consists of harmonized ideas and institutions, though of a different kind. Therefore, their character, after being transferred, is inevitably changed. As we have already said, a weapon in another society becomes a tool; a myth or legend changes its meaning; birds, animals, and plants are substituted for others in ceremonies; or an institution such as the blood feud, or head hunting, or ordeals, acquires a special significance.

This means that we always have to take into consideration the essential character of the social body.

§ 7. These sociological points of view have generally been ignored by ethnologists, especially those of the so-called 'Kulturkreislehre' and the 'kulturhistorische Methode'. Every custom, tradition, and object, all skills, take their character from their connexion with the whole culture. On the other hand, each of them moves in its own particular orbit, which, by intersecting with others, allows each to participate in various other communities. We have, moreover, to consider that their duration is unequal, and cannot, therefore, be calculated with mechanical accuracy. There is also a connexion between the nature of certain institutions and customs ensuring the permanence of one while the other survives. For instance, there is undoubtedly a certain relation between the blood feud and the custom of giving sanctuary. The latter can only last as long as the former continues, while the blood feuds themselves, as also the paying of composition for indemnity among the parties concerned, depend on a certain stage of political life, i.e. one without any effective central authority. This principle is equally valid for technical matters. Primitive methods of handicraft, for example, can only survive until more complicated or efficient machinery has come into use. Therefore, economic institutions and methods of social-economic exploitation must also keep pace with political conditions and the development of technical ability. Thus, slavery and the exacting of forced labour from tenants presuppose the rise of certain groups in authority, the stratification of society, and, further, the absence of money or its equivalent. Both phenomena are interdependent in their rise and their fall.

The origin of slavery may be conjectured from some phases of primitive life, and it is worth noticing that its appearance in its true form is the outcome of economic conditions. Captives among the hunting tribes of North-American Indians, for instance, or even among Polynesians, are not exploited economically. Their disposal, indeed, presents their conquerors with a difficult problem. Sometimes they are slaughtered or sacrificed, sometimes adopted into the tribe, and it may happen that they are married. When labour is asked from them, they are often treated, and even dressed, as women, because the special work of tilling the soil is the women's monopoly, and any man doing it becomes, so to speak, a woman. But in those tribes where men also labour, as in the hoe-cultivated parts of Africa, there is a strong tendency for the bulk of the work to devolve upon the slaves. On other occasions, the exchange of goods among tribes obtaining their food in different ways, such as herdsmen and tillers of the soil, has sometimes become one-sided. That is to say, one negotiator has insisted on receiving gifts from the others without giving adequate compensation for them; this, in the course of time, has meant at least the economic subjugation of the weaker party, and thus leads to the stratification of the two communities. Such a process may be observed among the Bakitara in East Africa. Taken in conjunction with the remarks in the preceding paragraph concerning their implications, the economic importance of these stratifications becomes clear. It is still further emphasized by the point next to be considered, the origin of kingship.

Even among hunting tribes, the headman, or chief, plays an important part in so far as he is the person who, although he must conform to tradition, disposes of the booty of the hunters and trappers, and he is often the finder of the way and leader of a successful migration. His wife is frequently the most influential person among the women. The position he holds is made stronger, in stratified communities, by his being the leader of the first clan, from which fact he acquires a great influence over his people. By the time that a large number of tribes have been united by the necessity of paying tribute to one headman and his family, the latter has grown into a dynasty with enormous power, of which the first member is called a king. Such was the case among the Incas of Peru, and in ancient Egypt of the so-called New Empire. Under certain conditions this function of kingship was of supreme importance for the building up of special economic institutions.

In all these aggregates of communities (i.e. stratified or united societies with one ruler) we find the original ethnical distinctions in a state of transition, mostly due to the increasing importance of wealth, and, as mentioned in the last paragraph, to the rise to power of an authoritative ruler. That is to say, the rivalry among the aristocratic clans led to one gaining the ascendancy, and eventually either absorbing or suppressing the others. While this was proceeding, the importance of political and military leaders made itself felt, so that it was possible for them to establish their personal authority within their own clan. In order, however, to make their position more secure, they tried to augment the number of their followers, and for this purpose were willing to accept all comers, whether slaves, captives, foreigners, or even volunteers from other aristocratic clans. This naturally led to a confusion in the original ethnical stratification, and its replacement by a social one, where the position of the individual was determined by the rank he held in relation to the despot, or to his family. Thus the aristocratic clans were undermined, and an officialdom arose in their place, dependent on the despot. Briefly stated, these are the processes which blurred the old ethnical distinctions and substituted for them the new social stratification.

§ 8. A special point must be made of the tendency towards amalgamation in stratified or graded communities, especially when these are of small dimensions and without a leader of recognized authority. A process occurs which tends to make the former ethnical distinctions disappear. But the idea of rank undoubtedly survives in some directions, although it manifests itself in unorthodox forms. We see it, for instance, in the aristocracies of wealth which arise and also in the organizations of secret societies. Both these are to be found among the Gunan-tuna of the Gazelle Peninsula (New Britain, South Seas, e.g. in Tahiti, and the Caroline Islands; in Western Africa, &c.). On Banks Island and in the New Hebrides they are combined in the *suque*, although this institution itself varies in each island (Speiser, pp. 338, 382, 397, 406, 416, 419 et seq.).

Suque is a ritualistic association for which the entrance fee is paid in pigs, mats, and shell money, the status of a member depending on the size and frequency of his contributions. A man's social standing depends upon the grade he succeeds in reaching in the *suque*. His rise, however, is slow, because it is difficult to acquire the necessary number of pigs, mats, and shells for the donations and feasts. Usually large debts have to be incurred if a member is to go far up in the society. Therefore it is a question, on the one hand, of wealth, on the other, of obtaining credit, since rank is expensive in exact proportion to its degree. The lending of pigs, &c., for such purposes, is connected with transactions of various kinds which are accompanied by mimetic performances.

Since pigs, mats, shell money, &c., are an indispensable condition for entrance to this society, they acquire a special value in the eyes of the community. Such a value can be given to any object by making it a qualification for membership. Thus we see how social and ritualistic customs and institutions have an enormous bearing on economics, by enhancing or depressing the standards of value. Thus economic values do not stand isolated in their own special field, but are closely interwoven with the whole texture of society.

§ 9. These changes have gone on everywhere on the same pattern, although at varying rates of speed, according to special circumstances. It is questionable, however, if we should call them progress, for they only denote development in the limited life of a community, and so are only a stage in it. Another appellation may, therefore, be more appropriate. In this case, we had better refer to certain aspects of political development, which do not, at the moment, come within our province. Here we are solely interested in the economic importance of the process, and this lies mainly on the side of organization. Economic organization in such a society is brought about by the king, who, relying on the old principle of the headman as distributor, demands revenue from his subjects in order to feed, house, clothe, and adorn his followers. In this way his court is extended and becomes one of the most important centres for the exchange of goods, a function carried out by his officials. Consequently, these despots come to be considered as the sole owners of cattle and of land. They are credited with the ability to dispose of the wealth of the community, and from such notions originates the feudal system, by which the king gives away cattle or land to those who maintain friendly relations with him, or whom he wishes to reward for services rendered.

These processes have occurred many times in various places, and we are confronted with the question whether they have been the result of a transfer of ideas, or whether similar causes have had similar effects in different places. Reference may be made, for instance, to the economic organization of the Inca regime in ancient Peru. We find forms of government more or less similar to it among the peoples of the ancient East—in Egypt, Mesopotamia, India, China, Further India, and so on. Here the question becomes acute, and perhaps we must find the answer, not in one theory or the other, but in an interaction between the two. If there is contact, of whatever kind it may be, a transference, as already mentioned, takes place within relatively narrow limits. A choice is exercised according to the dispositions of the accepting peoples, and all that is borrowed inevitably undergoes modification. It ought, perhaps, to be made clear how this process is concerned with social institutions. What can be transferred in the social or political realm? In seeking for an answer, we must start from certain ideas or principles which guide the actions and behaviour of men. We shall find that it is from these that customs and events have acquired their characteristic shape.

If we compare, for instance, the economic organization of Africa, of the ancient Mediterranean cultures, and of old Asia, we find that composite communities were built up on the stratification due to shepherds gaining superiority over the agricultural and hunting tribes. But how did similar composite states grow up in America, where there were no pastoral people? With the exception of the llama, which was used as a beast of burden, no large animal was tamed in pre-Columbian America. Could the idea of such a stratified state with its organization of a central power wielded by the chief, such as we find in old Egypt, be transferred to Mexico, Yucatan, or Peru? Or could anything else have been transferred? When the people of Kusae, of Jap, of Samoa, of Hawaii, or the ancient Maoris came to their final homes they could only have had a vague reminiscence of the institutions obtaining in the land where they had previously lived. We may suppose that the same would have been the case if the dominant people of the Inca had crossed the Pacific. Even the conceptions that were retained could only have been utilized if the conditions were favourable. When, for instance, as on the small Caroline Islands, voyagers from some of the Pacific islands landed on an uninhabited place, no stratified community arose.

But the institutions of primitive people differ in many ways from ours. Whereas ours are defined by written statutes and conditioned by a legal machinery, theirs consist in the customary practices and the traditional conduct of the people. Consequently they can be changed more smoothly without formalities and can adapt themselves to new circumstances without a formal break. In the second place, the distinctions between the various regulations are vague and in a greater state of flux, consequently there is more opportunity for individual adaptation of the decision to each case. To this also is due the wide variety of primitive institutions in form and colour.

In handling this enormous mass of material it will, perhaps, be best to sort it into several economic types which will be built up with reference to technical facilities and political forms. As we have seen, these are of the highest importance in all questions of economic life.

II

POPULATION AND ITS MEANS OF SUBSISTENCE

§ 1. Factors influencing increase and decrease of population.

§ **1.** In order to understand the differentiation of ranks in the progress of society, it is instructive to cast a glance over some factors which have a restrictive effect on the life of peoples with primitive technique and economics. It is especially important in this connexion to raise the question how the membership of the various associations is influenced. On the one hand, it is a question of how a certain technical process in given natural surroundings fixes the numbers of an association, while, on the other hand, we must take into consideration the fact that in consequence of increase in the population the associations may become numerically greater. In general, it may be said that (*a*) the wild products collected by the women do not provide sufficient suitable food for young children, so that the time of nursing is prolonged, and, consequently, the intervals between births become greater; (*b*) the dangers of sea-fishing increase mortality; (*c*) the circumstances of nomadic life in general have an influence on the frequency of births; (*d*) the hunting of dangerous beasts certainly develops skill in fighting, but also increases mortality; (*e*) the use of beasts of burden and boats is an asset for the nomadic life. The more stationary life necessitated by gardening or fishing in rivers causes an increase in birth statistics and also a decrease of mortality. The great efforts made by the women when at work (as among the Iroquois, Basonga, Baluba, Papuans, and Dayak tribes) also influence birth statistics, but they can be restricted by other factors (pleasures) as among the Bangala. The difficulties attending the spread of the tribe lead again to voluntary birth control, as in the case of certain Papuans and Melanesians. In more advanced societies, above all, the practice of polygamy by rulers, and the existence in some quarters of organized concubinage and prostitution, have an unfavourable effect on the increase of the population (Descamps, iii. 1 and 2, pp. 186 et seq., 405).

III

THE FOOD QUESTION

§ 1. The place given to eating in primitive society. § 2. Illustrations of the ceremonialism of eating: the Eskimo, the Bergdama, &c. § 3. Separation of men and women when eating. § 4. Banquets. § 5. Choice of dishes. § 6. Magic with remains of food.

§ **1.** Although the taking of nourishment is by us taken for granted as a matter of course, it is, nevertheless, a serious business for the 'primitive man', both from a practical and an emotional point of view. He is not only more dependent than we on nature's moods in obtaining his food, but also less well informed regarding the effect of food-stuffs. His attitude towards food is governed not only by the danger of starvation but also by its possibly poisonous and intoxicating action. Influenced by this feeling, his intellect has drawn the most remarkable inferences based on occasional similarities or resemblances. In particular, the process of eating is affected by trains of thought connected with mimetic or symbolic magic.

§ **2.** It is occasionally reported that when hunter tribes such as the Eskimos kill a large animal, a walrus or a white whale, they fling themselves with wild ravenous greed on the spoil, which they devour raw (Nansen, p. 95). Yet even among hunters and collectors the preparation of food appears to be connected with no little ceremonialism, an attitude based on traditional considerations. Apart from the making of fire, cooking itself among the Bergdama (Vedder, p. 29) is already conducted with scrupulous care. Two pots which have been put on the fire must never touch each other. That would be a misdemeanour entailing consequences that must be atoned for by special rites. In particular, it causes bad luck in hunting. In addition to the supreme head of the kraal, there is also a food-master, who has to taste the dishes before they are eaten (Vedder, p. 19). He also samples the berries, roots, and tubers collected before any one else is allowed to taste them, and large animals killed in hunting are cut up, cooked, and prepared either by him personally or according to his directions. He tastes a morsel from each of the pots on the fire and lays the meat on the wooden platters held in readiness in such a way that first the old men and then the hunters receive their portions, after which the chief is served. The liver and other viscera are sent by the food-master to his wife, whose duty it is to do the tasting for the female inhabitants of the kraal or encampment, and for the children of both sexes, and to distribute the food in the same way. This food-master seems to foreshadow the functions of the supervisor of tribal economics among digging-stick agriculturists. An old Bergdama gave the following explanation of the office of food-master: 'Do we not throw food unknown to us to a dog and wait to see if he eats it and if it hurts him? The chief, therefore, has all food-stuffs first tasted by the food-master, for he knows the herbs of the field. If he eats the dishes, the others can also eat them. If he were to die, the kraal (camp) has lost nothing, for he is an old man who must be fed by the kraal but no longer contributes to its upkeep'. Special behaviour is adopted in eating small animals, when they have been caught in a snare: the sandals must be removed from the feet and laid on one side, nor is it permissible to eat standing or lying down or crouching on the ground with drawn-up knees, or to lie on one side; but the eater must seat himself upon a stone or the trunk of a tree in order to consume the meat with decency. Impropriety at meal-times is 'seen by the fire', which causes the game to shun the snare if its laws have been disregarded. When the first catch of a new snare is eaten, the meat must be bitten off with the teeth or torn off without the help of a knife. In the case of wild animals killed with an arrow or a throwing club, it is permissible to seize the cooked piece of meat with the teeth, hold it firmly with the left hand, and then hack it off close to the lips with the knife held in the right hand.

From these examples we see the very varied sets of ideas which become connected with eating. The offering of food, in particular, is often considered a sign of love, as, for example, in Australia (Strehlow, p. 92) or in the Solomon Islands (Thurnwald ['12], i. 53). Among the Mafulu, a hill tribe in southern New Guinea, an unmarried youth may not eat in the presence of women (Williamson, p. 79). On the other hand, on the island of Ysabel, in the central Solomon Archipelago, a man may not marry a woman from whom he has received food (Rivers, i. 256).

§ 3. The men frequently eat separately from the women, a custom which must evidently be connected with the traditional distribution of work between the sexes and with the special way of obtaining food adopted by the men, who are principally hunters, as contrasted with the women, who collect fruit, tubers, and molluscs. Lumholtz says of the Australians, that the women provide for the daily food by collecting fruit and berries, digging up roots and tubers, or tapping larvae out of the tree-trunks; the man brings honey, occasionally eggs, lizards, or game; but he often keeps the animal food for himself, while the woman is confined to vegetable diet for herself and the children.

Among the South-African Bergdama (Vedder, pp. 25, 28) also the women and children eat separately from the men. This custom has, in many cases, been maintained even among the less primitive peoples; indeed it continues to prevail in the agricultural stage. On Yap, one of the Caroline Islands, the family is separated at meals (Müller-Wismar, p. 284). The reason given is that no one may eat the dishes of a man of higher or lower rank. As the wife is not included in this order of precedence, she and her children must eat separately from her husband. The dishes are prepared from raw materials specially laid aside and cooked on a separate hearth. In earlier times it was also usual on Kusae for the sexes to eat separately, and, moreover, it was the husband who attended to the cooking, the wife being forbidden to enter the cooking-house (Sarfert, pp. 119, 136).

Among the Mafulu of southern New Guinea, men and women eat together, seated in a circle. If they are by themselves, they help themselves from the platters with their fingers, but if guests are present they use chopsticks made from the bones of the cassowary and the kangaroo (Williamson, p. 69).

§ 4. Very special importance is attached to banquets, for which great preparations lasting for many months are often made, as, for instance, at the initiation of youths as practised in Australia and elsewhere, at funeral feasts, or at the inauguration of new canoes or houses, and the like. On such occasions they often accumulate enormous quantities of edible tubers, such as yams and taro, coconuts, sugar-cane, and bananas, pandanus, and other fruits, and especially pigs. At the same time, this accumulation of food-stuffs for feasts supplies an occasion for display on the part of the individual, as, for instance, on the Trobriand Islands, to the east of New Guinea, where they begin by holding an exhibition of the crops in the fields, when every one tries to make a better show than his neighbour. After this, enormous quantities of yams are piled up in storehouses, where they are not necessarily all eaten but often left to rot. Further, when a pig is to be killed, it is first carried round and shown in one or two villages, and finally roasted alive before the whole village and the neighbours. It is then cut into pieces in a ceremonial way and distributed. (Malinowski ['22], pp. 148, 168 et seq., 214.) As in the case of so many primitive peoples, so much is eaten at the feasts that they are sick, which is considered the height of enjoyment. The exhibition and the accumulation of food-stuffs are doubtless connected with these pleasures of the table.

§ 5. The choice of dishes is connected in a special way with the emotions. Certain food-stuffs are thought to give special strength derived from supernatural powers. Such are dishes that are either conspicuous as staple foods or considered as special delicacies, or else those eaten by neighbours and strangers. The attitude with regard to these special foods is connected in many cases with the imaginative complexes described as totemism.

(a) Among the Ainus of north-east Asia, the bear is the animal usually killed and eaten. On certain occasions a ceremonial eating of this animal takes place: the male members of the family drink its blood and the women and children eat the liver raw. The Gilyaks behave in the same way (Frazer, ii. 375, 385). The *juka* plant is the principal food of the Uitoto Indians. Great feasts and dances take place for the eating of the *juka* plant, and these are connected with the whole system of mythological beliefs held by these Indians. Their principal object is to produce an abundant crop of *juka* (Preuss, pp. 130 et seq.). The idea of increasing the amount of spoils or crops by a ceremonial feast is best known to us from Australian examples. Even in killing the animal certain rites must be observed, but many other restrictions are also observed. For instance, immoderate enjoyment must be avoided: among the Australian Aranda, members of the fish totem are allowed to eat only a small quantity of fish, and even this must be bad and stinking. The people of the water totem must be moderate in the use of water; but when it rains, they ought not to go into a hut, but must expose themselves to the rain (Strehlow, i. 2, p. 59).

(b) In many cases special delicacies are avoided or reserved for the old men of the group, for example, steenbok, hartebeest, and duiker among the Bergdama, or the fat and tail of the kangaroo among the Aranda of Australia. In many cases, each group has its own special forbidden dishes. In particular, women are often prohibited from eating certain dishes (Roth ['97], p. 69). On the other hand, a certain effect is ascribed to given dishes; thus, on Mota (Banks Islands) the woman eats the fruit of certain trees according to whether she wishes to give birth to a boy or a girl (Rivers, i. 150). It is believed, in many cases, that the child acquires the physical and mental qualities of the animal with which it is brought into totemistic connexion. The eating of such a totem animal would be considered as a kind of cannibalism (Rivers, i. 152).

(c) Among peoples dominated by a more complicated and sophisticated magico-religious thought, the point of view appears to shift. While the occasional ceremonial eating was originally done with the object of influencing the supernatural powers, the more advanced among the primitive peoples are even less influenced by rational views of eating, and respect for supernatural powers has become the main consideration. Eating becomes a means of attaining partnership with supernatural powers and thereby sharing in the control of destiny. Among peoples where the conditions of life are indicated by an improved technique in handiwork, agriculture, or cattle-keeping, the expectation becomes prominent that the course of destiny can be guided by certain manipulations, one of which is the consumption of food. It is only from such points of view, and by paying regard to the explanations and examples given above, that we can understand the remarkable institution which has become known as 'the food of the gods' or 'of the king'. The idea that the qualities of an organism can be acquired by eating its substance is very widespread, and doubtless connected with the conceptions mentioned in the foregoing paragraphs. Among the ancient Mexicans a representative of the god Tezcatlipoca was chosen annually and, after a year of luxurious existence, sacrificed on the occasion of a great feast. He bore the name and played the part of the god, decked in all his insignia. His heart was torn from his living body and offered to the sun, while his arms and legs were served on the tables of the nobles (Sahagun, p. 485 et seq.). We have similar information regarding Peru and Nigeria, and there are also traces of it in the Indian Vedas (Weber, i. 72 et seq.). Similar proceedings of killing and eating are known to us in ancient Egypt (Frazer, iii. 9 et seq.).

(d) Planting of cereals provided new forms of nourishment and thereby new relations to the nutritive powers. The ideas are, however, less directly connected with the grain than with the bread made from it. Not only among the Germanic tribes, but also among all agricultural peoples, bread had a certain sacred character. The process whereby the sheaf, in which strength was believed to be concentrated, was given a special form or distinguished in some way, was also applied to bread. Baked bread, in which it was believed that the force pervading the whole of living nature had been captured, was given a special shape, in particular bread baked for feasts. Specially baked bread is sometimes in the shape of an animal, sometimes of a human figure (Reuterskiöld, pp. 115 et seq.). In this case we already find a sequence of very complicated mental transferences and combinations, which obviously arose owing to the fact that, on the one hand, the memory of a time when animals and even men were eaten persisted, while, on the other, a connexion was established with bread, the new source of nourishment and strength.

(e) A special role falls to the first-fruits, whether of animal or vegetable products, which were originally considered to be imbued by the deity, and, later on, created by him, and which were then offered as thank-offerings or sacrifices to the god or chief.

§ 6. In conclusion, we must recall the magic performed with the scraps of food remaining after a meal. For instance, on the Solomon Islands and in the Bismarck Archipelago, the remains of betelnuts, or other scraps of food, are wrapped in leaves and stuck in the ground; earth is then heaped on them, the place stamped down and three hot stones laid on it. A charm may thus be prepared to kill the man who left the scraps (Thurnwald ['12], i. 443). Rivers reports similar proceedings from the Banks Islands, Motlav, and Mota. The idea that the influencing of a person's fate is connected with remains such as hair, nails, and the like is widespread, but cannot be considered here in full.

IV

SETTLEMENTS

§ **1.** The importance of the settlement from the sociological point of view consists in the fact that its form often reflects in a startling way the political and social structure of the group. For as the organization of the community is essentially founded on relationship, those more closely related, or those who consider themselves to be specially related, endeavour to remain near together. This is observed even among the large families of the hunting and trapping hordes, inasmuch as a special hearth is maintained by the individual small families or in the larger associations by every woman with, at least, her own children and, as a rule, her husband as well. This isolation of the fully-developed woman is carried out in temporary camping grounds, such as those in Australia, or those of the Kalahari of South Africa, as well as in the communal houses which serve for a whole sept.

§ **2.** In order to obtain an idea of primitive roving we may picture the mode of living of the hunting nomad tribes of the Bergdama (Vedder, p. 11). The Bergdama of South-West Africa uses suitable caves as a temporary dwelling when it suits him; they offer protection from cold or rain, and he puts up his wind-screens according to his need or inclination. A low-growing, thick bush, the gaps between the twigs being filled in case of need with bunches of grass, serves at first to protect the fire from the wind. This is followed by the development of an artificial wind-screen and, finally, of a hut. Women, who naturally have a greater inclination to permanent residence, have a special interest in housing conditions, and, as a matter of fact, among the Bergdama, the women erect the huts with but little assistance from the men, and the house is considered to be the woman's property. With regard to the Kubu, cf. Hagen, p. 156.

§ **3.** The case of pastoral nomads is naturally somewhat different.

Certain Arab tribes on the upper Euphrates build beehive huts of sun-dried bricks, which huts are arranged in rows. The life of these cattle-breeding nomads necessitates a complete change from summer to winter quarters. Two powerful tribes of the Bedouin, with a number of minor ones, migrate regularly in winter to the great desert which lies between the Jordan and the Tigris, extending from the Befuds to the hills of Kurdistân. In summer they move northwards to the Kurdish hills with their wives, children, camels, horses, and sheep. When the Shamar tribe is on the move, with its 30,000 sheep and 50,000 camels, its camp forms a line of tents seven miles long, occupied by 20,000 grown men with their families. The move to the south begins in autumn, and the winter is passed in Nejd. They carry everything they need with them.

§ 4. The conditions among agricultural tribes are different. But, notwithstanding, it would be a mistake to think that digging-stick agriculture necessarily implies permanent residence. On the contrary, their usual practice of letting the ground lie fallow causes the digging-stick cultivators and also the hoe agriculturists to change their gardens and fields. This occurs particularly often in mountain districts.

In settlements of hunters, collectors, and gardeners, it is characteristic that the social and economic unit is formed by the kinship association of the clan. An instance of the way in which this works is found among the Marind-anim of Dutch South New Guinea, where the men's hall is built by the members of a *boan*, a totemistic sect. In addition, several women's huts stand round the men's hall. The various *boans* in the immediate neighbourhood may happen to have their settlements close by, but each is quite independent of the rest. If the number of inhabitants increases, a new men's hall surrounded by women's huts grows up. The married woman usually goes to the hut of her mother-in-law; it is only when the hut which is shared with her sisters-in-law becomes too crowded, that she goes, with her children, to a hut of her own. The independence of each group of relations so settled is expressed by the fact that no name is applied to the settlement in its entirety, each individual group having a name of its own, which is applied in the first instance to the men's hall (Wirz ['25], ii. 162). For this reason the European often hears the most different names for what he regards as one village, according to the kinship group of which his informant is thinking. It may, however, happen that in some cases the men's hall possesses a name distinct from that of the kinship group, or that there is a common name for the whole ground on which the settlements of adjacent kinship groups are found, so that finally, in practice, something resembling a general name appears to exist. In many cases, however, the name of the oldest part of the village is applied to the whole.

In these aggregated settlements we find that the units are groups of persons related by blood, living side by side. They are, however, also important as associations of men based on friendship. In particular, a member of one sept can have himself admitted as a member of another. The aggregate forms an offensive-defensive association against the outer world, however loosely constituted it may be. It thus represents a political unit, while economic transactions are carried on inside the kinship group. (Cf. Wirz, pp. 115 et seq.)

§ 5. The social organization is illustrated in village life by the fact that every clan or sept has its special hamlet which is divided from those of the others, and that the dwellings of one sept are grouped together more closely than those which belong to another sept, as, for instance, in many Melanesian districts.

§ 6. In this connexion it is, of course, impossible to enter into details as to methods of building and the differentiation of houses according to the purposes to be served. The style of building is based, in the first instance, on ethnic tradition, for which reason the factor of collateral relationship is of paramount importance.

But it is not only the shape of the building which is important but also the care with which the design is carried out. Fülleborn (p. 147) points out that on Lake Nyasa, in East Africa, on the Kondeland shore, and on the Ikombe and Lumbira peninsulas, a type of round hut is to be seen which has been copied by the Konde people from those of a neighbouring tribe, and which lacks the accurate finish of the Konde houses. The style of dwelling is not only connected with different local conditions, but also with certain ethnic traditions. For what other explanation can there be of the fact that different tribes who live in the same district cling obstinately to different styles of dwelling and settlement. Such traditions as to the special form of dwelling or settlement may be occasionally determined by relations with adjacent tribes or by actual requirements of daily life. Thus, in South-West Africa, the Bushmen have more and more withdrawn themselves into inaccessible regions, to escape from the cruel hunts organized against them by the Hottentots and the Bastards. The families now live there, usually in caves or under overhanging cliffs on the mountains, just as the Veddas in Ceylon are known to do. The Bushmen from their heights can survey an extensive range of country, which is more important for them than living close to the much coveted water-holes.

Security plays a very important part in the choice of a site for a settlement. Even the number of those living together in one group is determined by the necessity of striking the average between the maximum provision of good food, which is favoured by reducing, and the maximum of safety, which is favoured by increasing the number of members of the settlement. The possibility of danger from more powerful neighbours, as might be expected, often leads to a breach of tradition in this respect.

Sometimes it is to forests, as on the Congo (dwarfs), in Ceylon (Veddas), or in Sumatra (Kubus), and to deserts (Bushmen, Damas) that the weaker and more timid hunters, trappers, and women collectors withdraw. In the Mbama district on Lake Nyasa the fishermen build their houses, which are only accessible by means of ladders and trap-doors, on gigantic blocks of granite. In this way they protect themselves from the marauding Wangoni herds-men. It appears that, in earlier times, buildings on piles were erected for safety on the shores of Lake Nyasa (Fülleborn, pp. 418 et seq.). These recesses allowed them to continue their traditional manner of living. In many cases the hunting and collecting tribes, unable to resist the more aggressive and enterprising herdsmen and fleeing before them, were thus cut off from the progressive influences radiating from the centres of civilization in other parts of the world.

Special forms of settlement have often become traditional owing to the need of security. Such are the dwellings in caves and on rocks which are found in all parts of the world, and also hiding-places excavated in the soil, such as are found in Tunis. This type of settlement, partly subterranean with a view to greater security, is represented by the East African *tembes* of the Wafiomi, which provide shelter for man and beast in underground excavations. Those of the Watataru of Mangati and Iraku are constructed in a similar manner. There are, however, different forms among different tribes, for in many cases only one family lives in a *tembe*, while with another people the *tembe* provides accommodation for a considerable number of families.

The large community houses, such as those met with in many parts of New Guinea and in eastern Sumatra, appear to be connected with matriarchal institutions. This is indicated by the fact of their also being found both in North and South America in matriarchal regions. The large blocks of community houses in the country of the Pueblo Indians, built in this case of stone, in conformity with the nature of the country, are well known (Fewkes ['10]). The gigantic fortress-like houses, the so-called *casas grandes* of Arizona, were not really dwelling-houses but places of refuge, also used for ceremonial trade. The population lived in small huts of a perishable type in the neighbourhood. The inhabitants had, however, already been driven out before the time of Columbus (Fewkes ['12], pp. 153 et seq.).

§ 7. Different ethnic groups often become intermingled. Where government by elders is found special halls are erected for the meetings of the men; or these are often held in special sacred places reserved outside the village, under trees.

§ 8. It is thus possible that different ethnic groups, settling in the immediate neighbourhood of each other, yet belong culturally to different groups, and thus often use different tools and utensils, and maintain, socially, different gradations of rank, while being, politically, under the same leadership. This point of view should be borne in mind in the study of prehistoric settlements.

In places where aristocracies have arisen, as at certain points in the coast-lands of New Guinea, or the Caroline Islands, Samoa, &c., the groups of different ethnic origin settle apart from each other.

Among the Dobuans (North Massim) the villages are scattered over wide stretches of country. Small compact hamlets of a dozen houses built on piles have quite a different character from that of the villages in the Trobriand Islands. Among the latter, a round space is enclosed by provision stores (yam houses), some of which, those belonging to the chief or to men of rank, are better and more spacious. The dwelling-houses are arranged in concentric circles round these store-houses, but separated from them by a road. The chiefs and men of rank have special houses next to those of their womenfolk, and there are, in addition, houses for bachelors and unmarried women (Malinowski ['22], p. 55).

§ 9. In places where a system of large despotic courts has arisen, as in certain regions of Africa, the settlement occupied by these courts is apart from those of the rest of the people, as, for example, among the Baziba of East Africa.

The special position of the prince finds expression in Eastern Africa in the complete detachment and independence of the prince's settlement. The people dependent on him live in a stronghold by themselves. While the ordinary village, among the Baziba of East Africa, for instance, is called *kiaro*, the prince's stronghold is called *kikare*. It consists of a large number of houses, all of which have different names according to the purpose they serve. Behind the prince's sleeping-house are the houses of his wives, a special house being reserved for his mother. The hall for the national assembly, which also serves as a law court, is usually near the prince's sleeping-house. The prince's band is housed in a music building. Special huts serve as dwellings for the brothers and relatives of the prince, the court hunters, cooks, guard, and also for various craftsmen, such as smiths, bark cloth workers, and also herdsmen. Stalls are provided for the cattle, and the whole complex is enclosed by a grove of banana trees. The stronghold is surrounded by various stockades, and, in addition, almost every house has its special defences. Between these a courtyard is left, the dimensions depending on the size of the house. A stranger entering the stronghold at first receives the impression of passing from one line of defence to the next, but any one familiar with them would have little difficulty in breaking through the numerous palisades with a few blows from an axe, and thus providing direct access to the prince's house. It is said that, even in earlier times, these defences were never very powerful (Rehse, p. 11 et seq.).

§ 10. The location of the settlement is apt to be determined by accidental circumstances. This applies above all to the difference between settlements regularly planned and more or less permanently located by a large body of men, and dwelling-places which have gradually grown up without any systematic plan, and which increase in size owing to the natural increase of the population or accretions from outside ('cumulative village'). The question arises whether a certain order in the arrangement of the houses is dependent on political conditions, as, for example, in a settlement resulting from a general emigration for the purpose of colonization. This gives rise to the various types, in particular to the so-called 'colonial villages' which are known to us in the history of settlements in Europe. As early as Carlovingian times the founding of villages was predominantly the business of the liege lords. This leads either to the village built in one row, or to the street village in accordance with varying local traditions (Braungart, pp. 43, 53).

§ 11. Regularly planned settlements are virtually limited to two possible designs, which within certain limits arise and persist as well among primitive tribes of the present day, as, for instance, in ancient Europe. These designs are represented, first, by the round village in which the houses are arranged in a circle or on a circular flat space (clearing), either without a real centre point (e.g. on the Trobriand Islands; cf. Malinowski ['15]) or by grouping the women's houses round the men's hall (e.g. in New Guinea; cf. Wirz ['25]). The idea of attributing the round villages in Europe solely to Wendic influence has been abandoned (Mielke). The other possible design consists of an arrangement in rows which again can be a single row (row village), something like the fen villages in which every homestead stands on its own strip of land, or the arrangement of the houses on two sides so that a street is formed, the street village. These forms of settlement are by no means rare, even among primitive peoples. It is not necessary in such cases that the streets should always intersect at right angles. This form of settlement occurs, for instance, on the islands Alu and Mono in the Solomon Islands, in the South Seas, and is due there to the ruling race of the black Solomon Islanders.

§ 12. A few representative instances are here taken from other tribes of low agriculturists (using the digging-stick) in the South Seas. In southern Bougainville (Solomon Islands) the first building to be erected in a new settlement is the men's house, which is named with a certain symbolic meaning. The erection of the houses, and, in particular, of the festival halls, is accompanied by many magical ceremonies, in which human sacrifices and offerings of skulls are not uncommon. The huts of each family or split of a clan (sept) are situated on a special clearing. This is also the case on the Gazelle peninsula of New Britain.

§ 13. The naming of the settlement is often connected, as, for instance, in New Guinea, with the names of the clearing. For, accord-

ing to my information, hitherto unpublished, regarding the lower
Potter River in New Guinea, and Buin in the Solomon Islands,
every strip of land there has its own traditional designation.
The settlements are often named after the general name of the
field, which, again, is taken from some peculiarity, such as an
outstanding tree, a good fishing-ground, a place where sago is
obtained, or from some local memory, as the place where some one
was murdered, or the like; all these are points of practical
importance (cf. also Lambert, p. 59). In the districts of Utah, in
North America, where water is scarce, the place names given by
the Gosiute Indians are mostly combinations with the words for
water, spring, or brook; but in one case the name recalls a great
fight (Chamberlain, p. 3). It is evident from this that the predominant points of view are the same under different conditions of
life.

§ 14. The removal of the settlement or the erection of new
dwellings may be due to various causes. Among peoples who
build huts not very difficult to erect, it is often the custom to
abandon the dwelling if a death has occurred in it. The house,
which is allowed to fall to pieces once it has been closed, thus
serves to a certain extent as a coffin for the deceased. A new house
is erected on an absolutely new clearing, according to personal
observations in the mountains of New Guinea, on the Mountain
River, the upper tributary of the Augusta River (Sepik) coming
from the right.

The information collected by Wirz (['25] ii. 153 et seq.) in
Dutch New Guinea is absolutely typical of the rhythmical alterna-
tion of migrations, fights, and expulsions; and numberless parallels
can be adduced, *mutatis mutandis*, from other places from the
earliest times. They indicate, among other things, that, in spite
of all coercion, institutions among primitive peoples are very much
exposed to the vicissitudes of fate and that no rigid classification
can therefore be perfect.

§ 15. According to their own traditions, the Marind people
were formerly resident in the British coastal district at the mouth
of the Fly River, whence they gradually pushed westwards. It
was probably a case of isolated migrations of smaller groups, septs,
or even individuals, whose fate, partly disguised in mythological
phrases, is still remembered. For instance, among the inhabitants
of Bian the first and earliest stratum of immigrants can be fairly

well defined by the difference in their dialect. These people settled at the mouth of the Bian, then, later, worked their way inland along the river, expelling and destroying the once great tribe of the Nak-leeu-anim, while adopting many of the peculiarities of their language (probably through the women whom they took captive). The Mahu-zé sept and part of the Geb-zé probably established themselves very early in the Imo and Méb settlements, which correspond to the Sangassé and Domandéh of the present day. Part of them went to the upper Bian. The Geb-zé formed the mythologico-totemistic relationship with the banana, while the Mahu-zé established a mythological relationship with the dog. Yet the backward Geb-zé developed a secret cult on the fabled island of Majo, which gave its name to the entire secret cult of the social group. They observed a mythological connexion with the coco-nut palm. Further migrations westward broke up the groups, which adopted mythologico-totemistic connexions or developed secret cults which cannot here be further analysed.

They took possession of the entire coast to the westward, as appears from the place names, which are all Marindinese. The Kanum-anim were driven back more and more by the Badé-anim, i.e. the Marind-anim coming from the Kumba and Maro rivers; for many years they were the victims of head-hunting expeditions, until, at last, the remnant withdrew, some of them into the interior, between the Maro and Torassi, and others into the inhospitable region to the southward, which is mostly under water in the rainy season, while there is a shortage of water during the dry season. The entire tribe of the Kanum-anim in Dutch territory only amounts to a few individuals whose former social classification is now completely unrecognizable. Some of them live in the great swamps, Paran, to the north of Kondo, and for this reason are also called Bob-anim, i.e. swamp-men. One of their settlements (Jamu) had, in 1918, only two inhabitants and another (Tamarau) only ten. The once great clan of the Badé-anim is completely broken up. At the present time, numerous spots with traces of former cultivation are only known by name, which reveals the fact that the region was once densely settled.

In settling inland, the first consideration was the finding of suitable dwelling-places, for the greater part of the country is under water during the rains. Besides this, it was important that there should be supplies of sago in the vicinity. Over and above this, they sought for their permanent settlements soil suitable for coco-nut plantations, the best soil in the interior being marine clay; but marine clay soil is rare in the hills. It was not as a rule possible to combine all these advantages. It was also desirable to have a river in the vicinity, as a suitable line of communication. In spite of all these requirements there was no lack of settlements in the interior. The location, in many places, was determined by the presence of drinking-water. On the lower and middle reaches of the river, high-lying stretches of land on the banks are rare, while, at the same time, brackish water often makes its presence felt further upstream. Settlements were always established by groups of relatives. The first sept to immigrate usually retained the leadership, as against those who came later, a fact which, in most cases, is accurately represented by the myths.

The original condition of the settlement can frequently be gathered from the name, which is often derived from that of a very early immigrant who founded the settlement, and whose name was often applied by his successors to the whole district. The newcomers established themselves in the neighbourhood of the existing settlement, erected huts for themselves and their women, and looked around for suitable soil for planting coco-nut or sago palms. In some cases, perhaps, possession could be taken of more distant stocks of sago, but, for safety's sake, they preferred to establish themselves in the neighbourhood of the existing settlement. In this way were formed the large settlements and agglomerations of settlements which, however, were composed of small individual hamlets, genetically and socially independent of each other. If the new immigrants settled on a fresh site, such as one suitable for cultivating coco-nuts, they had to share the surrounding country with the early settlers. In this way the original condition of the settlement gradually lost its character of an association confined to relatives. The areas occupied by the local groups are much larger in the interior than on the coast. It may be said, in general, that the further inland, the greater the area. In consequence of the sparse settlement of the country there is much more scope for various possibilities of change than on the coast. This finds expression in the character of the settlements and also in the entire mode of living of the natives, that of the coastal inhabitants being very different in many respects from that of the inland people. Both, however, possess, in addition to their permanent headquarters, minor settlements in the sago jungle or the plantations which are visited at certain times, as, for instance, when the plantations are laid out or the sago harvested. They also withdraw to them when the main settlement is suffering from a flood or, in the dry weather, from lack of drinking water, or when it is ravaged by disease.

V

TECHNICAL SKILL

§ 1. Technics the outcome of environment. § 2. Processes of development. § 3. Points of view and distinctions. § 4. Inventions and changes in treatment of material. § 5. Illustrations from South-American tribes. § 6. Further illustrations. § 7. The deterioration of technics. § 8. The Bergdama and their pots. § 9. The question of separate inventions. § 10. The status of the artisan. § 11. Magic. § 12. The technique of primitive navigation. § 13. The making of weapons.

§ 1. Does the development of technical skill depend exclusively on necessity? Were inventions made only because there was need for them? I think that a closer scrutiny of the facts shows such an explanation to be too simple. For with the development of technical skill, the needs themselves increase, while the satisfaction of one immediately gives rise to others. Technical ability, however, is relative to its environment. The kind of instruments, tools, and weapons required, depends on whether a man is surrounded by deserts or woods, whether he lives on the coast or in the mountains, in the polar regions or in the tropics. It is further determined by the kind of beasts he hunts, the species of domestic animals he keeps, the fertility of the soil, and the varieties of plants that he can grow. The question is what and how much any given group of men is able to extract from the country by its collective skill and knowledge.

In this case we had better ignore for the present the question whether the inventions have been made by the people themselves or acquired from others—a question which can only be settled by a detailed inquiry into each particular case. Perhaps its significance has been somewhat over-rated. For, when two peoples come into contact, they do not exchange all their technical resources, their stores of knowledge, or their social institutions. For instance, in spite of the hundred years of contact between the Bergdama hunters and the Herero herdsmen, the former have not become a pastoral people, nor have the latter devoted themselves exclusively to hunting. The dwarfs of the Congo again have not become husbandmen through visiting their neighbours, the agricultural Yaunde. The Bakitara and Banyankole cattlemen of East Africa have not devoted themselves to field-work, although they have been constantly associated with many agricultural tribes. It is only since the races have become to a certain extent mixed that they have acquired any culture elements from one another. The same is the case with the Tuareg camel-breeders who have come into contact with the Negroes of the Sudan. In general, one people takes from the other only what appeals to it and what fits in with its whole system of life. Mental and social processes of selection are always at work.

In the same way, again, a choice is exercised when utilizing inventions within the tribe. They are only accepted when they can easily be absorbed into the existing way of life. On this account, only those innovations are welcomed for which the community is ready.

§ 2. Technics are the outcome of an adjustment between man and his environment. The whole life of a society is planned on the basis of the traditional arts by which animals, plants, minerals, and climate are made to serve the purposes of its existence. This is not a peculiarity of man alone, but has been observed in many kinds of animals. But, in the case of man, there is the further factor, that he acquires fresh experience, alters his procedure where necessary, and stores up the knowledge so gained, whereas we have so far no information of anything similar in the animal kingdom.

This process of storing up knowledge, which is characteristic of man, has not, however, continued at the same rate at all times and among all peoples. For not only does the acquirement of the earliest arts appear to have extended over a particularly long period, but the growing mastery of nature did not always proceed at the same pace in historical times; epochs of great technical progress alternate with others of comparative stagnation. We are probably justified in assuming that such stagnations also took place in prehistoric times.

This rhythmical movement is not accidental, but can be attributed to the fact that man must first adapt himself socially and mentally to the technical processes evolved by himself. For the new technical processes bring with them new conditions of life for the community, thus affecting activities and the position of the individual, conditions which the inventor himself, perhaps, neither wished nor could have foreseen. Such periods of adaptation to the new technical conditions created by man appear in the form of ethical or social demands; they loosen the ties of communal life which depend on the limitations of a more primitive period, and also by mutual accommodation modify the viewpoint of the people forming the society. In earlier times such crises of adaptation were more especially connected with new methods of obtaining food; in the first place with the introduction of domestic animals and the cultivation of a variety of crops, and then with the invention of the hoe, the plough, and other agricultural implements, and, finally, with the development of manifold forms of craftsmanship, such as pottery, weaving, metal-smelting, &c.

It is difficult to over-estimate the influence of technical progress on political and social evolution, and also on mental processes. The size of primitive communities is limited, in the first instance, by the difficulty of obtaining food-stuffs with primitive tools. Hunting and collecting tribes require a comparatively large area from which to obtain their food. The cultivation of the soil or the keeping of animals enables denser settlements, and an augmented population, to live on the same area. But even in this case there are comparatively strict limits. It was agriculture, making use of the plough, and combined with cattle-breeding, in the stratified communities of early antiquity, which helped to concentrate the population in towns at the principal points of communal life. The size and importance of the settlement in itself brought about quite other conditions in political and social life. In many cases it was the possession of superior weapons and, above all, of superior technical knowledge and skill which placed one ethnical group permanently in a position of superiority to another. This position was reinforced by the idea that mystic magical powers were responsible for greater intelligence and skill. It is, above all, in societies where skill in craftsmanship is highly developed that importance is attached to magical precautions and ceremonies, rather than in communities with only slightly developed technical knowledge. Technical skill (digging the soil) is to be distinguished from magic (spells for fertility) by the first one being the more rational method and in the long run the more efficient one.

Technical knowledge is marked, as already mentioned, by the fact that higher and more developed skill improves and augments inferior and rougher forms of it. The plough is inconceivable without the hoe, and the hoe is inconceivable without the digging-stick and the stone-chisel. On the other hand, cattle-breeding presupposes that a large animal, an ox, a mule, or the like, must be harnessed to the plough. The full development of technique is due not only to discoveries but also to changes which make their appearance during migrations, owing to the necessity of adaptation to new local surroundings. The institutions and arts of alien tribes, more especially, are partly gained through women or prisoners of war, but often considerably altered in the process, so as to suit the cultural system of the adapters. This process of modification, acting in two directions, provides the impulse for further change, and thus, in many ways, also for progress and the acquisition of new arts and knowledge.

The union of different ethnic groups, each possessing its special arts, constitutes, again, the social factor which is favourable to advance in technique, because an exchange of arts among men who are politically and socially united and live comparatively close together is furthered by this process. A result of such intercourse is represented by the discovery of ploughing, already referred to.

To this must be added that every cultural system can only make a selection among the cultural features offered by alien civilizations, choosing what is suitable for the perfection of its own system. It is not rare for such acquisitions to deteriorate and for the art to be practised in a clumsy manner. But this may give rise to a reverse process, which does not necessarily exclude the possibility of this process being followed by other developments.

We gather from this that the non-reversible process of the accumulation of technical knowledge and skill neither follows a single line, nor even several straight lines but that it always passes through social systems of cultural horizons. By 'cultural horizon' is to be understood the entire state of technical knowledge which forms the necessary basis of certain political and social institutions (such as blood-feuds, trial by ordeal, asylum, the organization of septs, &c.) and also of mental concepts (e.g. 'mana', purification, oracles, and the like). We may thus speak of the cultural horizon of hunting and collecting, of that of herding, of elementary garden-cultivation, of hoe-cultivation, and of farming proper. In addition, the entire state of primitive technique up to farming or thereabouts may be taken collectively as a 'large horizon' of inferior technique. The single straight line which ideally represents technical progress is constantly interrupted by this gradual variation of cultural horizons which governs the cumulative character of technics.

But cultural horizons only represent generalized summaries of basic social and mental characteristics dependent on certain technical requisites. It is not until we can define cultural spheres that we can ascertain the exact limits of the spread of skill and knowledge. Such cultural spheres result, however, from the co-operation of people and technics within a certain area. The pastoral people who invaded Africa and mixed with the older inhabitants, forming a stratum above them, while trading and living with them, have thereby introduced a certain modification into the stock of their technical knowledge and formed certain cultural spheres within the cultural horizon of pastoral life, just as the waves of immigrants in the South Sea have there formed separate cultural spheres varying with the vicissitudes of their wanderings and the degree to which they have mingled with other races.

In discussing the diffusion of individual articles and arts we are surprised by resemblances found in widely separated countries and even continents. The question how such resemblances are to be explained, whether by parallelism, convergence, or transference, must be dealt with briefly in this connexion. We can no more apply cut and dried rules to concrete products than to social institutions. For material products are, as everybody knows, not merely made for exhibition in museums, but usually serve a special purpose in the cultural life of man. As has already been hinted, therefore, the same object, the same throwing-knife, may serve at one time as a weapon, at another as an object of worship, or yet again as a household utensil; the boomerang is a weapon in Australia but an object of worship in the New Hebrides and the Solomon Islands. Thus the mental background must not be lost sight of even in the case of material objects. And further, objects, such as pots, of which the occurrence is reported in any given region, have not necessarily been made where we find them. In addition to this, tribes vary greatly in their readiness to adopt innovations in implements for obtaining food, in weapons, dwellings, ornaments, means of locomotion, or manufactured products.

But even in the matter of obtaining food, we must take into consideration the whole tradition of life and the whole cultural system in estimating the readiness with which novelties are accepted. Attention must be drawn to the extraordinary difficulty found by hunter tribes in passing over to another cultural horizon, such as that of pastoral life or tillage, to the dread of agriculture felt by pastoral peoples, and to the fact that peoples in the digging-stick stage of agriculture have no skill in the treatment of flocks and herds. Hence, we can only expect new technical methods of obtaining food to be adopted by a tribe with the same cultural horizon as the innovators. The adoption of food technics alien to the system must be preceded by profound social dislocations, such as the acquisition of alien women and thereby blending with alien races. It is otherwise in the case of the acquisition of weapons. In this case geographical considerations may come into play, e.g., the need of special wood for making bows. If the suitable wood cannot be obtained, the throwing-stick may replace the bow. Social tradition certainly plays an important part in adoption of new designs in building.

§ 3. In order to gain a general idea of primitive technics it would be necessary to deal with the subject from different points of view.

(1) According to the function of the processes and articles in question. Here we have to consider in the first instance the obtaining of food, next, the cooking of food and all the preparations connected therewith, such as fire-making, the fabrication of vessels, and the like; then, means of transport: sledges, boats, beasts of burden, and the like. In this connexion, the mutual dependence of functions, such as food-procuring with house-building, or of clothing with ornament, already makes its appearance. The cultural horizon determined by the state of technics makes its influence most decisively felt in the manner of obtaining food, whereby the remaining arts of life are simultaneously determined to a very considerable extent. It is only necessary to recall what implements and weapons are required by hunting tribes where food is collected by the women, and in what way the more abundant technique afforded by the sedentary life of gardeners and hoe agriculturists again give rise to further requirements involving new arrangements (store-houses, conservation); and, further, how the different processes required by cattle-breeding, such as milking (pots, pails) or the employment of the animals for pack purposes and riding (halters, saddles, carts) have, to a certain extent, a fructifying effect on technique. From this arise certain associations between peoples who obtain their food in the same way. But the different forms of skill also overlap; the same articles can be employed in functionally different ways, as weapons used for hunting or battle; the large carrying-bags used by the Bergdama women for bringing in field produce are used at night as coverings; indeed, certain

forms of bows in New Guinea are used indifferently as digging-sticks or spears, the playing bow of the children, as a musical instrument, &c.

(2) Technical products can also be differentiated according to the material: whether made of wood, stone, earth, metal, vegetable fibre, skins, bones, or the like. In primitive technics the whole process of production is usually carried out by one person or in one family. For instance, in New Guinea the man takes the threads obtained from certain aerial roots in the forest and spins them, but he then hands them over to his wife to work into a net or for securing the finished net to a wooden frame. Various materials are employed for the same articles, as, for instance, arrow- and spear-heads of stone or bone, axe-heads of shell or stone and the like.

The distribution of the individual materials varies with the cultural horizon, with the state of development of technique, and also with the way in which life is built up. Thus we find soft wood principally among forest hunters in the tropics; bone, horn, and teeth among Arctic hunters or the cattle-keepers of the steppes; the more easily worked stones (flint, soap-stone) in other parts of the world; shells among coastal peoples, and so on.

(3) The available tools and implements can further be differentiated according as certain principles of physics are applied in the different processes. In this connexion such things as wedges and levers must be considered, and also the principle of elasticity in spring-traps or in bows and the like.

(4) Another differentiation consists in the primary purpose which an object has to serve, whether for cutting (knife), or for penetration (dagger, spear), or for throwing (boomerang), or for discharge (arrow), or as a trap, or as a cooking utensil, and so forth.

(5) A distinction must also be made between simple tools and implements and complicated machines, even such elementary ones as the plough, the cart, contrivances for drawing water or for irrigation, a tread-wheel, &c. These complicated machines are exclusively the products of archaic civilizations, and, where they have found their way into primitive forms of culture, they must be attributed to later transference.

(6) Finally, a distribution of implements according to socio-logical points of view would be apposite, namely to what extent they are connected with men's work and to what extent with women's work. For the separate working spheres of the sexes are

also connected with quite different implements and tools of their own. In places where ethnic agglomerations or stratification make their appearance and where, finally, social groups for separate forms of activity have been specialized, certain implements, tools, and forms of procedure are intimately connected with the families, septs, clans, and castes in question who practise a special art.

We must, however, also raise the question of what is to be understood by technics. The objects of what is called material culture are the products of technics, and the study of these products naturally begins with observing the appearance of these objects, of their shape and of the material from which they have been produced. It is only later that we turn our attention to the method and the processes employed in making implements and tools. The student of prehistoric times is denied direct observation of the different methods themselves, and, as regards the kind of skill and the dexterity employed in making an article, he is compelled to rely, to a very large extent, upon guess-work. And in doing this, the ethnographical investigation of still existing primitive arts can provide him with valuable hints.

It is much more difficult to gain information regarding fossilized forms of articles and, in particular, the connexion between their various stages and variants. And this information also requires supplementing by the study of methods and processes in the making of different shapes, which should be compared with each other and the relationship established, as in the case of pottery.

Individual articles can, again, be regarded from different points of view.

(*a*) According to shape, size, form, and proportions, and, further, according to the number and kind of accessory tools used in the making, such as casting moulds for pots or metal articles, scaffolding in the building of funeral mounds, and so forth. This includes detachable or undetachable, but still essential, parts of the article, such as the removable or irremovable tip of an arrow or spear, or the handle of a basket or pot.

(*b*) According to the suitability and quality of the material or materials for the article in question and its parts, and also according to alterations in these respects (stone, clay, metal).

(*c*) As regards the construction, the relation of the materials and the relative shapes of the separate parts must be considered, as to whether they are loosely or firmly attached to each other, as in the case of axes, bark canoes, or in the structure of stone graves and the like.

(*d*) In the use of an article, the movement made by it refers to the mechanism of its employment, whereby, under certain circumstances the question arises whether the relative position of the parts changes, and how the course of the effective process is arranged, as in the handling of harpoons, oars, hand-mills or rubbing-stones, and weaving appliances.

(*e*) Finally there arises the question of how the raw material is obtained and adapted for use; by reducing it to small pieces, chopping bits off, sorting, and the like. We will, therefore, have to differentiate, (1) the providing, which often necessitates longer or shorter journeys; (2) the preparation or cleaning, as that of potter's clay; (3) the formation and preparation of the raw material, e.g. the mixing of potter's clay with water, the preparation of pigments; (4) the binding and application of the prepared material, e.g. kneading of coils for the building up of the pot.

§ 4. Material objects do not change in the same way as do legends and myths or social institutions. While mental forms appear to be constantly in a state of flux, material formations are much more rigid. Under favourable circumstances the same shapes are retained for thousands of years, as in certain cases, for example, in Egypt and the Sudan.

On the other hand, the kind of material and the attitude of man in relation to it limit the number of ways in which it can be used; so that in this case, also, the law of limited possibilities easily becomes an urge toward converging shapes that must be investigated in each separate case.

Every single object, every needle or brooch, every vessel of vegetable fibre or basket-work, wood or clay, used in everyday life has its own history and its destination as a type in use. In its original and earlier forms it has played a formative part in the lives of successive generations and cultures, each of which had contributed its share, by head and hand, in shaping it.

For it is the peculiar fate of utensils that, once they have been produced and adopted among the traditional possessions of a society, they are accepted as part of natural order and hold man in their spell. We need not here think of the mechanical appliances which forcibly introduce an alien mechanical rhythm into man's work, for the tools and implements of primitive forms of culture have not yet reached this stage. They appear almost exclusively as prolongations or extensions of human organs; they demand, it is true, special skill in using them, even the digging-stick or the stone axe, but their employment is left to the discretion of the individual, and the work allowed to develop unhindered. This applies even to the primitive loom, the so-called small plank weaving. The origin of implements and forms of tools has a history of which the psychological and sociological roots and complications have so far been comparatively little investigated. For it is not sufficient to determine the purely technical changes, merely to explain the relationship to the natural surroundings, but the problem of invention, transference, modification, and adaptation can only be explained by the social and mental attitude of the individual in the conquest of nature. He, it must be remembered, does not stand alone, but is always connected in manifold ways, on the one hand, with the unnumbered generations who have gone before and, on the other, with those of his contemporaries who are in touch with him.

In any case we must imagine that the rate of progress of inventions is very slow in primitive forms of culture, the reason for this being that these small societies are usually in an excellent state of equilibrium. The adoption of inventions must, therefore, be generally regarded as resulting from a modification of this state of equilibrium which, especially in the case of transference to a new abode, produces certain changes in habits. There is, further, a second factor, the meeting with other human groups, which, especially through the acquisition of alien women by the group in question, tends to introduce alien habits and arts.

Both in the case of new inventions and of the acquisition of alien arts, a certain sifting process always comes into action which causes the group to select from among the numerous novelties offered, whether originating with its own members or outside, only those which are suited to its own culture. It is, therefore, not merely a question of inventions and more or less accidental ideas, nor yet only of the possibilities of contact with other forms of culture, but of an active choice among the novelties offered, which makes for technical progress and, further, for cultural change.

§ 5. To illustrate this, attention is invited to the standard works of Nordenskiöld ['18, '24]. A thorough investigation of the relations between several tribes and their South-American neighbours reveals a constantly changing distribution of the various elements of technical culture and, on the other hand, always raises the question whether, in the case of the extraordinarily sporadic occurrence of one or other form of technical knowledge, this is due to transference or to personal invention. But in this connexion it must be clearly understood that all processes of transference and adoption are much more complicated than we are apt to assume if we follow an *a priori* historical classification (Nordenskiöld ['24], p. 229). An article may be invented in one region while it has continuously existed in another. For technical processes can even be lost, in given circumstances, e.g. pottery-making or canoe-building, if the local or other conditions of existence are interfered with. There is no parallel in South America to spinning with a fork as practised by the Bororò. The same applies to the basket in which the spindle is kept, which still exists among the Baure and was formerly in use among the Mojo. It is possible that the chains of the Huari are an imitation of metal chains obtained from white men or Negroes; though it is remarkable that a different material was employed, and the chains were used as hair ornaments. Nevertheless, the Huari chain may after all have been an independent invention. The small measuring-stick with which the Yuracàre make their combs has not been observed anywhere else; but they may conceivably have adopted it from the Quichua. The Indians of this region probably hit upon the idea of making a substitute for grinding-stones out of burnt clay. Extraordinary importance attaches above all to the making of substitutes in the domain of technical innovations. This includes, for instance, the substitution of clay and melted glass in the manufacture of beads and other articles for stone, as in ancient Egypt.

A special invention must be recorded among the Yuracàre and Chimane, who attach the feathers to the arrow in a peculiar manner. In its extreme form, this little invention was, perhaps, not made until d'Orbigny had visited this region about ninety years ago. The duel arrows of the Yuracàre also appear to have no parallel elsewhere; they are really simple bird arrows of refined form. The peculiar grafting of a rodent's tooth on a very long shaft in order to give the arrow balance also probably occurs only among the Huanyam and Huari. The pipes of the Huari, which resemble Pan pipes, also appear to be found only among this tribe. A number of Indian tribes have climbing-rings, but only the Chama make such rings in advance and carry them about with them to be used when required. Whenever other Indians require a ring, they make it every time by bending the stem of a liana or any similar material. The way in which the Chimane tie up their canoes appears to be quite original: a hole is made in the bow of the boat through which a stick can be stuck, which is very practical in view of the many sandbanks, especially during the dry season. This arrangement has no parallel in South America. As the canoe is probably a comparatively recent cultural element in this region, this arrangement must also be considered as a comparatively recent invention. The tassel on the throwing-stick of the Mojo appears to be quite original. The use of the bamboo for blow-pipes is known to the Huanyam alone of all the Indian tribes now living.

Every tribe has made its own minor improvements or changes in weapons, ornaments, household utensils, &c. Small modifications in the form of the arrow-head, or the manner of fixing it, are not very noteworthy in themselves, but they must not be under-valued; for they are just the sort of processes that exhibit the incessant changes which go on in the construction and use of tools among primitive peoples. Besides this, individual tribes have, as might be expected, taken over a number of cultural elements from one another. For instance, a newly arrived tribe may at the present day encounter elements which are locally very old, but with which the newcomers were not yet familiar. Some of the Guarayù, for example, have exchanged their method of spinning for another since they settled in their present abode.

It is particularly worthy of note that, where languages differ greatly, this exchange of cultural elements does not, as a rule, produce an equal degree of culture in neighbouring tribes, as, for instance, in the Chaco, on the upper Xingù River, and so on. In this region only one zone has arrived at cultural assimilation, namely in the regions between the Rio Beni and the Rio Madre de Dios, where the Tacana-speaking Tambopata-Guarayo (Chama) and the Pano-speaking Atsahuaca and Yamiaca have a uniform culture. On the other hand, tribes with closely related languages, like the Atsahuaca and Chacobo, on the one hand, and the Tacana-speaking Tambopata-Guarayo and Cavina, on the other, have very different forms of culture, although living under similar natural conditions. The Atsahuaca have a much poorer culture than the Chacobo, although the two tribes are closely related. The latter have made permanent settlements and build large four-cornered or eight-cornered huts, while the former incline to be nomadic and only erect temporary huts. The Chacobo use large flat roasting platters, bark canoes, the Pan pipes; they have a process for making baskets, the cotton bow, stools made of laths nailed together, a wooden peg at the lower end of the arrow, and build store-rooms on piles, &c. All these cultural components are lacking among the Atsahuaca. It may be conjectured that the Atsahuaca and the Chacobo were disrupted before the introduction of the banana into these regions, as they have quite different words for this plant. This also applies to tobacco. On the other hand, they have very similar expressions for cotton, maize, sweet potatoes, and manioc. The question therefore arises whether the cultural differences between the Atsahuaca and the Chacobo are to be attributed to their having altered their culture under the influence of the neighbouring tribes, or whether the one tribe does not really belong to the Pano but has only been 'pano-ized'. Without going into this question, which is merely of local interest, attention will only be drawn to the fact that another hunting tribe, for instance, the Siriono, speak a Guarani language which is probably not their original speech but was only subsequently adopted by them (Nordenskiöld ['24], pp. 225 et seq.). We have similar information regarding hunting and female-collector tribes in other continents, in Africa and in the Sunda Islands. Here the problem of the possession of technical skill and material culture is involved with that of the language, but, especially, with the whole conduct of living.

§ 6. The investigations of Nordenskiöld regarding the South-American tribes above mentioned have been reproduced in such detail because they are thoroughly typical for other continents and countries and because, in this one case, unusually searching and reliable inquiries made by an investigator on the spot illuminate the whole problem of invention, transference, influence, and cultural connexions. They show, however, also how important it is not to select individual details, but to investigate the entire culture, and, indeed, not only to compare the objects which are being collected to-day, but also to pursue the technical processes themselves in detail, to pay regard to the modifications these have undergone in each tribe, and to ascertain how articles have been acquired, either by exchange or purchase. Nothing but such a really carefully conducted registration of the distribution of individual objects and also of the little modifications and discoveries can provide us, on the one hand, with clear insight into the history of the material culture of a district and, on the other, explain the general problem to which allusion has already been made.

Loewenthal (p. 231), for instance, arrives at the conclusion that the most important economic antiquities of the Iroquois are of alien origin: the maize knife and the maize store-room are Mexican, the rubbing-stones have their origin in the Antilles and in South America, the maize mortar, perhaps, and the maize receptacle, probably are north-eastern Asiatic, and he believes that he is justified in describing the spoon with chain links and a carved bowl as Swedish. As the date for the borrowing he takes a period before A.D. 1003 for the maize store-room, and the year A.D. 1638 for the spoon with the chain as a *terminus post quem*. He considers the cultural stream from the Antilles and South America as the most important, the next being the influence from north-eastern Asia. Where early Scandinavian influence is found in the area influenced by the Iroquois, it has made its way in from the Arctic, and then only sporadically. The track followed about the year A.D. 986 appears to have been from South Sweden, via Iceland, the west coast of Greenland, Hudson Strait, Hudson Bay, the Nelson River, the Red River, and Lake Superior.

With regard to inventions, we must also consider, in addition to the more or less gradual variations already described and the cautious feeling in different directions, some other modes of invention. Harrison has described these (*Man*, 26, 27) as 'mutations' and subdivides them again into either 'free' mutations or cross-wise mutations. As instances of the first he gives the transition from the spear with a rigid tip to a harpoon with a removable head and catching-rope; the use of a strap for the borer whereby this becomes a 'twirling-stick', the addition of a second attachment to the steering rudder which converted it into a 'steering gear' with only circular motion, &c. The rubbing and polishing of flint, which probably arose as the result of the working on softer stones, and thus represents the employment of experience gained on another material, may be considered as the result of a cross-wise mutation.

A special form of invention is the endeavour to obtain certain results, and in this case we may speak of 'guiding' factors. How far such guiding factors, which play a prominent part at the present time, may have been decisive in primitive technics is, however, a question which must remain undecided. For instance, the transference of pottery-making from women to men and to the head of the family in particular, owing to the intensification of the work due to agglomeration, stratification, and the obligation to make contributions, may have led to improvements.

Great importance doubtless attaches, as already mentioned, to the replacement of one material by another, and often gives the fresh products the appearance of an invention, for instance, the replacement of stone or gourd receptacles by those made of clay, metal, or basket-work, or that of flint axe-heads or knives by those of the same shape made of metal.

§ 7. Finally, the deterioration and retrogression of technics must be taken into consideration.

(*a*) The shape may be affected by inadequate substitutes (e.g. when a change of habitat occurs), or the quality impaired by faulty constructions (e.g. imitation by people of inferior skill). Within the same people a shifting of attention (either over a long period of time or by some sudden event) may bring about another mental attitude and other interests may result in a neglect of traditional skill.

(*b*) The loss of whole groups of arts is also possible in a society, as, for instance, owing to the dying-out of families in which a technical process was principally or exclusively practised. This can happen without substantial modification of the way of living, as it did for instance on the islands of Torres Strait, owing to the dying-out of the families who were able to make the large canoes which formerly traded far away on the south coast of New Guinea; or owing to tribes which formerly lived on the coast withdrawing to the interior.

The utensils of the Bergdama people of South-West Africa consist principally of vessels made of soft wood, which is obtained from a low tree which attains a considerable girth and has a pale green bark. It is dry, and thus becomes tolerably hard without splitting. Should a crack appear, a small red root is looked for, which is reduced to powder and put into the crack, after which the vessel is bound with a leather thong until the parts have united. The vessels are used as troughs or pails for keeping seed-corn or fetching water or for goat's milk. Bottle gourds are obtained from the Ovambo, but the clay pot is the most valuable utensil. Besides the small spoons used in preparing and eating porridge and other food, the digging-stick of the collecting woman is of the greatest importance, and also the traps and snares, the bow and arrows of the hunters (Vedder, pp. 60 et seq.).

§ 8. The making of pots, the most valuable utensils of the Bergdama, appears to have been learned from the neighbouring Herero, but by no means every Bergdama is an expert potter. Only a few of the men have acquired a certain skill in this art. That the pottery-making is done by men in this case may well be connected with the fact that it is probably a question of farm-hands who have come back after working among the Herero and brought the art of pottery-making to the Bergdama. They are unwilling to reveal where they obtain the potter's clay. An ant-hill often provides suitable material. This is broken up and stamped into lumps, all hard portions being carefully removed. The clay is then mixed with water and kneaded until it is smooth. The vessel is first dried in the open air and then baked at a blazing fire (Vedder, pp. 61 et seq.).

It is, indeed, not improbable that the method of making pots provided the impulse for the discovery of the smelting of metals (cf. Linné, pp. 123 et seq.).

§ 9. In Peru there were found not only large quantities of bronze utensils and tools but also much pure metallic tin which proves that the Incas (at least Machu Picchu) were familiar with the use of tin and obtained it by smelting kassiterite ore, which they discovered, along with copper, in the seams of Bolivia. It is, therefore, probable that the inhabitants of the Inca Empire themselves discovered how to alloy tin with copper and the fact that bronze can be better cast and worked and is more suitable for utensils than either tin or copper alone. The comparative regularity of the mixtures appears, in any case, to indicate that the alloys were made on purpose. (Phillips. For the goldsmith's art before the time of Columbus, cf. Rivet.)

The wooden horn used in various neighbourhoods in the interior of New Guinea appears to be an imitation of the shell horn, the use of which is fairly common among the coastal tribes and, to a certain extent, has made its way through barter into the interior. The breaking off of relations between the interior and the coastal tribes, or the middlemen, may, indeed, have led to the substitution of the wooden horn. This horn is extraordinarily widespread and is used for giving the same signals as the shell horn, namely, to announce a death, or the murder of a man, as a call to arms. It is also used when a pig is killed (Beaver, Seligman ['10]). I have often found such horns in northern New Guinea, in the region of the tributaries of the Sepik River. (May they be interpreted as referring in some remote way to connexions with cattle-breeders?)

§ 10. The greatest respect is paid to a man or woman who shows skill in any kind of work and accomplishes it successfully. Among the Maori for example, the skilled wood-carver was a respected and important person in his own village, even if he was a slave. His work was considered as a dignified employment. Even chiefs busied themselves with the carving of wooden beakers, axe-heads, and so forth, and were often absorbed in their work. Although everybody understood this art there were only a few really expert carvers. The knowledge of individual arts was here, as elsewhere, derived from ancestors and particular spirits (Firth ['26]).

§ 11. In order to obtain a conception of the ideas held by graded societies regarding their own activities, attention may be directed to the fact that it is precisely these graded peoples, with more developed handicrafts, who encompass their activities with all sorts of so-called magical accessories. Yet we must not forget that these societies themselves are not aware of any difference between magical and practical means. The distinction between magical accessories and essential functions is made by us. Among the Maoris of New Zealand the practical action had to be supplemented by the magical, if successful results were desired. Regarded from a psychological point of view it is here a question of various things, very frequently of exercises in concentration.

Similar procedure is observed among the Maoris in connexion with various arts used in obtaining food, such as spearing fish, setting rat- and bird-traps, climbing trees, and the like. The magical rites (so called by us) which accompany all forms of activity, tattooing and cutting, house- and canoe-building, &c., are not without a useful effect on the working process and the mentality of the work-people, whom they inspire with confidence in the success of the work, and so ensure its completion (cf. Firth ['26]).

§ 12. In conquering nature, a knowledge of navigation and skill in its practice are of great importance, not only in building vessels

E

but also in guiding and steering them, especially on the open sea. Observation of the heavens and setting a course according to the position of the constellations and the sun are the only available data.

It is not possible here to go into the question whether the knowledge of this system of orientation was first gained by the Micronesians in the course of their migrations or brought with them, at least in part, from the country of their origin. The knowledge possessed by the present natives of the Marshall Islands is, therefore, specially worthy of note, for it not only exists in the range of their ideas but has been given concrete form in maps drawn to scale. Kubary ['85, '95] was the first to draw attention to their astronomical knowledge and its application to navigation. Sarfert's ['19–20] investigations (cf. Erdland, pp. 16 et seq.) showed that the inhabitants of the Marshall and Caroline Islands have given names to nearly three dozen stars, the greater number representing constellations; that myths exist regarding these stars and constellations and their relationship to one another; and, further, that the names of the months are taken from constellations. The regular appearance and disappearance of certain constellations in the course of the year were connected with the regular changes of wind and weather.

To the position of the stars a system of orientation on the open sea was attached. This was favoured by the fact that in equatorial regions the courses of the stars are principally east and west, while the meridian is given by the remarkable behaviour of the Pole Star in relation with the other fixed stars. From this fixed point they constructed, on the principle of our compass card, a chart in the form of a radiating star, on which the lines coincide with the points of rising and setting of the fixed stars. It is probable that consideration of the main east–west and north–south movements recognized by them led them to draw the horizon not as a circle but square, as is done in a co-ordination system. In constructing this quadrangular chart, only nineteen of the known and named stars were chosen and in such a way as to place their points of rising and setting at approximately equal intervals.

This system naturally leads to many inaccuracies. The east–west line lies about $8\frac{1}{2}$ degrees too far to the north and, further, the constellations do not provide lines of mathematical regularity. Even the natives are aware of these irregularities. This chart is not identical on all the Central Caroline Islands; indeed, on some of them the knowledge of it seems to have been lost. The number of lines south of Palau is 36, in the Central Carolines 28, and on the Coral Islands, in the neighbourhood of Ruk, 32; but the constellations on which the scheme is based are, in general, the same. On the islands lying to the south of Palau the number of the lines has been increased and new constellations inserted, probably on account of the north-eastern and north-western courses. The lack of large fixed stars in the neighbourhood of the South Pole has caused the Central Caroline Islanders to use various stars of the Southern Cross for fixing the lines in that area. In this way they generally lay down three, but sometimes five, lines. The difference in the attitude of the Caroline Islanders and of that of the inhabitants of the Marshall Islands consists, as has been said, in the kind of orientation. It is only on some of the islands south of Palau that it is customary to mark the lines of the star and the position of the islands with little stones, for instructional purposes. Under these circumstances the knowledge of the chart is confined to comparatively few families, within which it is transmitted from father to son.

As they are unacquainted with the magnetic needle, they have to depend on the visibility of a point of which the direction has been determined, or with the help of which such a direction can be determined as a natural directive constant. When the sky is clear this can be obtained from the stars; but when the sky is cloudy the system of orientation connected with the stars is of no assistance. Among the number of stars visible at the same time there is generally one near the horizon of which the point of rising and setting is thus immediately obvious. In this way they have at once a line on the chart and its opposite line on the horizon, a direction by means of which the chart can be mentally reconstructed. The employment of the chart is more difficult by day than by night, as the sun provides the only means of orientation. But the Caroline Islanders know exactly at what point on the horizon the sun rises or sets at any time in relation to the points of rising and setting of the constellations; in this way one or two lines of the chart are determined and the rest added mentally.

For every journey between any two islands, the Micronesian captain knows by heart, through long experience, the positions of the islands with reference to the lines on the chart. The number of courses outside these is, comparatively speaking, not very large, yet there are very great differences in this respect. The captains of the Central Caroline Islands know as many as one hundred courses.

The Caroline Islanders supply the deficiencies in their chart by advancing from one island to the next by stages, limiting their voyages to the months when wind, weather, and astronomical conditions are favourable, by interrupting a voyage when the wind is against them, and, finally, on a voyage, between two given islands, by having in mind a third island which may be called an 'emergency island'. Should unfavourable conditions make it impossible to reach either the starting-point or the goal of the journey they take refuge on this island, which lies off the course.

Such a deviation to reach the emergency island naturally compels the captain, on the ground of his experience of the normal time taken for the journey, and of his estimate of the speed, to change his course to the necessary direction. This expedient, which is known as 'dead reckoning', was also used in Europe before the introduction of the log at the end of the sixteenth century.

The usefulness of the emergency island is naturally dependent on its position relative to the course. The method of calculating the length of the journey should be noted in this connexion; it is reckoned according to a measure of length called *etak*. The number of *etak* is identical with the number of the lines over which the emergency island apparently passes on the horizon in the course of the voyage. In doing this, the first line passed at the beginning of the voyage is not counted. Thus the *etak* represents a circular measure of the size of one line or an angular measure of the size of the angle at the centre of the circle belonging to the curve. The captains remember the number of *etak* for most journeys. There is naturally no relation between *etak* and nautical miles, i.e. between the angle and the actual length of the voyage. The frequent cases of loss of bearings and consequent disasters at sea are doubtless attributable in part to the inadequacy of their navigation. On the other hand, this system makes it possible, in spite of very limited technical resources, to steer a course with sufficient accuracy when out of sight of land (see also Sarfert ['19], pp. 218 et seq.). (For knowledge of the stars and constellations in the Malay Archipelago see Maass. For the different kinds of canoes and boats, which are of great importance for migrations, especially across the Pacific Ocean, see Friederici ['29], pp. 27 et seq.)

§ 13. In addition to the method of trapping by pitfalls, practised by the ancient palaeolithic hunters, we must not forget that of hunting with sharp arrows, or spears either sharpened with fire and smoothed with stones or provided with stone heads. As a matter of fact, wood can be cut and worked with flint implements with comparatively little trouble (cf. Pfeiffer). The way in which the Baining people of New Britain make wooden spears is described by Parkinson as follows: the shaft is scraped till roughly cylindrical and its end cut to a point and then hardened in fire. In spite of their coarse workmanship, they are dangerous weapons in the hands of the Baining people, who practice throwing them from early youth and, in time, attain astonishing skill and dexterity. The date of the first manufacture of such weapons must be assigned to the Chelléan period, or even earlier, and they have obviously been improved with the development of flint implements. It is not until neo-palaeolithic times that bone and horn tips to weapons made their appearance. The Tasmanians, though their implements were extraordinarily clumsy, were yet able to make long wooden spears, pointed boomerangs 20 inches long, &c. La Billardière speaks of a throwing-spear 16 to 18 feet long, and says that this weapon was nothing more than a long, straight stick which they had not even troubled to make quite smooth, but which was pointed at one end. Melville describes the spear as a straight stick from 5 to 8 feet long, made of the hard wood of certain trees, the bark being removed and the stick pointed at the thicker end. Widowson describes it as being about 12 feet long and as thick as a man's little finger, made of the wood of the tea-tree, hardened at one end, and provided with a sharp point by burning and scraping with a flint. Fourneaux mentions sharpening with shells. Henderson states that straight branches of various bushes are selected for use as spears. After they had been dried, hardened over a fire, and carefully pointed, it required but little effort to produce a serious wound. Backhouse mentions that the Tasmanians carefully try the balance of their spears, shaped like a well-made fishing rod, by holding them in their teeth. The notched spears and shields were confined to the northern tribes. There is only one mention of a poisoned spear (Ling Roth ['90], p. 79 et seq.).

It must be remarked that bows and arrows were lacking among the Tasmanians, and also among most of the Australian tribes except those in the north. It is, therefore, a mistake to suppose that early palaeolithic man was acquainted with the bow or with traps depending on the elasticity of wood. These can, at the earliest, be ascribed to the neo-palaeolithic age. For this reason it is quite out of place to emphasize the bow as a weapon specially characteristic of present-day primitive hunters. The idea of transference makes it clear that these tribes adopted the bow from their neighbours at some period in their history. For the bow and arrow were well adapted to the life of a hunter tribe, and there existed from the start a readiness to adopt them and include them in the culture of these tribes who were otherwise poorly provided with technical knowledge.

As regards the boomerang, there are various forms of it in Australia and the adjacent parts of the world. The fact that the distribution of the boomerang was quite different in earlier times, when it must have played an important part, is proved not only by the evidence of its existence in ancient Egypt, but also by its inclusion as a symbol in the cuneiform script.

The distribution of the boomerang, which is erroneously taken to be confined to Australia, can be proved to extend to the New Hebrides and even to the Solomon Islands, in particular to the southern point of Bougainville. In these regions special ceremonial importance is attached to this weapon. This circumstance, in particular, indicates that the object has long been associated with at least some part of the population from which a community, or an agglomeration of communities, is descended. In Australia, the so-called native land of the boomerang, it is only used as a weapon. Similarly, the throwing-knife of the Sudan tribes in Africa has become a religious object among some Bantu tribes and a household utensil among others.

The boomerang of Espiritu Santo on the New Hebrides is so constructed that it does not return to the thrower, yet it makes turns in its flight like those made by the Australian boomerang. A special feature of its flight is that it touches the ground a few metres in front of the thrower. The people maintain that they have always possessed the boomerang; it also occurs in their legends. It is particularly prominent in a ceremony called *wōs*, in which *kava* is drunk at intervals of five days, the young men throwing the boomerang while the old men drink *kava*. This ceremony, which is held at intervals of more than a year, is connected with the secret societies locally called *suqwe*. This is the same designation as *sukwe* or *suque* on the Banks Islands. One of the septs of Nogugu, called Taliu, is believed to be descended from the boomerang. According to tradition, the Taliu are a branch of another sept, the Tapulu. It is said that the Tapulu were throwers of boomerangs, and attempted to throw them in a valley over a hill called Liu. One man finally succeeded in throwing his boomerang as far as Liu; but when the people went to look for the boomerang they did not find it, but a woman instead. When they asked her if she had seen the boomerang, she replied, 'No, I am the boomerang'. She became the ancestress of the Taliu.

The boomerang occurs characteristically in a part of Santa Cruz where the bisection of a tribe forms the basis of their marriage rules. On the other hand, the boomerang, as representative of Australian culture, has so far been connected with totemism and patriarchal institutions. The connexion with the secret society and the drinking of *kava* makes it seem very doubtful whether there is any justification for regarding the boomerang as a characteristic of Australian culture. It seems much more likely that the boomerang was introduced into Australia and into the Melanesian regions above mentioned from the same source (Rivers ['14], ii. 83; ['15], No. 59).

PART II
TYPES OF ECONOMIC LIFE

I

HOMOGENEOUS COMMUNITIES OF MEN AS HUNTERS AND TRAPPERS, WOMEN AS COLLECTORS

§ 1. Common traits and variations. § 2. Methods of hunting. § 3. Mutual help of Eskimo. § 4. Two points of interest. § 5. Bergdama women as food collectors.

§ **1.** The lives of hunters and trappers show more variety of form than we should expect, for these people are essentially dependent on the animals and plants of the country where they live. Therefore, they must act differently according to whether they live in the tropical forests of the Congo, Ceylon, or Sumatra, in the polar regions of Greenland or Alaska, or in the deserts or steppes of Africa or Asia. In prehistoric times also, their life in different parts of Europe or Asia must undoubtedly have been largely determined by the local peculiarities of climate, flora, and fauna. They have, moreover, a tendency to specialize in some degree, some people, for instance, preferring to live on big game, while others have a partiality for fish.

But in spite of this, their lives are, nevertheless, dominated by certain common traits. Their communities can never be very large, but, in fact, vary from twelve or twenty to fifty head. They consist of a number of small families, a family being made up of a mother with her children, who uses a special hearth and is protected by a man. The men more or less live together on their hunting expeditions and, as in the case of the Veddas of Ceylon, are often away for many days, weeks, or even months before they return to the more stable camp of the women. Among other tribes, as, for instance, the Bergdama or the Australian aborigines, as also among those hunters who live in deserts and steppes, the whole community has a fairly permanent camp, though this has to be moved from time to time according to the movements of the game, the ripening of wild fruits and other produce, or the season when crabs, shrimps, or small fish are abundant.

§ **2.** Let us consider the economic life of hunting-tribes. The methods of hunting are numerous and always depend on the conditions of local life. Baiting, stalking, enticing, snaring, and the setting of traps or laying down of poison are known almost everywhere.

Livingstone's account of the Bushmen who hunted disguised as ostriches is well known. The feathers of an ostrich are made into a disguise and the head of the animal stuck on a stick, in order to approach a herd while imitating the movements of the bird. Then the Bushmen shoot them with arrows at short range.

All this shows a certain technique, and is by no means a mere individual search for food. It is usually small family associations (clans or septs) who go hunting as a group within a certain area, as, for instance, among the different Algonquin tribes (cf. MacLeod, p. 448), or among the Eskimo or the Bushmen.

§ 3. Mutual help also constitutes a characteristic of Eskimo economics in Greenland. In particular, in times of distress, no one can suffer from hunger, while, on the other hand, every one has a share in the surplus. In these tiny groups, bound together by kinship, it is, of course, easy to carry out these principles. The spoil must, therefore, belong to the whole village so that the bread-winner of each separate family may not have to go out every day; and when the catch fails, there is no privation. With this goes the willingness to lend one another boats, arrows, fishing-rods, or other tackle. If anything is damaged, the owner bears the full loss, without compensation from the borrower. It is only if some one has borrowed something without the knowledge of the owner, that he is compelled to make restitution for the object lost. These communistic traits, as with all hunters and collectors, imply the absence of private property, the place of which is taken by the right of the sovereign tribe to the hunting-ground. There is, however, no bar to ownership on the part of families or private persons. In rivers where salmon are abundant, dams are built to gather the fish, and any interference with these by strangers is strongly resented. Floating timber belongs to him who first finds it in the water. In order to maintain his right, he must bring it to shore, draw it up beyond the water-mark, and put some kind of sign on it. Should any one take it, he would ever after be despised. The tent belongs to all who live in it. The father of the family has the disposal of the women's boats. But the things with which private ownership is especially concerned are the kayak (a light sealskin boat), the kayak dress, and the requisites for trapping. These no one is allowed to take away, because it is by their means that the man feeds himself and his family. He must always find them where he left them. They are very rarely lent. Snowshoes are treated in a similar manner; so are household implements: knives, hatchets, saws, and scrapers. In the same way, the women consider their sewing materials as their personal belongings. But what the Eskimos lack is the desire to amass riches, for everything brought home from the hunt goes to be divided among the community, according to rules supported by long tradition. There are only a few kinds of animals which the hunter is allowed to keep back for himself and his family. One of these is the Atak or Greenland seal. But even from these he is expected to give a small piece of fat to the kayak man who greets him immediately after the take, and also to every child in the settlement. Other kinds of seals are shared, according to certain rules, among those who were present, or assisted at, the catch. Sometimes, even, every house in the settlement receives a piece. This last rule applies more especially to the walrus and several kinds of whale. Other rules, again, obtain when several men have attacked a reindeer, or a seal, with arrows or other weapons, or when they go fishing.

It is clear that this economic arrangement has the effect of binding the small Eskimo communities strongly together in good and bad times. These communal tendencies are not affected by the wife being considered the property of her husband, or by his right to lend or exchange her. Nevertheless, as a rule, she is well treated. She carries home the booty, prepares the food, cures the hides, makes the clothes, and takes care of the house or tent.

§ 4. Women only catch the Kapelan fish, which occasionally come in such dense swarms that they can be ladled with buckets into the boats. They are dried on the rocks, and are chiefly gathered as a winter store. As among all hunting and fishing peoples, the men's only occupation when at home is to clean and repair their hunting and trapping gear, at most to do a little bone-carving. For the rest, they tell stories, eat, loaf, and sleep (Nansen, p. 90 et seq.). The severe strain of hunting is followed at home by utter relaxation.

The statement of A. Radcliffe-Brown (['22], p. 50) concerning the inhabitants of the Andaman Islands is worth noticing. He finds that laziness is considered as anti-social behaviour. Every man is expected to contribute his share towards providing the rest with food. If any one evades this obligation, nothing further is said, except when a young unmarried man is in question. He continues to receive food from the others, but he sinks in the

estimation of his camp comrades, and finally loses the respect of
his people.

§ 5. The report on the Bergdama of South-West Africa gives us
some particulars about the life of the women who gather food. The
camp sib has to thank her for more or less regular nourishment. It
is she, not the hunter, who comes home every day with a well-filled
bag. From this springs the proverb: the sib is a woman's affair,
that is to say, without the woman's activity, the sib would not be
able to exist. Nevertheless, she takes care in the first place of herself and her children, but she regularly gives something of her
store to the man. In exchange for this, she has the right to certain
pieces of the game brought in by him, after it has first been carried
to the sacred fire. Here again, the maintenance of several wives
eases rather than increases the burden of providing a livelihood.
The most important part of the woman's equipment is the leather
bag which she slings over her left shoulder before starting. In it
she brings home the produce of the fields. To her outfit belongs
the digging-stick, with which she roots up tubers, &c., out of the
ground. (In spite of the poverty of the households, there are
plenty of wooden utensils, buckets, pots, tubs, spoons, and so on.)
When collecting, she knows the places where, at certain seasons, it
is possible to find tubers, roots, bulbs, and fruit. The shovel-like
end of the digging-stick, which is easily blunted, she sharpens on
a flat stone which is not too rough. She is usually accompanied
by her daughters, who from their earliest childhood begin to learn
where the most produce is to be found. But this produce is always
considered as the common property of all members of the family,
among whom it is divided according to certain rules, young and
old each obtaining a share. After the rainy season, when the small
bulbs, which form the bulk of the provender, are ripe, a certain
day is fixed, on which nothing else may be taken from the places
where it is customary to dig. The bulbs so brought home must
first be ceremonially roasted, and tasted by the 'food-master',
before the new crops are licensed for general use. On other
occasions, food is divided by the woman who has brought it home,
and the man is not allowed to take anything from her store without
her permission. For in his wife's hut, the husband is a guest so far
as eating and drinking are concerned. His special sphere is connected with the sacred fire (Vedder, pp. 39, 57 et seq.).

II

HOMOGENEOUS COMMUNITIES OF HUNTERS, TRAPPERS, AND AGRICULTURISTS

§ 1. An illustration from New Guinea, the Kai people. § 2. In the temperate zones. § 3. The significance of plants.

§ **1.** The community of the Kai people (Papuans), in the interior of the Saddle Mountains on the north coast of New Guinea, may serve as a representative of an unstratified society of hunters, trappers, and women collectors. Like other Papuans, they chiefly subsist on yams, taro, and other tubers which are planted everywhere, while potatoes are little known and seldom found. When the community thinks of cultivating a piece of land, every dweller in the village pegs out his claim in advance. First the men cut down the small trees and undergrowth, let it dry, and then set fire to it. In this way the larger trees are also destroyed, and after the burning only the bare trunks are left. Sometimes they first kill the trees by peeling off their bark in rings round the stem. They usually leave the larger charred stumps in the ground, because it would take too much trouble to pull them up. It is some months before they start to clear the place of leaves, twigs, and branches in order to prepare it for the planting. The men loosen the ground with pointed stakes, while the women put in the seedlings they have already prepared. The fields are by no means uniformly well cultivated. Individual allotments are often separated by a rough fencing of sticks. The Kai people finally surround the whole field with a barrier of stakes or bamboo canes in order to defend it from the pigs, who are in the habit of rooting up the tubers. Every part owner of the field has to build a part of this fence. In addition to the staple fruits they also usually cultivate sugar-cane, bananas, and other vegetables. By the time of harvest, the weeds, which are not too often cleared away by the women, have already grown to a considerable extent. Pulling up taro and yams when ripe often takes much trouble. From the former the women do not usually obtain provisions for more than a few days, but the yams, which keep better, they preserve in pits or on stands. After the harvest the land is allowed to lie fallow and soon returns to jungle. The natives are fond of returning after a few years to previously cultivated fields, as they are comparatively easy to clear. Fruit trees, such as coco-nut palms, sago palms, pandanus, mango, and almond trees, as well as betel palms and tobacco, are principally planted by the men; bananas and sugar-cane by either sex, and in some cases tobacco also. The wild animals used for food include the kangaroo, the cassowary, the bush turkey or buzzard (*Talegallus*), also fishes, crabs, eels, and large snakes, as well as frogs, toads, termites, caterpillars, certain spiders, grasshoppers, and such-like. The most highly esteemed food, which forms the staple dish at every feast, is the flesh of pigs, which run wild in the primeval forest, but are also kept after a primitive fashion in the villages. It is extremely probable that pigs were first brought to this neighbourhood by the explorers—except in so far as the cultivators of the terraced and irrigated fields (as in many of the Micronesian and Polynesian islands) already possessed them. Dogs, which are also much appreciated as food (Keysser, pp. 12 et seq., and also the personal observation of the writer), are almost certainly contemporaneous with the first human immigration.

§ 2. The pre-Columbian races of the New World did not progress beyond the stage of the digging-stick and the hoe, because they knew nothing about cattle-breeding. In Europe, and the greater part of Asia, domestic animals, such as oxen, horses, camels, and buffaloes, were used in tilling the soil, while in America the ground was entirely cultivated by manual labour. The lack of wheeled vehicles is another consequence of the same fact (Boas ['24], p. 25).

In general the temperate zones have favoured the cultivation of grain. In Asia and Europe wheat, barley, oats, and rye were available, and rice in the southern parts of Asia. A similar situation existed in America, where the principal cereal was maize, a plant probably indigenous to Mexico, whence it spread northward and southward. Beans and marrows are also native to America, so that in this respect the influence of the Old World cannot be accepted (Boas ['24], pp. 23 et seq.). It was only the deserts and the Arctic regions where the cultivation of grain was impossible.

§ 3. From plants used for food various other parts, leaves, fibre, wood, &c., are employed for making implements, ornaments, clothing, and used as building materials, just as the bones, horns, and skins of animals are increasingly used for purposes other than food.

As the relation of man to wild animals or to the flocks which support him is governed to a certain extent by personal feeling, so similar ideas are developed in connexion with plants. The South-American Jibaros of Ecuador speak to plants as if they were human, for when they are under the influence of tobacco or two other narcotics, which produce a hypnotic state, the spirits of their ancestors appear to them in the form of plants. They attribute to every plant either male or female sex, the majority being regarded as female. The distribution of work between the sexes with relation to the cultivation of plants is connected with this. The male plants must be cultivated by men and the female by women. The really important food-plants of the Jibaro are considered as female, for the tilling of the fields is regarded as above all a woman's occupation. The men do the heavy work in clearing the forest, but even when they do the planting, the women sing magical songs in order to further the growth of the trees, for they believe that women have a special mystical influence on the growth of the fruit. (Karsten, pp. 4 et seq. For forestry, cf. also Pechuël-Lösche, pp. 213, 215.)

F

III

GRADED SOCIETY OF HUNTERS, TRAPPERS, AGRICULTURISTS, AND ARTISANS

§ 1. Variations in development. § 2. A case of symbiosis. § 3. Instances
of varied activities. § 4. The economics of the Maori (New Zealand).
§ 5. The stars and Maori agriculture. § 6. The initiation of Maori girls
in the art of weaving.

§ 1. While, in pursuing our subject, we are about to deal with
a form of economics, similar in certain main points to the obtaining
of food, it is not intended to suggest that the concrete existing
forms always developed directly from those dealt with in the preceding paragraphs. In Oceania, for example, many apparently
homogeneous Melanesian communities exhibit the decay of stratifications which, owing to an intensive mixing process, have in the
course of time lost their original peculiarities as regards position
and mode of life. Among the Papuans, on the contrary, we can cite
many cases of alien economic elements being adopted, e.g. the
planting of coco-nuts or tobacco, or the keeping of pigs, without
implying stratification at all. On the other hand, the Micronesian
and the Polynesian world have retained their stratifications and
thus developed economically to a much greater extent. In spite
of this, there is an unmistakable weakening, even in the pre-
European period. It is more especially on the dividing line
between the Melanesian and Polynesian civilizations that we find
such stratifications weakening, as, for instance, apparently, among
the Trobriand Islanders. Local peculiarities never allow such processes to remain stationary and always indicate a transitional state
of affairs, starting from a certain historically determined situation.
Among all stratified and graded societies there is a tendency towards recuperating homogeneity. This is effected sooner or later
according to the circumstances (e.g., if a small aristocracy is faced
with an overwhelming mass of indigenous people, or if the blending
of races is progressing rapidly on account of intermarriage, &c.).
In spite of this tendency, the idea of social distinction, once born,
does not die, but shifts only its connexion. Instead of its primary
association with kinship it becomes correlated with political and
economic power, with the possession of land, cattle, and wealth in
general. In other cases social distinction is maintained by an

intellectual aristocracy that has withdrawn into secret societies or into the priesthood.

§ 2. Let us first of all consider a clear case of symbiosis.

In a society which has not become stratified, the Pigmy hunters supply the Yaunde agriculturists in the south of the Cameroons with meat and receive agricultural produce in return (Heepe, p. 123). These agriculturists, who have taken to a sedentary life, are able to congregate in large settlements and, owing to their more regular food, have a better prospect of rearing their children than hunters or collectors. Compared with them, the position of the hunters is constantly becoming less favourable (Meinhof, p. 35).

Among other Pigmy tribes different processes appear to have taken place. According to Torday the Pigmies from the Kasai district abandoned the forests generations ago and devoted themselves to agriculture. This is probably superficially recorded, being a question of more complicated processes. As a living example, the Kubus of Sumatra may be cited, who, when they have mixed with the Malays, become sedentary and cultivate their fields. The fact that these agricultural Pigmies are taller than their fellows who have remained in the forests also indicates a mixture of races. Similar processes have doubtless also taken place among the Papuan tribes. For instance, among the agriculturists in the region between the Augusta River and the coast mountains of New Guinea, many persons of small stature are met with, but among them about one-third are of normal height and of a different type (according to my own observations). The communal life of the coastal population in the Gazelle Peninsula (in New Britain, Oceania) has the features of a society in which, as is indicated by the institution of slavery, the idea of stratification was active but, owing to increasing racial mixture with Europeans, has now begun to weaken. As recently as the end of the last century slaves were captured from the Baining, the mountain people of the interior, and resold by middlemen. The price of a slave among the coastal population was ten strings of shell money, sometimes more. The kidnapping of children was especially prevalent. The slaves were not allowed to marry, but had to do women's work; in particular the tilling of the plantations. Taulil people from the interior were also carried off as slaves (Hahl, p. 77).

For the effects, both economic and linguistic of a former stratification which has disappeared, see Paasonen (p. 34).

§ 3. The secret societies in particular, such as we find on the Gazelle Peninsula or in the New Hebrides and the Banks Islands, permit us to recognize the waning of such earlier stratifications. This is also in accordance with the comparatively varied forms of activity in agriculture, hunting, craftsmanship, trade, &c., such as we find, for example, in the New Hebrides and the Banks Islands. In some points conditions there are similar to those in the Papuan communities, but their whole cultural stock is richer and more varied. In the New Hebrides agriculture is also mainly the duty of the women, who are only helped by the men in the heavy work of clearing the ground and planting the seedlings. The ground belongs to the sept, and a large field is either worked by the sept in common or sections are handed over to individual families. In many cases a special share of the field is allotted to each adult. The fields are usually situated in the neighbourhood of the villages. Flimsy huts in which the women rest and chat in the intervals of work are frequently erected near the fields. If the fields are far from the village more permanent huts are put up, where the night can be spent (Speiser, pp. 145 et seq.).

§ 4. The economics of the New Zealand Maoris were based on the village community. All the inhabitants of a village, who were usually related to each other and claimed to be of common descent, belonged to the same clan (*hapū*). The division of labour between the sexes was shown by the fact that nearly every man was a fisherman, bird-catcher, collector of certain forest fruits, agriculturist, or maker of utensils, weapons, nets, ropes, and ornaments; he also built houses and generally had some skill in wood- or bone-carving. Every one had naturally a certain preference for the form of activity in which he excelled, although he could do other things as well. Besides these there were also specialists, tattooers, carvers, and priest-magicians (*tohunga*) who were compensated for the practice of their arts by the gift of food, basket-work, or ornaments; but these things were always considered as presents, not as payment. In the same way there was always certain specialization between the coastal tribes and the peoples of the interior, who exchanged fish and edible seaweed for birds or river crayfish, but always in the form of ceremonial presents. If special admiration for the good qualities of an article was expressed this was a hint that the article in question was desired. Real trading and bargaining was contrary to Maori feeling and was considered a breach of good manners (*Tika*). If the return present was not of a suitable kind nothing was said in the presence of the giver, but, later on, free and general expression was given to his dissatisfaction by the receiver which, when reported to his own clan, tended to the disadvantage of the man in question. For hospitality and generosity are counted among the principal virtues in Maori society. In all such matters the power of public opinion was a stimulus for every laggard and determined his economic behaviour.

Side by side with the clan (*hapū*), the village (*kainga*) and the tribe (*whanau*) formed the social foundations of the economic constitution based on relationship. The chief, as leader of his people (*teina*), organized the obtaining of food, the craftsmanship, and the exchange of goods. He did not owe his position to his wealth or his descent. Certain products belong to the village community and not to his family or his descendants. This was especially the case with regard to food, for instance in relation to the catching of fish or birds. When the annual hunting season had been opened with the necessary ceremonies each man went for one day to the special place where he had the right to cast his line or his net, to spear birds or catch them in a snare. After their return in the late afternoon, each man laid down what he had caught on a heap in the village square (*marei*) where the booty was examined, praised, and discussed by the population, after which some of it was cooked and the rest stored in the communal village store-house. From this stock food was taken as needed. All meals were partaken of in common on this village square, and each man received his share of the food in a newly woven basket. This share, however, bore no relation to the contribution of the individual. All persons in the village had the same claim to the food supplies, and only those who, like the sacred chiefs and the priests (*tohunga*), were entitled to special treatment, received specially succulent morsels in their baskets. Other work was also undertaken in common by the members of the village under the leadership of the chiefs, such as the building of houses, the felling of trees, the clearing of forest land in order to prepare fields for sweet potatoes, the knotting of eel traps and drag nets. Similarly, when a canoe was to be made, or the main pillar in a large assembly hall to be put up, the logs were carried from the forest by all the men of the village. Indeed, the help of other villages or septs was invited for such purposes. Other kinds of work, on the other hand, were carried out by individual craftsmen; thus every one prepared his own stone axes, cut his bird-spears, his pigeon-troughs, his fish-hooks, his floats, nets, wooden utensils, greenstone neck- and ear-ornaments, &c. All these articles formed the private property of the individual and might be presented to friends and relations in accordance with certain customs (Firth ['26], pp. 13 et seq.).

The belief in the intervention of supernatural powers in all economic activity, whether in the getting of food-stuffs or the preparation of tools and utensils, of weapons, boats, or houses, led to the peculiar regard paid to all possible influences, whether helpful or harmful, which we describe briefly as 'magical'. It may be said that the richer and more manifold the technique in its preliminary stages, the greater will be the disposition, on the part of minds groping in all directions for guidance to success, to accept the possibility of such magical intervention. This means the tentative establishment of (in our opinion) non-essential conditions for the accomplishment of success.

§ 5. The planting of the crops, particularly that of *kumara* (sweet potato), is determined among the Maoris by the position of the stars, those observed being the Pleiades, the bright stars in Orion's belt, and two more. The prospects of the year's crops are estimated according to the position of these stars on rising, and the seedlings are planted in September. If the position of these stars is un-favourable, which indicates a late spring, the planting is post-poned for a month. Another important star is Atutaki (Canopus), which stands apart from the Milky Way; its southward movement is also taken as a guide for the planting of *kumara*. Such observa-tions of the stars in connexion with planting are also made by the Kajans and other tribes in Borneo, particularly when the Pleiades appear above the horizon before dawn. According to an old popular legend, a *makuru* (personification of spring) who lived in Hawaiki, the earlier home of the Maoris, sent the cuckoo to New Zealand as a messenger to announce to the Maoris the time for planting out *kumara*; but the bird arrived too soon. *Kumara* was only planted on certain days or nights with special names which have reference to the phases of the moon (Best ['25], p. 75).

§ 6. The priestly expert or *tohunga* was trained in magical pro-cedures of all kinds, incantations, and ritual. He was also the authority consulted by the hunter, the agriculturist, and the craftsman in economic matters. The initiation ceremonies are partly connected with this, as, for example, those performed in initiating Maori girls into the art of weaving. In all these initiation ceremonies the priest first pronounced an incantation to induce clear thinking on the part of the candidate, and give her a receptive mind, a reliable memory, and a capacity for grasping the new knowledge. In the weaving initiation the girl was made to sit down in front of the weaving sticks, and materials of various kinds with handsome patterns and borders of coloured threads, which had been made by practised hands, were spread out before her. These were to serve as masterpieces which the girl was to take as a model, not merely for the moment but during the whole course of her training. She then took a prepared thread in her hand and held it, while the priest pronounced an invocation (*karakia*) to implant the new knowledge firmly in her mind. The girl then advanced and bit the upper part of the weaving stick which she held in her right hand and which was sacred (*tapu*). She then wove the first and sacred set across the frame with the thread in her hand. She had then entered on her career as a weaver and began to make her first piece of cloth. This was followed by the *whakanoa* ceremony with which were connected the pronouncing of another magical formula and the ritualistic tasting of certain dishes. During these proceedings and until the candidate had completed her first piece of cloth, she was not allowed to eat ordinary food, set foot on a place where food was cooked, or associate with her family. (The aim, therefore, in this case is to produce intense concentration and avoid distraction of any kind.) After the initiation ceremony the woman weaver did not cease to observe magical precautions. Even now the women do not eat their meals in the house where they weave, without covering their work. If a stranger enters the room in which a woman is weaving, the weaving sticks are at once unshipped, the work covered up and laid on one side. Even if a near relative enters the room, work is immediately stopped and the stick laid down next to the work on the right until the visitor is seated. If any one goes behind the weaving apparatus, i.e. opposite the weaver, to examine the work, this is considered to be a bad omen (*aroakapa*). It is also a bad omen for the weaver, if she has not finished a set (*aho*) by sundown. It is believed that her power of concentration and her memory are put to the test by this and that she will never be able to finish the piece of cloth she has begun (Best ['98], pp. 627–32). Te Rangihiroa (P. H. Buck, p. 85) is of opinion that the weaving is hidden from strangers so that others may not be able to imitate the pattern. For a weaver would lose her reputation for skill and her pattern would no longer be admired if copied. If the set is not complete she can easily unravel what had been woven (Firth ['26], pp. 18 et seq.). (The loss of material was associated with mystical ideas of evil omens in general.) All other forms of activity, such as bird-catching, fishing, carving, and tattooing, house- and boat-building, were performed in conjunction with spell and magical ritual, to ensure the success of the work. The neglect of certain rites caused failure just as much as the omission of any practical detail of the work or any necessary precaution. To the mind of the Maori there was no difference between the practical and the magical measures which were considered to supplement each other if real success was desired. They firmly believed that the invocation (*karakia*) really strengthened the capacity of learning the work and retaining one's skill in it when learnt. In reality, this led to concentration, alertness, and self-confidence, which were all of benefit to the work. This is also the case with various arts connected with getting food—spearing fish, setting bird- and rat-traps, climbing trees, &c. It may thus be said that the ceremonies which accompany the work, and which we usually describe as magical, are by no means without effect on the working process and the mentality of the workman, and that, since they create confidence in the success of the work, they benefit it and also those taking part in it (Firth ['26], pp. 18 et seq., and ['25]).

IV

THE HERDSMEN

§ 1. The significance of herdsmen's work. § 2. The Banyankole of East Africa.

§ 1. In the history of the human race the domestication of animals has played a very important part in shaping social organization. In this respect discoveries were made, although the tendency to symbiosis of certain animals, notably the dog, undoubtedly met man's efforts half-way. Having later discovered that animals could be used for drawing or carrying burdens, man was able to enter new fields of labour, as he does whenever fresh technical facilities arise, which in their turn make him dependent on that which he has created. This new factor in his conditions of existence naturally influences his mode of social life, for example by imposing the necessity of caring for the animals.

For this reason the use made of animals is by no means to be overlooked in tracing the history of pastoral tribes. The importance of animals differs according to their kind, whether they provide food (fat, meat, milk), clothes (skins, fur, wool), or labour-saving devices (riding, carrying, drawing, guarding, &c.). As a consequence of these divergences, even apart from other influential factors, such as race, climate, the physical features of the country, the keeping of animals developed on different lines in different places. Nevertheless, a whole series of similar circumstances exercised a similar influence on pastoral peoples: the fact of being dependent on certain grazing grounds, in spite of a nomadic existence and the seasonal change of pasture leads to the pre-emption of a definite territory necessary for the animals' sustenance. The intensive cropping of the land by the herds restricts the size of the groups moving with their stock, and the population consequently consists of small scattered communities, entirely independent of each other, but which in the course of their wanderings come in touch and so keep up cultural relations. The sense of dependence on the animals and their produce (i.e. milk, fat, blood) induces a special religious conception, a particular respect for the higher powers. A number of rites and ceremonies, or traditionally defined modes of procedure was the outcome of the care for animals, their pasture, and everything concerned with them.

Among cattle-keepers the consumption of the animals' meat is not always the principal reason for their maintenance, as, for instance, in eastern Asia; among the western and African pastoral tribes the enjoyment of the milk is, on the contrary, the paramount consideration. Among many tribes there is a tendency to regard the most important foods with respect, mingled with the fear of causing the supply to diminish through their behaviour. The tribes to whom milk is imparted accordingly arrange their life with this end in view. Some of the Indian tribes, the Todas for instance, are a notable example of this; the tribe is divided into two parts, one of which is responsible to the other half for the care of the sacred buffalo milk (Rivers, p. 680).

Moreover, the paramount importance of the animals' milk as against their flesh gains added significance in that milk promotes more favourable conditions for the rearing of the coming generation, enabling a larger proportion of children to be kept alive. The greater proportional increase in the population of such communities is a vitally important factor, which has engaged the attention even of uncivilized peoples.

From yet another point of view, cattle-breeding seems to have exerted a widespread influence on the ideas and outlook of peoples, correspondingly affecting their everyday life in certain special ways. For instance, among some matrilineal agricultural peoples (Trobriand Islanders) and among some hunting, trapping, or root-gathering tribes (Australians) the definite connexion between cohabitation and conception does not yet seem to have been recognized even to-day. At any rate it is ignored. Consequently we have even more reason to suppose that in earlier times this lack of knowledge existed. Observers of animal life, such as herdsmen, would naturally draw their own conclusions sooner or later and reason out the connexion between the two. Among hunting peoples the tendency, already present, to emphasize the father's authority was probably strengthened by the fact that the care of the animals was the man's province. Moreover, the constant wanderings kept the woman's activities in the background. Where, on the contrary, hoe-cultivation existed, the plenteous and certain supply of food which the woman was capable of supplying to the hunter strengthened female influence, and as it entailed a more or less fixed place of residence it made woman's existence easier.

§ 2. A typical example of a pastoral tribe which has overlaid an agricultural people are the Banyankole of Eastern Africa. The nobles and chiefs are drawn from the pastoral section of the tribe and employ the peasants to take care of the goats and sheep and the dogs, and they are also expected to supply their betters with corn and beer. These peoples seldom remain in one spot more than two or three years, as a frequent change of habitation is considered necessary for the health of the animals. The habitation is also changed on the occurrence of a death of a person. Only members of the pastoral section of the tribe, those who have no cattle of their own, or too few to support their own families, are employed to look after the herds. These underlings, should they so desire, may leave their employers at any time. A number of ceremonies are connected with milking, with the drinking of milk, its distribution, milk-sacrifices, the form of the milk-containers and the mode of cleaning and preserving them. The milking is done by the men under the protection of a charm. The care of the milk-vessels and of such milk as is not immediately consumed is the women's province (Roscoe ['23/a], pp. 15, 17, 66 et seq.). Similar conditions prevail in Ruanda (Czekanowski, 141 et seq.).

The Mongolian herdsmen live in small scattered family groups whose economic centre is the *yurta*, the felt tent; the possession of the herds is vested in the family unit as a whole. Horses, saddles, clothes, and arms, are the only kinds of individual property recognized. People in this higher stage of pastoral life possess more than one kind of animal; in addition to horses, they have camels, sheep, and goats which are accompanied by dogs. Pigs are never found. The possession of these various animals necessitates knowledge of the different kinds of treatment required, and leads to class distinctions based on property. A family group owning roughly 1,000 horses, 100 camels, and a corresponding number of goats and sheep, passes for rich. In spite of the scattered and individualistic mode of life of these tribes, they are in constant cultural contact. From time to time one clan might establish its dominion over the rest, or one man might rise to supreme power and carry the whole tribe with him, as has sometimes happened among the Arabian nomads.

The strong personal sense of independence possessed by hunters is also found among herdsmen, as is also the dislike of any kind of subordination and of what we should call a settled government. The intense opposition which Muhammad encountered among the Arabs testifies to this fact.

V

HOMOGENEOUS HUNTERS AND HERDSMEN

§ 1. The habit of keeping domestic animals. § 2. The tribe confines itself to one kind of game. § 3. A point to notice. § 4. The use of animal products.

§ 1. The question of how the keeping of domestic animals first originated is a peculiar problem. We can only visualize its far-reaching significance when we consider what difficulty the hunting tribes (even such as have been in contact with pastoral tribes) experience when they take to cattle-breeding. Although the Bergdama have had intercourse with the Hereros for centuries, they have not yet made the transition; though a few of them have begun keeping goats. The cows which the Bergdamas who had been servants of the Hereros sometimes brought back with them, were not kept long, but were soon slaughtered and eaten. Such Bergdama as began to breed goats were forced into a completely different mode of life from those who remained exclusively hunters. (Vedder, pp. 9, 173, 187.) The work of tending the flocks is found so burdensome by this tribe of hunters that, when their goats have to be pastured away from the settlement, they prefer to engage the services of a man living by himself at a distance, as a precaution against raids on the part of predatory neighbours. He is repaid by making use of their milk, and is obliged to produce the skins of any animals which have died or been killed by wild beasts and, if his post is not too remote, the flesh also. He has to account for every head, keeping tally by means of notches in a stick, as an aid to memory, when the owner comes to inspect the stock. No separate mark is made for lambs born during the interval. The owner does not count the flock, as he remembers each individual animal by its colour and markings. At the end of the year, the shepherd receives a she-goat as his wage, so that he can gradually acquire a flock of his own and thus gain the right to join the tribal settlement and sit beside the sacred fire.

The habit of keeping domestic animals must obviously have arisen in several ways, differing according to the kind of animal. The dog, the earliest animal domesticated, may originally have been attracted by the refuse-heaps of the village (cf. Studer). This may also be the case as regards the pig, which is associated with early agriculture in fens and marshes. In both cases it was probably a question of 'family-taming', of the young being kept and fed, so that they eventually became accustomed to man. The process must have been entirely different with regard to the large herds of pasturing ruminants. Without doubt the initial stage was that of rounding up a herd, as, for example, is done by the reindeer hunters of Siberia, who follow the wild herds of these animals.

§ 2. The stage when a hunting tribe begins to confine itself to one particular kind of game, as, for example, when the North-American Indians followed the herds of bison from place to place, is the first in the transition to a nomadic life combined with herding. Compared with the true hunters such nomads are relatively more certain of their subsistence, and their community is, consequently, more closely knit. The herds represent a permanent possession, and, in some cases, rapidly increasing riches.

Such groups as attached themselves in this way to the herds of animals on which they subsisted eventually had to adapt themselves, more or less, to the habits and character of these animals, and it became imperative, not only to protect them against their enemies, but also to discover suitable pasture grounds, and provide against times of famine. This recognition of personal dependence on the animals on which he subsisted more than probably induced in primitive man an egocentric view of the universe, and in due course resulted in the animal being regarded as a supernatural being which must be protected in order to secure his own personal safety and continued existence. This gave rise to the most varied ceremonies, such as we find in use by all tribes who have been long in possession of cattle, although we must regard the deification of domestic animals in particular as a secondary phenomenon, similar to that which took place with regard to wild animals, but not quite the same.

§ 3. It is worth noticing that when the New World was discovered cattle-breeding was unknown; the dog alone seems to have accompanied the tribes who crossed to America. There were, it is true, some attempts at keeping particular animals as pets, which were of no economic importance. Such attempts may be observed in Australia and the South Seas to-day. The flocks of turkeys and herds of lamas in Peru were the only exceptions (Boas ['24], p. 25).

The North-American Indians and the Eskimo were ignorant of reindeer-herding. In Europe the natives were in the habit of catching reindeer, and tamed females were used as an aid to the hunt. It is possible that this custom of hunting reindeer, and also the fact that they move in herds, largely influenced their domestication. It is certain that reindeer were already in use as beasts of burden during the Finnish Stone Age (Sirelius ['16–20]; see also Hatt ['20]).

§ 4. The use of animal products, such as cow's milk or sheep's wool, can only be regarded as a secondary derivative when animals had already been domesticated for some time. Not only is milking quite unknown in the whole of Eastern Asia, but even the gathering of wool has not yet been introduced among some sheep-breeding peoples. In this process, awkward methods were employed in ancient Babylonia, the wool being plucked from the living sheep by hand, and only that taken off which could be easily detached, which can be done when the animals have been short of food for some time. Even at the beginning of the nineteenth century this way of getting wool was quite usual on the Faroe Islands; in ancient Italy it had not yet been entirely abandoned in the time of Pliny (Meissner ['11], pp. 96 et seq.).

In Egypt, the sheep were not deprived of their wool at all, as they were only used for slaughter. The oldest finds of wool were made in the Greek tombs in Egypt. (As regards horses, cf. v. Negelein.) It is particularly significant that even the horse was only used at first as a draught animal and comparatively late for riding (Kornemann, p. 6). We are justified in assuming that the reindeer, as far as our information goes, was first used as a draught animal. The use of animals as food may be considered as the oldest form of economic use. This was probably followed by further attempts which led to their use, at first as draught animals and beasts of burden, and only later for riding, or for the sake of their milk and wool.

We may say that, from the economic point of view—allowing for the standards of their time and culture—the primitive people acted with the greatest care in order to avoid all possible harm due to unexpected events, such as epidemics, and so as to get the best return from the herd. The whole mass of ceremonies and 'magical' performances appears 'irrational' to us. Yet in this behaviour, which appears to us 'irrational', there lies a perfectly sound sequence of reasoning. Such ceremonies, and the motives dictating them have been, e.g., studied and described by Roscoe among the Bakitara and the Banyankole.

VI

ETHNICALLY STRATIFIED CATTLE-BREEDERS AND TRADERS

§ 1. Introductory. § 2. The Tuareg as an illustration. § 3. Significance of their conditions. § 4. The Xosa Kaffirs of South Africa. § 5. Milk rather than meat. § 6. Economics of cattle-breeding. § 7. Predatory tendencies of herdsmen.

§ **1.** The unstratified herdsmen who live in homogeneous hordes and communities must be differentiated from those among whom the stratification of society, by aristocracy or by the keeping of bondsmen and slaves, can be distinguished. Such stratifications may, again, be found among other pastoral peoples, as has happened with the Mongol tribes or among the Arabs, or they may include ethnic groups with a completely different basis for their food supply, such as agriculturists or primitive hunters.

Among stratified pastoral peoples the keeping of several kinds of animals is usually a prominent feature. As a rule it is·those who keep cattle who have succeeded in establishing their superiority to those who have only sheep and goats. It is also worthy of remark that the introduction (usually attributable to alien influence) of a different animal disturbs the traditional organization and places the economic system on another basis, as in the case of the Jakuts.

§ **2.** We will begin by considering the conditions of life among stratified pastoral tribes. For this purpose, the Tuareg tribes of North Africa will serve. It is comparatively easy to obtain a survey of their history, which enables us to visualize the migrations that gave rise to a certain form of economics and mode of life existing to-day. The Tuareg are not one tribe but a people, that is to say, they are composed of various elements of varying origin. The separate parts of this race consist of historical and geographical groups. Each of these groups contains nobles (*imajeghan*) and slaves (*imghad*). They lead the life of nomads, but the conquest of foreign elements in battle, and their assimilation in course of time, has led to certain physical modifications and, in individual groups, even to their permanent settlement. Yet the Tuareg are strongly differentiated from their neighbours, especially from the Berbers. They lead a nomadic life. Only the Negroes and the domiciled Libyans till the soil, while the towns are governed by a different people, who may be the descendants of the ancient Garamantes. Successive waves of Tuareg spread, for instance, over the Air district (to the east of Timbuktu) and drove the old agricultural Negro population southwards. But, as always happens in such cases, the invaders became mixed with the negroid population of the Sudan and, further, their half-breed descendants adopted a sedentary and agricultural mode of life. In consequence of these successive invasions, the separate tribes of the Tuareg, already more or less mixed, are differentiated among themselves, owing to the fact that a number of Negro tribes were reduced to dependence by different conquerors.

The tribes of the Tuareg make a distinction among themselves based on social superiority. The economic basis of the Tuareg is the camel. The respect paid to a man is measured by the number of camels he possesses, although he may also have donkeys, goats, sheep, and houses, gardens, and slaves. The camels were distinguished, apart from being provided with marks of ownership, by very minute gradations of size and colour. Horses are not found, and only a few cattle are imported from the south, also donkeys, sheep, goats, and dogs. Every village has, in particular, large herds of sheep and goats; they form, after the camel, the most important possession of the Tuareg. The main food supply of the villages is derived from goat's milk, but the hair of these animals is never made use of. The connexion of the Tuareg with the camel as their most important domestic animal is worthy of note, because the camel became common in Africa only in the second century of our era, and this ancient people can only have taken to camel breeding at a comparatively late date. Being real camel nomads, they live on the milk of these animals and on that of the goats which formerly, perhaps, were the most important part of their flocks. In addition to their milk diet they eat millet porridge seasoned with salt, both of which are bartered from neighbouring tribes. Their main interest is in the great caravan journeys undertaken in autumn, principally in order to buy salt. The crafts practised by them are those needed for the fitting out of the caravans and providing the fighting men with weapons. The principal craftsman is the smith, who also does carpenter's work and occupies a leading position.

The season for fighting begins after the first rains, when water is plentiful in the northern Sahara. As a rule, the Tuareg in these forays do not kill the members of a tribe or the inhabitants of a village unnecessarily, for a sharp distinction is made between such forays and war. Their principal object is lifting cattle and horses and, above all, camels. The raid is kept strictly secret. They do not make slaves of each other except in case of war, but it is no breach of custom to steal the slaves of outsiders as well as their camels.

Among these people the great independence of the women is worthy of remark and quite contrary to Muhammadan custom. A Tuareg woman can dispose of property in her own name even when she is married, and, indeed, without the interference of her husband, and make provision for its disposal after her death. It sometimes happens that when the tribe abandons its original territory, the community assigns the unoccupied land to the leading women, who thus, to a certain extent, receive a kind of annuity. Even in war, women have sometimes played a leading part. In spite of Muhammadan influence, monogamy appears to have been an old tradition.

§ 3. What is worthy of note in these conditions is the importance of racial tendencies and habit, and their influence on the economic system, for, in the same geographical surroundings and in the same climate, the tribes adjacent to the Tuareg, the Berber and the Negroes, behave, as has been mentioned, quite differently. Their mode of obtaining food from natural sources differs according to their habits and their historical traditions. We have seen how hard it is for a pastoral people to adapt itself to a settled existence and the tilling of the soil, and can thus realize the difficulties involved in such changes where there is no mixture of tribes, difficulties usually passed over too lightly in the speculations of economic writers. It is further economically important that when large animals are kept the principal point is not the eating of the meat but other uses which can be made of the animal; thus the camel both supplies milk and serves as a beast of burden. In keeping goats, milk is also an important factor, and perhaps the use of goat's milk suggested that of the milk of large animals, i.e. cows, mares, and camels could be used. In order to obtain vegetable food the Tuareg adopt three courses: direct attack and robbery, the theft of slaves for the purpose of laying out gardens, and the subjugation of agricultural tribes. But even among individual herdsmen, especially those who are not Tuareg, fights take place which lead to dependence. The Tuareg account for their

G

aristocracy by attributing to themselves a slighter admixture of alien blood; on the other hand, a Tuareg who has been taken prisoner in war occupies ever after an inferior position, and even his descendants, who take their place again in the tribe, never attain the respect enjoyed by their elders. Similar points of view are also applicable to the different classes of slaves, from whom, again, the Negroes are differentiated (Rodd, pp. 128, 138, 360, 426 et seq.).

§ 4. Among the Xosa Kafirs, of South Africa, the man alone does all the work connected with the cattle, including the milking. He also cuts and prepares the posts and wattles for the cattle kraal, and makes skewers, spoons, pipes, and sticks. Apart from this he cures skins and sews them together, makes the milk-sacks and shoes, but he also digs the corn-pits (silos) in the cattle kraal. In addition to this he goes out hunting and strolls about to hear the news. The principal work of the woman consists in tilling the field, which keeps her occupied for two or three weeks in spring. Two months later she has to hoe it, which takes from three to four weeks. (It is, therefore, a question of hoe agriculture by the woman; the plough was only introduced at the end of last century and has been used since then by the men and boys.) Wives and daughters make it a point of honour to work in the fields in order to provide abundance of food for the house. The heaviest woman's work consists in carrying home on her head the materials for house-building, poles, wattles, and grass, and in moving to another place, when she often has to walk long distances, carrying the household utensils on her head and, in addition, the smallest child on her back. The man goes either on horseback or on foot carrying the lighter articles. Waggons were not used until recent times. In addition, the women and girls plait eating-mats for the cooked meat and the maize porridge, as well as water-tight milk-vessels of grass or rushes. Rougher mats made of rushes or tree fibres are made for sleeping on. Besides cooking, the women undertake the grinding of the grain and the brewing of beer, and also the washing-up of the eating-mats, the milk-baskets, and the other vessels, in so far as this is not done by the dog. The care of the cattle, which is exclusively a man's occupation, has something of a religious character, and special relations between the ox and the man are assumed to exist. The bull was in earlier times the property of the chief alone and a symbol of his power, while the cow symbolized wealth, happiness, and generosity. Every tribe

has a tribal ox from which it takes its name; besides every prominent man also has such an ox as a pet to which he gives all sorts of
titles and honours, and which must be spared in war and never
killed, but returned to the owner because of its magical associations. The sickness and death of a favourite ox often causes
mourning and lamentation expressed in these words: 'Death has
broken into our midst with much greater power than if he only
wished to carry off a man. Our great ox is ill, and if he who is
stronger than all should die, what will become of us? It will be
the end of us all!' In earlier times oxen were only used for carrying
loads and riding, and it is only of late that they have been yoked to
waggons. The cows give very little milk, at most three quarts
a day. They do not give milk until the calf has had enough, and
as the calf is left with the mother until she calves again, a great
part of the milk is lost. If a young calf dies the cow cannot be
milked, unless they adopt the subterfuge of wrapping the skin of
the dead calf round a Kafir boy who, by sucking the cow, causes
her to give her milk. All these cows (in primitive cattle-breeding)
do not give milk unless first sucked by the calf. Every animal has
a name to which it answers. The calf is called by the name of its
mother. The milking is done by boys and men, and also the herding and guarding of the cattle. The Kafir never has all his cattle
in his own kraal, but has always a few head hidden with friends,
so that in case of necessity, or when he has to pay for thefts, or is
robbed in war, he always has something in reserve and is not quite
impoverished (Kropf, pp. 107 et seq., 147 et seq.).

§ 5. In general all these pastoral peoples, especially in warmer
climates, live, as has already been mentioned, on the milk of their
herds and it is only occasionally that they kill animals for meat.
When meat is eaten it is usually the flesh of smaller animals, that
of the large animals being reserved for feasts. The cattle form, in
a certain sense, the capital on the return of which, in milk or at
most in the increase of stock, the people live, while some tribes
use them also as beasts of transportation. Inroads on capital,
however, as has already been shown, are made unwillingly, even
among meat-eating herdsmen. (Compare with regard to the
Kalmuks, Pallas [1771], pp. 319, 514 et seq.).

§ 6. The tending of animals, especially in pastoral life, originated from a close association and observation of the animals. It
undoubtedly required considerable time, milleniums, for men to

isolate the conditions essential for the life and prosperity of the animals so that man could make adequate use of them. The magic devices gradually gave place to more rational ones. The mental attitude had to be changed also, in so far as the idea of prey had to be abandoned in favour of protection of the animals. This alteration marks possibly a most important step in human thinking. It is the more notable as predatory tribes of our age can hardly be induced to care for animals. The Bergdama were partially used as serfs for the keeping of the cattle of the Herero and were often sent home with some cows, but they strangely never made up their mind to keep cattle themselves. It may have been the disproportion between the number of men and that of the animals upon which they were living that finally led to the protection of them. The way in which these men reacted to the growing disproportion shows a most remarkable faculty of adaptation, an outstanding plasticity of mind. The picking out of a species for particular tending with the aim of living upon it enhanced the feeling of economic dependence upon the chosen animal. This emotion compares with any sentiment of dependence on superhuman powers. Similar methods were therefore used for obtaining omens, oracles, ordeals, for taking advantage of them as mediators (scapegoat), &c. In fact the religious and magical relations of the herdsmen show entirely different features from those of predatory tribes in regard to their animals.

§ 7. The predatory tendencies exhibited especially by herdsmen in contrast to agriculturists is connected with their nomadic life, which secures for them comparatively greater freedom of movement. In this connexion the need for vegetable food, at least as a relish, appears to have been a motive which should not be underestimated. However, as has already been hinted, the keeping of cattle has economically a much greater educational effect than the tilling of the fields, for cattle are productive, permanent, and movable capital, the increase of which tends to increase the numbers, influence, and power of the group. Agriculturists only need to cultivate crops sufficient for one year, and the cultivated area cannot be increased, at least not so long as a scattered population has surplus land at its disposal.

VII

SOCIALLY GRADED HERDSMEN WITH HUNTING, AGRICULTURAL, AND ARTISAN POPULATION

§ 1. Cultural connexion of small communities. § 2. Union of self-governing bodies into a compact body. § 3. Illustration: the Nilotic Lango. § 4. And the Ovambo. § 5. Exploitation by traders. § 6. The Bakitara. § 7. European point of view misleading.

§ **1.** A matter of extraordinary importance for a certain line of economic development is the cultural connexion of small communities on the basis of equality, such as we find between specialists in food and others in handicraft, for instance between potters and those who provide sago and yams in the South Seas, regarding which more will be said later. Hence, there arises a tendency to depreciate those who are under the necessity of buying their food, so that, as on the Trobriand Islands, the craftsmen find themselves in a despised and dependent position. The frequently unfavourable position of the smiths is doubtless connected with this. (Where they are respected it is due to the magical powers ascribed to them if, in addition, they can make provision for their food by means of their own gardens or fields.)

In general, the difference in the means by which food is obtained has largely contributed to a difference in the mutual estimation and the behaviour of the groups coming into ethnical contact. This close association, when the groups are sharply divided from each other, tends to stratification in which the herdsmen have the advantage, as has been already explained. On the other hand, there may be a tendency towards mixture, principally in cases where the superior ethnic groups are numerically weaker and especially when wives are taken from the other group. This often produces a false appearance of homogeneity, though it really represents the result of an assimilation due to mixture. The special position of racial components as, for example, that of the hunters in Ufipa, East Africa (Fromm, p. 87), shows such a process in the making.

§ **2.** By the formation of an upper layer, the economic area outgrows small self-governing communities and the process of uniting a number of them into a compact body begins. The ethnic grouping is transformed into a professional-social one.

There is thus created an organization based, on the one hand, on the contributions and services of the dependent class, and, on the other, on the power of distribution possessed by the heads of families in the leading stratum. The circulation of goods caused in this way affects the distribution of usufruct and possession in a decisive manner. The specialization already begun in the domain of handicraft, to which is now added the ethnically cultural specialization in food-production, is rendered more acute by means of the organization. For the power of distribution, which depends in the first instance on the absence of restraint and the consequent tradition, unifies the various ethnic elements to a certain degree and modifies their attitude towards each other, in part according to the relations to their ruler and in part according to the possession of economic key property (e.g. cattle). It has thus a disintegrating effect on the aristocratic-ethnic stratification and, in time, substitutes for it a new social structure based on the individual possession of economic or religious power, which arose in particular by the fusion of ethnic peculiarities. In this way is laid the foundation-stone of a new social unit based upon individualized families. The emancipation from the bonds of clan and sept mark the encroaching individualization. This process, however, affected the various strata in a different way. Among the ruling layer existed a rivalry for power and its symbols that became 'wealth' (captives of war, cows, ornaments, &c.). Ambitious persons were enabled to get influence over other people—slaves, agriculturists, and later also over herdsmen.

Overwhelming individual influence as an institution was not possible in a homogeneous democratic society as, e.g., among predatory tribes. But by the fact that the heads of families repartitioned the captives of war and the agricultural communities among each other, they became recognized and institutional leaders of other people. On the other hand they lost their interest in closer clan relations of which perhaps only religious or ceremonial ties survived. The lowest stratum, the captives of war and their offspring, faced another fate. They of course had to disconnect their traditional kinship adhesions and were 'detribalized'—to use a modern term. The agriculturists could perhaps preserve their clan life the longest time. But sooner or later they were exposed to the administrative requirements of the ruling stratum for collecting taxes. Their clans were transformed in one way or another, and in their place castes, guilds, and similar institutions were established. In these the families' economic influence predominated. Thus here also at last individual families became paramount in their importance. The commonwealth of the archaic states consists of aggregations of such families graded and assigned to castes, guilds, corporations of officials, &c., headed by a supreme family, the dynasty. This permits a specialization of skill and ability apt to provoke individual competition. By that, exchange of goods is promoted among a large number of families of various origin, skill, and affiliations. An immense economic unit thus comes into existence. As peace reigns in that comparatively vast area, exchange is carried on, and thus a kind of 'national economy' is made practicable.

§ 3. An example of a people in whose case cattle-keeping is combined with agriculture and various crafts is provided by the Nilotic Lango, of Uganda, in East Africa. They love their cattle like true herdsmen. They distinguish about thirty varieties, according to the colour, the build, the shape of the horns, &c., and have separate names for each variety. If a beast dies, or is carried off in a raid, the women raise the cry of mourning as if a man had met his death. This is not only due to the fact that the animal is an object of value but also arises from their genuine affection for the animals, as is also the case among the Dinka, Masai, and many other tribes. Every man knows exactly which cattle, goats, and sheep belong to him and can pick them out of a strange herd at once; he also knows which cow was the dam of each calf, although the calves are never branded with marks of ownership. The owner of a cow milks her himself, as is customary among herdsmen. In his absence the cow is milked by his children or by a hired herdsman, but in no case by a woman. They are not so greatly attached to the goats and sheep as to the cattle, but even these are distinguished by different names according to their colour and build. The relations between pastoralism and agriculture are characteristically expressed by the relative values of cattle and grain. Although these relative values fluctuate, a few examples for the year 1916 may be given. Six loads of grain (about 350 lb.) are equivalent to one he-goat; 11 loads of grain are equivalent to one young she-goat; 15 loads of grain are equivalent to one full-grown she-goat; 25 loads of grain are equivalent to a bull; a store-room full of grain (about $1\frac{1}{2}$ tons) is equivalent to a young heifer.

Among the Lango, agriculture is less developed than, for instance, that of their neighbours, the Akum. They use a long hoe. About a month before the sowing, the grassland is broken up and the trees felled or pollarded. After this the brushwood is burned and the soil cleaned and turned over to a slight depth. This breaking up of the soil is an important advance on digging-stick agriculture. This work is done by the men, in contrast to the practice among the Bantu. The hoe is used either standing or kneeling, the shaft being grasped low down and held away from the body, while the strokes are made towards the worker. The hoe, and not the axe, is used for digging out or cutting off the remaining small roots. The seed is scattered broadcast, the procedure already resembling that adopted in plough agriculture. Before sowing, the leaves of the sacred *alenga* plant are taken, divided, and strewn over the seed-corn in order to cause good germination, just as a little grain is thrown under the plant after the harvest. As soon as the blades shoot up, a stick or a bamboo-like grass is stuck in the ground, in order to protect the crop from the evil eye. Like a scapegoat, it attracts to itself the evil influences which might affect the harvest. The women and children have to clear the weeds and, while the crops are ripening, help the men to keep the fields clean. The crops are never planted in rows but are scattered at random, sometimes, even, more than one sort together. Thus millet and sesame are occasionally sown together, beans and millet are regularly planted together, and sorghum is often mixed with millet and maize.

A man does not undertake the cultivation single-handed except in case of great need, or when no assistance is available owing to a famine. Otherwise he obtains the help of his friends and neighbours, whom he recompenses with food and drink at the end of the day's work. The extent and nature of the assistance are assessed in a traditional way according to various forms of agreement. The helpers have to work hard for long hours, but they do so willingly, as they make similar claims when their turn comes. The groups that regularly offer each other such friendly assistance are called *wangtich*. Several kinds of such groups are distinguished. Those of 15 to 20 (*pur kongo*) cultivate a large field from sunrise to sundown, each man working for himself, no fixed task being apportioned to him. At the end of the day the workers are liberally rewarded with beer. To groups of three or four helpers (*pur gweno*) certain tasks are assigned by the owner. Each man must work a certain strip, about 100 yards long and as broad as the shaft of his hoe is long, being rewarded with poultry. In a case of *pur adwe* (or *pur poto adili*) the procedure used in *pur kongo* is adopted, but the amount of beer is only sufficient for two or three helpers. If only two or three helpers are used for a small field (*pur boyo aonya*), the payment—in bean-leaves cooked with sesame—must not be made at once. When this dish is prepared the helpers are invited to eat it with the owner's family. An arrangement for mutual help between two men, without payment, is called *pur aleya*.

There is no question of a regular rotation of crops. A plot of land is cultivated and, as a rule, since unlimited land is available, another plot is cultivated on the next occasion. It is usual, however, to sow millet where they have already grown sesame and, at the present day, the crop to follow this is potatoes. Where cotton has been planted they are in the habit of cultivating millet as the next crop. As the ravages of the white ants make it necessary to renew the huts about every three years, the site of the settlement is occasionally changed—as in digging-stick agriculture—and new huts erected, as a rule, not far off. Now and then they migrate for considerable distances, perhaps in order to settle near old friends.

The most important crop is millet, which provides food and also drink in the form of beer. The millet is mostly ground to meal and cooked as a kind of porridge which is eaten with vegetables. Old people mix buttermilk with it, and a kind of barley water is also made from it. Although the Lango live principally on cereals, they are very fond of meat. On ceremonial occasions animals are always slaughtered, cattle being speared above the third rib and goats and sheep stabbed in the throat with a knife; but for certain ceremonies other ritual procedure is employed, as for instance, suffocation by closing all bodily orifices.

In addition to breeding cattle and tilling the soil, hunting is practised, and nearly all wild beasts and birds are eaten, with the exception of carrion eaters and birds of prey. Women are never allowed to eat the flesh of chickens or goats till after the birth of the third child, and only those women who are too old to bear children are allowed to eat mutton.

The Lango practise various handicrafts. It is noteworthy that the Lango smiths have no knowledge of the art of smelting iron, though the ore is available in plenty in their country. They obtain iron from imported hoes, and brass, which is worked into rings and bracelets, from imported brass wire. The smith always lives outside the village. Pots are made by the men of the family, the clay being obtained by the women from the river beds. Pottery-making is not a special calling.

Families and septs do not always live in one village but are often widely scattered about the country as a result of wars and migrations. The eldest son usually continues to live in his father's village and also the younger sons, at least until they marry. Several families usually keep together in order to increase the village's power of resistance. The man erects a special hut for each of his wives and also special grain stores, for each wife tills her own fields. The woman does not receive her special hut until she has borne a child; until then she sleeps in the man's hut; if she continues to remain barren she is given back to her family. In each village a special pen is erected for the whole of the cattle (Driberg, pp. 71, 80, 87, 90 et seq.).

§ 4. Among the Ovambo, of South-West Africa, the main work of the year consists in cultivating the fields with the hoe. The men attend to the repairing of the fence round the gardens when it has become damaged in spots, so as to give passage to man and beast. The women and children clear the soil of the last year's stubble and other refuse, all of which is burned. The soil is neither profitably worked nor rationally manured. Manuring is mostly only done here and there in the fields, which are often very large; it is undertaken on a more extensive scale when a homestead is moved, when it also becomes possible to use the manure collected in the large cattle kraal. The women cultivate the garden, the master of the house assigning a certain limited portion to each of them. In most cases the children of the family also have their own little garden. The man and his sons attend to the pasturing of the cattle. Large and small animals are pastured separately, calves and goats being left to the care of the youngest. Milking is done twice: in the morning, before the animals go out to graze, and in the evening when they come home. Before the man begins milking he pours some water into the pail as a precaution, for he considers that if he failed to do so he would lose the cow in one way or another. The Ovambo also practise various handicrafts, such as wood-carving, pottery, basket-making, and smith's work (Tönjes, pp. 59 et seq.; pp. 66 et seq.).

Trading goes on briskly among the various tribes in the Ovambo country. Large and small stock, garden produce, grain and beans, the products of the smith's and the wood-carver's art, baskets, mats, and pottery, and also all kinds of weapons, articles of clothing, and ornaments are bartered in exchange for the two articles for which there is most demand, salt and tobacco, which thus acquire money value (Tönjes, pp. 84 et seq.).

§ 5. Traders intending to exploit certain areas find it most profitable to direct their operations to peoples of widely different race and culture. The most favourable region in this respect was East Africa during the nineteenth century, which had already been visited for centuries by Arab traders who obtained ivory and slaves from the interior by more or less violent methods, and settled at various points on the coast, where small despotic states came into being. The increased influx of Europeans, the spread of fire-arms, and the growing demand for the treasures of the interior, including cattle and grain, led to a notable increase in acts of violence during the nineteenth century.

§ 6. Among the East-African Bakitara such forays were usually accompanied by all sorts of atrocities which, however, were based on superstitious ideas (Roscoe ['231 b], pp. 310 et seq.). If the leaders of a raid did not meet with the desired success, they did not venture to return home until they had made a fresh attempt to obtain booty. Otherwise they ran the risk of being deprived of the whole of their property or even put to death at the hands of the enraged king. In spite of various limitations imposed on the kingship among the Bakitara, usurpers sometimes made their appearance, usually in the person of a brother of the king. Such risings, which were of the nature of palace revolutions, were conducted with the aid of local chiefs. These risings were particularly important at the beginning of a new reign (op. cit., pp. 313 et seq.).

§ 7. Many misunderstandings have arisen owing to a rationalistic explanation by Europeans unfamiliar with the mode of thought of primitive people. As an instance of this we hear of a 'monopolization of cattle ownership' by the Batutsi, in Ruanda (East Africa), 'in order to exercise their power'. As a matter of fact, this only appears to be the case when regarded from a European point of view. If due regard is paid to local conditions from an historical standpoint, it is seen that the development has followed the reverse direction. The exercise of a form of rulership under which cows are lent and taxes imposed on the agricultural population is a constantly repeated process which arises of necessity out of the overlaying of an agricultural by a pastoral people, as is evident from Roscoe's reports regarding the Bakitara and Banyankole. It cannot, therefore, be said that the land has 'come into' the king's possession, but rather that control over the land arises out of the immigration of the more powerful tribe. Conflicts within the ruling caste have finally led to one of the aristocratic families gaining the supreme power. The existence of a pastoral aristocracy, moreover, is the reason why wealth is reckoned in terms of the cattle possessed and not according to the extent of the cultivated ground.

VIII

FEUDAL STATES AND SOCIALLY GRADED
COMMUNITIES

§ 1. The plough and irrigation systems. § 2. Distribution centres.
§ 3. Pastoral life superseded by agriculture. § 4. 'Business on a large
scale.' § 5. Among the Sumerians. § 6. The yield of harvest. § 7. Cattle,
goats, and swine. § 8. Organized expeditions. § 9. Estates and temples.
§ 10. Distribution of tithes and offerings.

§ 1. The transition from the primitive state to a higher cultural
life is marked by the plough (preceded by the wheel and the
waggon) as an economic implement; the distinction is marked
politically by the form of the state. The earliest forms of civilization in the ancient East of which history gives us a glimpse already
have these characteristics. Both in the Nile Valley and in Mesopotamia, India, and China we find further characteristics of the
economic methods formerly prevalent, that is to say the irrigation
systems. The water of the large rivers which overflow their banks
every year is retained and stored by canalization in the districts
with insufficient rainfall, so that it can be used to promote the
growth of the crops and increase the fertility of the soil.

Waterworks of this kind are also found in places where cultivation is in use and for draining swampy country, as for instance
among the Maori of New Zealand (Wilson ['22]).

§ 2. The irrigation systems were of great importance in drawing
together the communities situated on a river, of whom the greater
part may well have consisted of the same social elements and have
had to reckon with the same economic conditions of existence
(Westermann, W. L. ['19]; Erkes ['19]). In ancient Sumeria we
observe within the individual communities two main kinds of
distribution-centre: (1) the priestly farms grouped round the
temple, and (2) the farms held and distributed by secular princes,
alongside of whom an upper stratum of 'great ones' or nobles
occupied, no longer by their own right but by delegation, a privileged position, which soon tended to assume more and more of an
official character.

§ 3. The ethnic groups appear in this case already socially stratified and the expressions for man-servant and woman-servant indicate that they originated among the hill tribes (according to Professor

E. Unger). Pastoral life has clearly been superseded by agriculture, under changed economic conditions, since the latter provides larger returns, feeds a larger number of people, and can, as time goes on, be made more productive. In the conditions then prevailing in the comparatively densely populated lands of the Sumerians, which we shall next consider, agriculture had already become extremely important. For this reason cattle appear to have passed into the possession of the priests, into which order the pastoral class had withdrawn, and also of the princes living in the towns, who displayed their power and wealth in this way. On the other hand, agriculture became more important in consequence of the increased importance of the peasant stratum with which the pastoral immigrants had doubtless already become inextricably intermingled.

We thus perceive in Mesopotamia and in Egypt a tendency for the pastoral class to become agricultural, while in the course of history fresh pastoral tribes from the vicinity endeavour to conquer the country, forming at first a superstratum which, however, thanks to the entire economic conditions, is always absorbed through amalgamation and the adoption of agriculture (cf. also Meissner ['20], i.).

§ 4. The new feature in agriculture viewed in contrast with digging-stick culture, in which the individual plants are reared as seedlings, is that the crop is obtained from seeds sown broadcast. Thus agriculture technically represents a kind of 'business on a large scale'. The plough, though a simple implement regarded from our point of view, is a much more complicated one than the digging-stick or even the hoe. The fact that a large animal (ox or donkey) is harnessed to it is a technical symbol expressing the connexion between cattle-breeding and agriculture. For the sickle and gleaning cf. Maurizio ['271 b], p. 185 et seq., and ['271 a]; cf. ['26].

It is known that America had no knowledge of the plough drawn by animals and only of a kind of 'foot-plough', more correctly called a digging-stick, which was used in the ancient land of the Incas for loosening the soil. It thus represents a remarkable variation in the stage preceding the plough (Cook ['20]; Means ['23], p. 397 et seq.).

§ 5. The following summary based on existing documents has been made in order to gain an insight into the working of economic forces in the oldest available combination of agriculture and cattle-keeping among the Sumerians. The high degree to which economic methods had been developed is surprising, especially in view of the comparative shortage of technical tools and expedients. There is evidence that, along with a widely prevalent belief in magic, their economic proceedings were very rational. We must thus be on our guard against attaching too much importance to magic. The present tendency is to exaggerate its influence on the origin of agriculture; but in fact there is no lack of common sense and clear insight into economic relations among the Sumerians, the oldest civilized people of whom we have any knowledge.

§ 6. In ancient Sumeria the plough was drawn by oxen, donkeys, or mules guided by the ploughman. The plough was furnished with a tubular seed-drill for scattering the grain, which was sown very thinly, one-twelfth of a *gur* of barley on one *gan* of land or 10·10 litres[1] on 35·28 ares.[2] This means the infinitesimal amount of 0·003 litres per square metre, and about 28·6 litres per hectare.[3] The soil was extremely fertile, yielding between 80- and 100-fold, or about 2,800 litres per hectare. This yield, in spite of the great fertility of the soil, is not equal, in comparison, to that attained by our home agriculture. In Germany, in 1914, an average of 19·8 double centners or 3,300 litres (1 kg. = $1\frac{2}{3}$ litres) per hectare was harvested. The amount sown is, however, correspondingly greater, being 200 litres of barley per hectare as compared with 28·6 litres in Babylonia. The texts so far examined have not afforded any evidence of a second barley harvest in one year. If this were assumed to be the case, the amount received by individual families from their shares of land would have been proportionately greater (Schneider [201 a], p. 47).

§ 7. The number of cattle was not very great in relation to the land farmed by the temple itself. The highest figures given in a census of cattle are 190 cows, 73 bulls, 65 oxen, making 328 head of cattle, with, in addition, 17 male, 67 female, and 39 draught donkeys, making a total of 123. These comparatively small figures for the large agricultural operations of the temples are explained by the lack of suitable grazing land. The great amount of labour expended

[1] 1 'litre'=61·022 cubic inches; 0·908 U.S. dry quart, or 1·0567 liquid quarts.
[2] 'Are' is the area of a square of which each side is ten metres in length; about 119·6 square yards, or 0·025 acre.
[3] 1 'hectare'=100 acres.

on irrigating the land which was brought under cultivation made it better worth while to grow grain, than to use it as pasture. Grazing on non-irrigated land only lasted a short time, as the intense heat of summer soon withered the grass. The cattle had therefore to be fed on grain for the greater part of the year, which was possible with small herds but would have entailed heavy expenditure if the stock of cattle had been large. The cattle were largely used for work. The draught oxen of the temple, and the donkeys which were destined for field-work, were distributed among the peasants or *sag apin*. Some texts state that one or two donkeys were entrusted to other temple functionaries, such as the business manager (*nubanda*), the merchant (*damkar*), the brewer (*lu kas gar*), and the smith (*simug*). The draught donkeys of the temple were looked after by drivers and assistant drivers. Some of the four-horse teams belonging to the temple were placed at the disposal of the *nubanda* for his work as business manager. For the remaining animals, the temple maintained herdsmen with their assistants: cowherds and ass-herds. All these were freemen to whom a share of land was assigned. Indeed it appears that they were reckoned among the important people of the country (cf. in this connexion Roscoe's ['23] description of the institutions among the Bakitara and Banyankole). The cattle reserved for fattening, of which the number was very small, were fed on the waste from the brewery and were therefore handed over to the brewers. Small stock, i.e. sheep and goats, were kept by the temple in large numbers on account of their wool which, after grain, was the second most important product of Sumeria. One text alone records 660 sheep, the shepherds also being freemen, helped by some slaves. Long-haired goats, too, were pastured in the gardens, the goat-herd being supplied with barley from the storehouse as additional fodder for them. Even the swineherd was a freeman holding a plot of land called *kur*. Under him worked several groups of female slaves employed in fattening the pigs and in tending them when they were driven out on the reed beds and swamps. The products of stock-breeding had to be delivered by the herdsmen to the temple. Cheese, butter, and milk were brought in large quantities and handed over to the business manager or the superintendent of the oil and fat house (*Ka Sagan*). The hides of cattle and donkeys were only delivered in small quantities, which indicates that these animals were considered very valuable and only rarely slaughtered, so that beef was not considered an ordinary article of diet. On the other hand, the number of sheep- and goat-skins handed in was very large, indicating that these animals were used for food. The annual shearing of the sheep and goats was performed under the supervision of the temple officials, generally near the palace. The large number of documents dealing with wool is a proof of the large quantities produced.

§ 8. Wars and forays were very rare among the ancient Sumerians, in contrast with such peoples as the Assyrians, but there were occasional collisions between the different city-states. In order to obtain wood and stone from the neighbouring mountains, some of the Sumerian governors organized expeditions for felling trees, quarrying stone, and digging for ore, although their members were compelled, at the same time, to defend themselves against warlike tribes of hillmen. It is known that the Egyptians made similar expeditions to the Sinai region. These expeditions were supplemented by barter with the hill people, from whom wood, metal, and stone were obtained in exchange for grain. There were also professional traders (*damkar*), who visited neighbouring countries and maintained communication with the neighbouring towns. This commerce was supplemented by an exchange of presents, such as female donkeys for copper, bronze, and lead. The *damkar* had his share of the temple lands and was one of the principal personages in the city (Schneider ['20/a], p. 73 et seq.).

§ 9. It is not possible here to examine in detail the conditions of land-holding, leases, the position of the free labourer, and the organization of handicrafts, but it appears advisable to cast a glance at the relations of the governor (*patesi*) to the temple. The endeavours of these functionaries were directed towards the advancement of their private fortunes at the expense of the temple. Max Weber's supposition that the economic development of Babylonia had its source in the personal administration of the Sumerian governors appears to be untenable. It cannot be seriously maintained that the economics of the temple originated in the establishment of the governor (*patesi*), and the course of development must have been just the reverse. This becomes perfectly clear if we consider for purposes of comparison the more primitive economic forms and the question of political development. We know, for instance, that the estates managed by the temples were converted by Urukagina into his private holdings. The process by

H

which the administration of the governor (*patesi*) became detached from the communal administration of the temple is perfectly plain. The temple itself was obviously in the hands of a group of inter-related families who practised a common economic system of distribution. The real rulers of the country whose influence carried any weight are doubtless to be sought in these families. But, side by side with these, there already appear private businesses belonging to various influential persons who had made themselves independent of the temple association. Among these, that of the governor, who may well be compared with the primitive village chief, became in course of time the most important. His court was modelled on the administrative system of the temple. The special private business of the wife of the *patesi* should also be noted as indicating that women enjoyed great independence. Monogamy was predominant in principle. Women appear as buyers and sellers in trading contracts, they made contributions to the temples, and could even receive a share of the public land and fill economic posts.

§ 10. The tithes and offerings, in the shape of grain, cattle, flour, bread, beer, cheese, fish, dates, metals, &c., which poured into the temple storehouses were distributed again. The most important distributions were those which took place on the occasion of festivals and sacrifices, the first served being probably the worshippers. Distributions of this kind were made in the same way on the occasion of funeral ceremonies. The temple had, moreover, to provide for its large staff of employees and slaves who, again, received their rations of barley, milk, dates, oil, beer, &c., in very different ways. Finally, the temple community lived on these supplies, this community being the large family directly busied in carrying out the different ceremonies (Schneider ['20/a], pp. 29 et seq., 33, 36 et seq., 86 et seq., 90 et seq., 98).

IX

THE DEVELOPMENT OF THE 'FAMILIA' AND THE 'MANOR'

§ 1. Economic system in Western Europe. § 2. Municipal economics.
§ 3. Racial communism. § 4. Other illustrations.

§ 1. The relative position of the various decisive factors—one unique in history—led to the rise in western Europe (in Greece and Rome, as well as in the Germanic countries), of other formations. In these, owing in part to the superstratification of society and the introduction of agriculture, an economic system, in which the extended family among the ruling class was the unit, persisted for a much longer period than in the old large communities of the dry zones where tillage was dependent on irrigation. The geographical and climatic conditions were different in the whole of western Europe: there were no large rivers and perhaps, also, the cultural tension between adjacent ethnic groups was not so considerable as in countries with negroid neighbours. Here, moreover, all peoples of whom we have any knowledge within the historical period already possess the plough and keep herds of cattle. We find, more especially, that the horse was already in use, while it seems to have been unknown in the Nile Valley in early times, though present in ancient Sumeria, where, however, it was crossed with the ass to produce mules.

§ 2. Municipal economics in ancient Europe, though somewhat of the type prevalent in early Sumerian times, took a different line of development from that followed in the East. The struggles for hegemony in Greece were never so decisive as they had been, thousands of years earlier, in Mesopotamia. The development of Roman institutions, again, assumed another form as, from the time of the emperors onwards, oriental traditions were freely utilized.

For the economic history of antiquity cf. Neurath ['18]; Rostovtzeff ['26]; Meyer ['10], pp. 79, 169.

A different state of things, again, prevailed in ancient Germany, though our earliest information dates from a time when Roman influence was already making itself felt.

In his essay on the original Germanic aristocracy, Ernst Mayer (['11], p. 226 et seq.; cf. ['16] and ['24]) arrives at the conclusion that a peculiar form of racial communism applied to the cultivation of the soil was connected with large holdings. Since the Ice Age most of the Germanic tribes, as well as the Celts, who were culturally related to them, had, he considers, tilled the land assigned to the racial unit in common. It was due to this arrangement that draught animals were inalienable by the peasant in both groups. The matriarchal features are probably due to agriculturists superstratified by patriarchal herdsmen. Such superstratification had presumably already occurred in early times, when the small ploughs were exclusively used, as is shown by the Swedish rock pictures dating from the Bronze Age (Montelius, p. 86). The change to the use of the large plough seems to have taken place later, at the time of the westward migration of the Teutonic tribes, but it was of great importance for economic organization. Like the co-operative threshing-machine of modern times, it required the services of more draught animals and workpeople and contributed to the development of the large aristocratic farmsteads. The large plough was at the disposal of the senior of the sept, and he appears to have derived considerable privileges from this circumstance. It is not surprising to learn that, in consequence, among the Celts, Slavs, Eastern Aryans, and also among all Germanic peoples and, presumably, at first among the Italo-Greeks, the association was under the leadership of the elders. Development, however, did not proceed regularly. It was different in Friesland, and in Scandinavia, where we find everywhere a special association of settlers, described as *hafnae*, *byr*, or *bol*. It corresponds to the racial association and represents, economically, an agrarian community. All over Sweden and Denmark the holders of the *bol* quotas handed over part of the seed-corn as a contribution, exactly in the same way as the *villani* on the English *hide*. This was the legal service rendered by the heads of houses of the junior line of the racial association to the racial leaders. Racial leadership, and not the enfeoffment of land, was the basis of territorial rule among both Danes and Swedes (Mayer ['16], p. 130).

§ 3. The economics of distribution underwent a special development in the later despotisms of the ancient East. The kingdom of Hammurabi in Babylonia (Thurnwald ['03/04]) and, in particular, the New Kingdom in Egypt (Thurnwald ['01/02]) were centralized official despotisms which, based on economics in kind, had enormously extended the old system of communal economics of family groups, and developed it in accordance with a kind of communistic, but sharply graded, process of distribution. These kingdoms bore an entirely different character from the Sumerian municipal states which existed side by side on a basis of equality. In the New Kingdom the old aristocracy was entirely replaced by a body of officials dependent on the despot. Strangers (in Egypt, Syrian prisoners) were frequently settled in place of the native peasants. An enormous number of storehouses received the products of the peasants' activities from cattle-breeding and hunting, brewing and baking, pottery-making and weaving, &c. The produce was accurately registered, transferred from the smaller storehouses to the larger, in so far as it was not consumed locally, and finally reached the central administration at the court of Pharaoh. From there, the corresponding distributions were made, the Pharaoh's court was an administration in itself, formed out of the various offices and occupations. There were separate treasure-houses for cloth, works of art, ornaments, cosmetics, silver, the royal wardrobe, and so on, and also grain-stores, arsenals, wine-cellars, &c.

This organization, which reached its highest stage of development in the New Kingdom under the Ramessides, and provided employment for thousands of clerks, employees, workmen, and slaves, had, however, considerable disadvantages, the principal of which were that the official class always endeavoured to conduct the administration to their own advantage, arbitrarily oppressed those under them, were guilty of all sorts of encroachments, and failed to issue the sanctioned rations regularly. These irregularities led in the time of Ramses III to risings and civil wars which continued for at least a century (Spiegelberg ['95]) and provide us with a picture of the problems arising from the great technical advance of agriculture and the organization of the gigantic archaic kingdoms.

§ 4. In the absence of a genuine economic system of agriculture, we find in America—in Mexico, and, above all, in Peru—a similar gigantic centralized political organization, based on transactions in kind (Trimborn ['25] and ['27]; Joyce ['12]). As regards the economic system of storehouses in Mexico cf. Joyce ['14]; also, referring to the agrarian system of the Spartans, cf. Kahrstedt ['19].

Side by side with the great collective economic system, private enterprise of various kinds has always existed, and indeed, in the ancient East, attained a high degree of development and importance after the introduction of metals as a standard of value (Schwenzner ['15] and ['17]).—This may complete the characterization of the types mentioned above. We will now glance at the functional components of primitive economics.

PART III

FORMS OF ECONOMIC ACTIVITY

I

GENERAL TRAITS

BEFORE dealing with the particular forms of economic activity a few considerations with reference to some general traits may be appropriate. They can be compressed into the following statements.

§ 1. Primitive economics are mostly direct, i.e. no money, in the modern sense of a universally recognized and exchangeable standard of value (such as gold) is employed. If anything in the nature of money is in use, it takes the form of such actual standards of value as cattle, hoes, mats, so-called shell-money, &c. These cannot, as in our modern world, be exchanged indiscriminately for any other commodity, as there is only a limited number of objects which can be taken in exchange for them. Besides, there are often several different standards. This exchange has, primarily, no economic meaning at all, but a social one, as when women are given for cows in Africa, or boars' tusks for pigs (in New Guinea), or in the so-called Kula-trade (in the Trobriands).

§ 2. In a society mostly governed by single clans or by associated sections of clans, the acquisition of money is superfluous. The earning of money only becomes important at a later stage when the clans break up. This is a consequence partly because of the political power exercised by the ruling patriarchal families, and partly because of the increase in the number and influence of detribalized prisoners-of-war. The latter, by coming under the protection of the patriarchs, ultimately increase their power, a process which, in time, develops an 'aristocratic plutocracy', since the poorer members of the upper stratum (of herdsmen) need the protection of the 'men of more consequence' who are the richer ones. Rivalry among the wealthy aristocratic families leads at last to the success of one person. Thus 'despots' with their 'dynasties' are established, relying chiefly on the support of clients, servants, and slaves recruited from all strata of the population, even from foreigners. States, such as the so-called 'New Empire' of ancient Egypt, which have evolved a complicated hierarchy of officials, may serve as an example. At this stage it becomes possible for a man belonging to any section of the community, or even an alien, to overthrow such a state from within, and establish a 'tyranny'. He has at his disposal a population not composed of one tribe, or of related clans only, but made up of the most various elements. The peasants and some of the artisans may still form clans, or castes, or guilds, but a considerable part of the population is detribalized, individualized.

This is the point where money and economics become important. It is noteworthy that it had already been reached by the ancient Sumerians, and, incidentally, it indicates the abundant and varied character of their past social experience.

From all these data emerges the conclusion that the economic constitution of a people cannot be inferred solely from their technique or from certain prior stages of economic configuration, but must necessarily be founded on political conditions as well.

§ 3. The economic units of the lower 'horizons' (levels) are excessively small. Each clan or part of it, each village community, has its own 'national economy' and its own method of solving its problems.

On the higher 'horizons' (levels) we find agglomerations of a number of clans or parts of clans. These may be on the footing of equality (e.g. where they consist of agriculturists only) or on that of a stratification, especially of pastoral tribes over agriculturists and hunters. In this case *distribution* begins to play an important part.

§ 4. Distribution has its own particular history, starting from the most primitive life of the hunting tribes. The Eskimo or the Bergdama returning from his hunting excursion, the woman from her search for roots, tubers, fruits, berries, leaves, &c., are each bound to offer the greater part of their spoil for the use of the whole community. This means practically that the produce of their activity is given to the persons living together with the hunter or collector in question. The idea is that the person receiving his or her share will be ready to-morrow to give the same to the distributor of to-day. To-day's giving will be recompensed by to-morrow's taking. This is the outcome of the principle of reciprocity which pervades every relation of primitive life and is exemplified in many other ways.

Among some tribes, however, as among the Dama, there is an intermediary in the person of a headman, or other prominent member of the community. He receives and distributes all supplies. The consequences arising from this fact appear to be far-reaching. With these people distribution is still effected on a democratic basis, but in graded and stratified societies distribution is the function of powerful families of influential men, of the ruling aristocracy, or of the administrative bureaucracy; and it is often abused. The distributors of any political power reserve a percentage of the profits for themselves.

In the great potlach distribution it is a point of honour with a chief to display his wealth of hides and to distribute them. But he does this in order to place the men who receive them under an obligation and to make them compensate him by becoming his debtors, and, being dependent on him, his permanent retainers. A very similar procedure can be observed among the long-settled Polynesian and Micronesian tribes of the Pacific. Under these conditions the receiving of gifts in the form of mats, &c., and the distribution of others is rather a matter of establishing and strengthening social relations and obligations, than one of economic importance, intended to serve any practical end. The mats, for instance, are stored up and represent social wealth much in the same way as the possession of jewels is regarded by us. In this form the distributing function only serves for the display of power and for the accumulation of treasure.

This society is not essentially homogeneous; it probably arose from the blending of several different tribes. Apart from a certain number of privileged families, the rest of the people have been reduced to a new race of mixed origin, who have no recollection of any ethnic differences.

The case is different in societies with a more recent and more pronounced stratification, in which the incoming race formed a larger proportion, and used different ways of procuring food. The most impressive example is furnished by the contact of herdsmen with agricultural people. Here the gifts take the form of commodities which can be consumed, i.e. cereals, beer, &c., as in Central Africa. Compensation is given in animals, especially sheep and goats. The distribution, however, takes place among the members of the aristocratic clans only.

The conditions in these societies differ considerably. But the distributing function increases with the growing political power of a few families and the rise of despots. The chief receives the gifts of the peasants, which have now become 'taxes', and distributes them among his officials, especially those attached to his court.

§ 5. This development involves more complicated systems of distribution. A more extensive area controlled by a despot necessitates an increase in the number of warehouses, granaries, and treasuries, and a corresponding increase in the number of officials required for their management. All archaic states—ancient China, the empire of the Incas, the Indian kingdoms, Egypt, Babylonia—made use of a metal currency for taxes and salaries, but relied mainly on payments in kind, stored in granaries and warehouses for pottery, clothing, ornaments, carvings, &c., of various capacity, and distributed to officials, warriors, and the leisured classes, i.e. to the non-producing part of the population. In this case distribution fulfils an essentially economic function.

§ 6. The procedure just sketched must, however, not induce us to lose sight of the fact that, while a certain proportion of commodities circulate after this collective fashion, barter and trade are going on at the same time, either associated with social exchanges of the potlach type, or as a private affair distinct from the paying of taxes in kind. Private barter and trade become more important as the clan régime breaks down, as pointed out in section 1. But we have to bear in mind that the importance of trade is persistent throughout. Even concurrently with the system of distribution we observe a considerable, both extensive and intensive, development of trade. This must be regarded as consequent upon the rise of patriarchal families, each having its separate status within the community. It is precisely at this stage that an increasing number of commodities attain a recognized standard of value in relation to each other, e.g. meat and milk against corn, beans, and other cereals (as with the Herero and Ovambo). In the archaic states of the East the number of objects so recognized has been reduced to a minimum. The importance of exchange is emphasized in the markets of all these tribes. Their function in the economic development of these cultures will now be described.

§ 7. It might seem strange to speak of 'capital' among primitive people. But if by 'capital' is meant commodities which, by their own inherent nature, can not only maintain themselves but increase themselves, such natural sources of supply could more accurately be designated as 'capital' than the abstract money-values to which we are in the habit of restricting the term. The substance, however, of this 'natural capital' seems still more important than that represented by bonds or securities in our economic world. It occurs in two main forms: capital in plants and capital in domestic animals, especially cattle.

(*a*) Capital in the form of plants undergoes a kind of cyclical process. The cultivator puts his or her seedlings or seeds into the ground and in due time reaps many times the amount. The capital of the seedlings or the seeds is thus increased within the year. The capital, it is true, undergoes a metamorphosis in the meantime, but we are only concerned with the result.

The important thing here is the labour: the clearing, the working of the soil, the planting, the weeding, the harvesting, and the storing. A considerable part of it is done by the women. Consequently the possession of women is essential, as indeed has already been shown when dealing with the culture-zones in question. At a later stage, the work of the men, especially in connexion with irrigation systems in the zone of plough culture, is transferred to captives of war and their offspring, the household slaves.

In the early stages of agriculture, as long as plenty of land is available, wealth takes the form of stored seed grain, or of the crops, not of the land. There is no private ownership of land, so long as the clans exercise their power. Private property in land originates very late, especially after the establishment of patriarchal family-manors with serfs and bondwomen.

(*b*) The case is different when the capital consists in cattle, camels, sheep, and goats—to name the domestic animals which are most important, especially in Africa. In this case the stock, as capital, constitutes a permanent nucleus. The young are the interest yielded by the capital. The increase of this is not nearly so great as that of the plant-capital. In the absence of accidents, diseases, or fights, the increase, though limited, is more regular than that of the crops. The essential minimum of production is maintained by the increase. It requires good husbandry to increase the stock. Whereas the planter consumes the result of his labour every year, things are different among pastoral people, who preserve the stock and live on milk and butter or cheese, make use of the wool, or employ their animals (donkeys, camels, &c.) mainly for purposes of transport. In these cases consumption is replaced by the utilization of the living animal. The herd being no longer a direct source of food-supply, the individual animal, which can be used while living, acquires new importance. Thus a slight change takes place towards a certain individualization of the capital.

This change from consumption to use implies an intensification of the economic process, which is also emphasized by care taken to improve the pastures, as by burning the grass. Moreover, contact between different tribes introduces new varieties of domestic animals.

§ 8. The importance of women, especially in connexion with agriculture, has been repeatedly hinted at. Labour in our sense, especially that involved in cultivation, was primarily performed by women. This means that a series of operations has to be carried out with the utmost care and the most minute accuracy. The crops must be reaped, stored, and preserved; often complicated processes are required, such as that adopted in South America, for freeing the roots of manioc from poisonous juices.

These operations are most important where the man goes out hunting and trapping and only plants a few fruit trees (as in Melanesia or among many South American tribes). Men of position become more desirous of possessing women, in order to display the abundance of their crops, and to emphasize their social standing, by distributing fruits, roots, and other edibles, and entertaining friends at feasts. This results in the importance accorded to women and the complex of institutions generally summed up as mother right.

Conditions, however, change when the clans begin to dissolve into families and standard values appear; social reputation and social position is measured by certain standards of value. These valuables are given in the beginning by foreign tribes in order to acquire wives. This, being found more convenient than working with the father-in-law's family, becomes the general habit. Sheep, goats, cattle, hoes, &c., in Africa; armrings, necklaces, mats, &c., in other areas, are the friendly presents, the valuables given in exchange for the woman.

These 'valuables' are not, originally, estimated from an economic point of view, but considered as tokens of friendship; it is only at a later time that they are regarded in a more utilitarian manner. Together with this shifting in the meaning of the 'valuables', the position of the woman exchanged for them is correspondingly altered. It deteriorates at least juridically. In spite of this, her real position may remain untouched. Traces of mother-right are preserved, even in societies with strong patriarchal power.

Another change, however, is remarkable. The children of the woman exchanged for gifts, reckoned by certain standard values, are now claimed by the father of the family that helped to 'buy' her. This indicates 'father-right'. But if the bride-price is not paid the children generally remain with the mother's family. The patriarchal families, growing independent and self-reliant, begin to make use of women's labour and their production of children from a different motive, one determined by economic considerations.

We encounter the fact that women are captured or bought, especially from pastoral tribes, in order to get female agriculturists. Among the conquering herdsmen the clans dissolve into individual families with their own serfs and bondwomen, attached to the manor.

§ 9. The use of male labour has a different history. It originated with the captives taken in war. In the life of the primitive hunters and trappers there was no place for a slave. As there existed no labour in the strict sense of the word, there would have been nothing for him to do. The fate of a captive taken in war varied according to circumstances; sometimes he was killed outright or kept for sacrifice, but on other occasions he was given a wife and received into the community of the clan. In societies where agriculture is the province of women we find occasionally a captive doing a woman's work, in which case he dresses like a woman and uses feminine gestures—probably for magical reasons. With this exception slaves play no really important part in the tribal economy.

It is only with the splitting up of the clan-states that the use of slaves becomes a significant feature of the growing patriarchal family. First the prisoners-of-war become attached to their new master, who under these conditions is the guardian of his followers. They may be employed in various kinds of work, e.g. in constructing irrigation channels or in handicrafts. When past work they may be rewarded by plots of land, or by having cattle given to them for herding. These functions give rise to different grades of household slaves, or certain classes of tenants. As they may, perhaps unknown to themselves, derive their origin from different races, they are without clan ties. They are also used for various services in the manor, and most of the officials are recruited from among them—that is, those whose occupations are of an economic rather than a political character.

In a later stage when despotic rulers have united the small manors into states, and the upper and lower strata of society are individualized and detribalized—only the peasants and perhaps some of the artisans having preserved their clan organization—the economic process becomes more important. A large number of non-producing persons have to be provided for; the ruler's body-guard, the military class, officials, priests, &c. Labour becomes necessary and is furnished by slaves. Wars are waged for obtaining slaves, as in the ancient oriental states. In this case the slave, as well as his labour, is commercialized.

§ 10. These few hints may suffice to show how the political life is inextricably intertwined with the economic one. In fact, without taking this into account, it is impossible to understand economic organizations. For political systems, no less than economic developments, are based on the organization of human beings. The same men are politically organized who serve an economic purpose, and not infrequently, political ends are served by economic means. *Panem et circenses*, the feeding and amusing of the masses, was not only a feature of the late Roman Empire, but already appeared in the displays and distributions of powerful chiefs in an earlier stage of society; it was and is a means for making others dependent on them.

II

HANDICRAFT

§ 1. Early specialization. § 2. Work of men and of women. § 3. Professional utilization of handicraft. § 4. The spread of the potter's art. § 5. The use of metals. § 6. Influence of supernatural powers.

IN detailing the different types in the first part of this book attention was principally focused on methods of procuring food, the organization of which is, to a considerable extent, determined by the political and social constitution. In doing so, we have selected a few of the most important causes which determined the course of economic development in each particular case. No more than a casual reference was made to handicraft.

§ 1. Attention at this point will be devoted to the functional arrangement of the practice of handicrafts in various types of economic life. Specialization in handicraft, as already explained, begins very early and must, in fact, be characterized as primitive. Attention has already been directed to the division of labour between the sexes, and it was pointed out that the making of certain implements and tools is connected with the respective activities of man and woman. Further, the making of stone axes, the carving of daggers, arrows, or spears, the knotting of pouches, the plaiting of bags and nets, are the privilege of individuals or families who have a special preference for practising these manual arts, even if the other members of the group should be able to make the articles in question. The importance of special dexterity is even more apparent in the carving of platters and wooden vessels, the kneading and firing of pots or the plaiting of special mats, the weaving of belts, and the like.

§ 2. The practice of handicraft is not carried on in isolation (see Descamps, 4/i ['23], pp. 351 et seq., 374) as the older economic theorists imagined, but usually in the house; the making of smaller things, such as plaited articles, and minor repairs, the cutting of arrows and the like are also carried on in the men's house. It is either the case that one implement is made by men or by women only, or else certain stages of the working process are regularly assigned to men or to women only. On the Augusta River (Sepik) in New Guinea, for example (according to my own researches), the threads from which nets are made are obtained by the men, who

I

break off the aerial roots in the forest, bring them home and pull out the threads, which they twist by rubbing on their thighs. They hand over the twisted threads to the women, who then knot the net. We also find a similar traditional distribution of work between the sexes (which, however, varies from tribe to tribe), in connexion with the preparation of sago meal. The practice of handicrafts is firmly established in families, in which it is handed down either from father to son or from uncle to nephew, or by the women to their corresponding female relatives. In larger undertakings, such as the building of canoes or houses, the whole community, and often even neighbours, take part in 'solicited work', yet the work is superintended by a master-builder, and also in the case of a large undertaking by one or more magic-working priests, to oversee the technical and ceremonial minutiae (cf. also Malinowski).

§ 3. The practice of handicraft with a view to trade cannot be brought into immediate relation with any of the types of political constitution. The Melanesian potters make a stock of their wares and carry them on long canoe voyages to the people with whom they have established business relations, and exchange them for foodstuffs, in particular, sago, yams, and pigs. During the dry season, as their country is not very fertile, they are dependent on foodstuffs obtained by barter and on the profit they make on their pots by transactions in kind. They can therefore be correctly described as a community of craftsmen, although during part of the year they are able to earn a livelihood from their own land.

Such cases are certainly rare, but they show that a professional utilization of a handicraft can arise from a certain state of affairs in economic life, without necessarily being bound to a certain manner of procuring food or to the development of money. It must only be possible regularly to dispose of the products, for which foodstuffs or other needs are demanded in exchange. Within the sphere of transactions in kind and of the self-sufficing practice of handicrafts by people who have their own gardens and keep domestic animals themselves, it is not, as a rule, necessary to purchase foodstuffs. It is only when population has increased and become more closely settled, with a more highly developed technique, and the workers are further specialized into professional groups, that we find a concentration by means of large distributing centres, which facilitates the development of barter and a system of marketing. The conditions necessary for such an elaboration of professional groups are, in the first place, the joint settlement of various ethnic groups under a strong government which, on the one hand, favours a widespread system of economic distribution (thus creating the conditions requisite for the professionally specialized practice of handicrafts rendered possible by the state of peace brought about by authority) and, on the other, provides the opportunity of visiting the markets to dispose of products.

Among craftsmen, the potter and the smith are of special importance. All that can be done in this place is briefly to compare the spread of their art in the Old World with what took place in the New.

§ 4. The distribution of pottery almost coincides with the agricultural regions both in the Old World and in America. South Africa and Australia have no pottery; in America this art is lacking among the tribes north-west of California as far as the Great Lakes, with the exception of the agricultural tribes of the Missouri River and the neighbouring Shoshone and Kutenai Indians. It is also lacking in the extreme southern part of South America. The exceptional occurrence of pottery on the Yukon River in Alaska and on the Arctic coast may well be ascribed to influences from north-eastern Asia. The invention of pottery may therefore have its origin in two independent centres, one of which is situated in the Old World and the other in the central part of America. The question is more difficult in the case of weaving, which, indeed, is lacking among the Eskimos and the Fuegians. An exception must, however, be made in the plaiting of baskets and mats (Boas ['24], pp. 23 et seq.).

§ 5. In ancient America the use of metals was extraordinarily limited. Copper was in use in the neighbourhood of the great North-American lakes, in some Arctic regions, on the northern section of the Pacific coast, and in some South-American areas, but it was not won from ore and smelted. The utensils were hammered out of natural pure copper. The making of bronze articles was confined to a small area, principally in Peru and the southern part of Mexico; the use made of it was unimportant, in comparison with that in the Old World. If the discovery had been introduced from the Old World we should have to assume that it came, during the Bronze Age of south-eastern Asia, across the broadest part of the Pacific Ocean, without coming into contact with the island world of the South Seas; and that it spread no farther in the New World during the long period preceding the discovery of America. It would also have to be assumed that no other essential cultural components were introduced at the same time. It therefore appears more probable, as Boas says (['24], pp. 24 et seq.), that bronzes were made independently in the limited areas referred to, at a comparatively short time before the discovery of America, that there had not yet been an opportunity for them to spread, and that bronze had not been extensively adopted for weapons and utensils. (It is known that the earliest Egyptian copper articles are needles and ornaments, and that copper was only utilized later for weapons and utensils.)

§ 6. The work of the craftsman, like the procuring of foodstuffs, is considered to be constantly connected with the influence of supernatural powers (Lenoir, p. 43). It would, however, be incorrect to take an exaggerated view of the matter. It is not usual, in everyday work, to pay so much attention to these transcendental relations, and only when extraordinary measures are required—and in this case the conception of what is 'extraordinary' is by no means the same in every tribe—or on festal occasions, that a carefully thought-out ritual accompanies the whole ceremony, in order that the building of a house or a canoe, or the weaving of a splendid piece of cloth, may be 'correctly' carried out (as to the Caroline island Yap, see Müller, p. 37). In this connexion secret cults, involving the use of certain instruments, such as the fire-drill, the bullroarer, wooden drums, bows, fishing-tackle, and the like, are of special importance (referring to south-western New Guinea, cf. Wirz, pp. 31, 33, 40, 105, 108, 111). It is said that on such occasions a thoroughly business-like ceremony is carried out in an exemplary manner.

III

HANDICRAFT (*continued*)

§ **1.** Industrial handicraft has not reached a high level of development among the Kai people (see Keysser, ['11]) of New Guinea. Yet it is noticeable that, as a result of increasing contact with other tribes, they have to some extent grown familiar with articles manufactured by these tribes, and from some of them have even acquired the skill to make the things. This circumstance proves that the objects found with a tribe are by no means necessarily made by the tribe itself, and, further, that the skill to produce them can be taught with comparative ease by one tribe to another, when both are at the same level of culture. Only a few mats made of broad pandanus leaves reach the Kai people from the Tami islanders, but they are often imitated with the leaves of the kind of pandanus found in the mountains. The Kai obtain pots by barter from two tribes in the neighbourhood, but they themselves make none. They manufacture rough wooden platters copied from those traded by the Tami people.

The larger carvings on wooden posts are only to be found in the villages near the sea, and have doubtless been suggested by similar carvings done by the Yabim and Tami people. This is probably also the case with the drums and the head-rests. The clubs, ending in sharp points, or with ball or star-shaped heads, which the Kai people formerly possessed, are said to have come from the distant west. The Kai people themselves usually carve their long shields out of easily-split wood. They make carrying-nets and decorate them with patterns, but they also obtain certain knitted nets from the Poum people north of the Saddle Mountain. The handles of the carrying-nets are knitted by the men. All these things are the products of home industry carried on by individuals or families whose special province they are.

§ 2. The Bergdama copy the pottery of the Herero shepherds. The potter fetches the clay, which he has broken off with a digging-stick, in a skin from a distant locality, which he keeps secret. Suitable material is often provided by a termite-hill. On returning to the kraal (the tribal camp) he breaks up and crushes the lumps, and mixes the clay with water. The mass is kneaded until it is tough. He then takes a small quantity in his hand, rolls it, kneads it with his finger-tips, rolls it again and twists it into a tightly-closed spiral of the size of a five-shilling piece. He then begins to build up the sides of the pot at an obtuse angle to this little base. The sides widen out until the pot is half formed, and from this point they narrow in again, a neck as thick as a fist being formed on the top. The upper edge is somewhat widened out so that the pot is given the form of a vase or urn. During the work the parts already completed are constantly moistened and smoothed. When the pot is completed it is put to dry in shadow in the open air for some days. If no cracks are then visible it is laid on a blazing fire, turned in every direction and allowed to cool slowly near the fire. As the pot has no real base underneath, i.e. no flat surface which would permit of its standing upright once it is made, great care is necessary to provide a socket for it in the hot charcoal which will prevent it from falling over. If necessary three stones are used which are placed at the sides to prevent it from upsetting. The finished pots are sold for a goat or a sleeping-rug of skins, &c. (see Vedder, pp. 56, 61).

Apart from this the Bergdama make all they need themselves. The women's armlets are made by the men from the skins of the animals they have killed, so that the ornaments on the arms of the wife provide a record of the husband's prowess as a hunter, for he may only cut one ring out of the skin of each animal he has secured. The women alone make the karosses. These are made by sewing together a number of prepared skins of the smaller animals. During the day they are worn by the women, tied round the waist, so that the fold serves as a bag in which the produce of the veld is carried home, and at night they serve as coverlets. The men, however, do not use these karosses. The man carries home the game he has killed on a carrying-stick. As domestic utensils they use wooden tubs, bowls, pails, and spoons all made by the members of the kraal themselves. The digging-stick is the most important implement used by the women in collecting, and she constantly re-sharpens it on a flat stone, not too rough.

§ 3. The pots and stone axes of southern New Guinea are manufactured at home, chiefly for the use of the family or the sib. There are, however, usually a good many left over for disposal to outsiders. Pots are manufactured with varying skill among the Tubetube, Wari, and in the Amphletts group and traded thence in various directions. The Mailu also make pots, but these are not of very good quality and are only used to a limited extent in the immediate neighbourhood. The Koita women, on the contrary, make excellent pots, which are taken on trading expeditions to the Gulf of Papua (Seligman, pp. 15, 25, 45, 114, 526).

The tribes of central Brazil have specialized their activities to a noticeable degree, and it may be said that this devoting of themselves to individual handicrafts has tended to unite the tribes, as it furthers the exchange of products. The specialization is only partly affected by the natural resources of any particular locality. Thus in the Kajabi country they find the necessary raw material for making stone hatchets. These are supplied to the Bakairi, the Nahukua, the Auets, and other tribes. In the Trumai country diabase is available for the same purpose, to meet the requirements of their neighbours. The Bakairi did not possess a single pot that was not of Kustenau or Mekinaku origin. But they had calabashes which, again, were absent among the potter tribes.

§ 4. On Yap the potter's trade is followed exclusively by the lowest caste, the Milingai. Pottery-making is the work of women only. The women retire completely naked to work in a special house used in common by the female inhabitants of the village. The only mechanical aid possessed by the worker is a plank upon which a massive clay cylinder is placed, on which the potter gradually builds up larger clay rings. The construction by experts of larger and more important objects, such as a canoe or a house, is also at certain stages accompanied by a magical ceremony.

The way in which special knowledge is further artificially restricted is shown, for instance, by the Marshall Islanders' star and weather lore. This is not the common property of all the natives, nor yet the monopoly of the ruling families, but the secret of certain special sections of the tribe who hand it down among themselves. Nor does every member of such a section possess the same degree of knowledge. A father imparts the information to his favourite child, whether boy or girl. The information is often withheld by way of a punishment. No one outside the sectional association is allowed to possess this knowledge, and even the chief will entrust himself to none but a skilled expert of the recognized seafarer's guild (Erdland, p. 76 et seq.).

Similar reports come from Truk, where all arts and crafts are considered the private property of families, and are handed down from the father to his children, and especially to the eldest son. The latter is treated as the master of the craft (*rong*) and called *popinrong* (*popun* = trunk), i.e. the upholder of the craft. The other members of the family are the *panen rong* (pan = branch), i.e. helpers in the craft. The crafts include all the skilled work done in the island, such as the building of houses, canoes, and wharves, the carving of dishes, the cutting of trees, divination, the practice of magic, and all kinds of medicine. The following of a craft demands a special mode of behaviour from the workman. He must follow certain rules of conduct and observe a number of taboos. He must be well versed in the prayers, charms, incantations, and sacrifices of his particular calling, otherwise his work will never succeed. Both men and women may practise a *rong*, but most of the important ones are in hands of the men. The love *rong* and some medicine *rongs*, however, are the prerogatives of the women. One person may carry on several *rongs*. All *rongs* are treated as secrets, and when they are practised the doors of the house are locked. In very exceptional cases, the craftsman (*sowrong*) will teach his secret knowledge to a pupil for money and good words. Certain fish are sacred to particular *rongs* and may only be eaten by the *popinrong*. They also possess holy trees, which nobody may approach and whose fruits are forbidden. Under their shade is hidden the medicine chest, containing the mixtures sacred to the craft. The heart of the coco-nut palm also plays an important part in craft magic.

The principal masters (*idang*) exert an enormous influence over the Truk people: they are the sole possessors of religious, magical, and medical traditions and of skill in handicrafts. Among themselves they use a secret language which serves to strengthen their extraordinary moral prestige. Each *idang* gathers round him a flock of disciples whom he initiates into the secret language, rites, prescriptions, and tabus. The schools formed in this way compete with one another for the promulgation of their ideas and the increase of their influence. Their most sacred instruments are spears, fire, and conch shells. In time of war the *idang* plan the campaign. In fact, they are the chiefs and rule the tribal assembly, where they gain influence through their superior eloquence (Bollig, p. 43 et seq.).

Even in Melanesian countries, where arts and crafts are less well developed, special skills belong to certain families. This explains the sudden fall in standard dexterity in a tribe when even one or two families have become extinct, if these happen to have been the holders of traditional skill. On the islands in Torres Strait there was only one family of skilled canoe builders. When this family died out, in 1896, the inhabitants of these islands were no longer able to build canoes for themselves. Since then canoes have been obtained by means of complicated intermediate trading, from the adjacent coast districts of southern New Guinea (cf. Haddon, p. 296).

§ 5. When several communities are welded together under one powerful authority, the economic result is a circulation of goods either directly, or by payment and subsequent redistribution of gifts. Moreover, there is often an organization of work among these communities. Consequently each community becomes acquainted with the manners and customs of the others, the more so, as craftsmen can travel easily and have peculiar opportunities of meeting together at the seat of the central power.

In the extremely centralized Inca state of ancient Peru, with its graded organization and officialdom, the artisans were supplied with the materials from which they produced the admirable pottery, woven materials, wood carvings, stone sculpture, and vessels of gold, silver, and copper. The people in an artisan village received wool to spin and weave for themselves and their families, but they had to hand over a certain surplus to the officials and to the court. These amounts were exactly prescribed and registered. Every province and every village had special traditions as to the shape and style of its products. But the Incas also transferred artisans from the coast to the capital, Cuzco, in order that the arts of the potter and the smith should be practised at the seat of government. This brought about a confusion of styles which influenced the shape of the objects. Woollen fabrics were originally only woven on the coast, but the transfer of craftsmen mentioned above and the exchange of products caused a certain blurring, so that, later, the dividing line could no longer be so clearly defined (Joyce ['12], pp. 109, 198 et seq.).

§ 6. When communities of various origins were consolidated into a stratified and graded society under a despotic power, skilled industries flourished in an increasing degree. Since each community within the whole keeps, to a greater or less degree, to its own ethnic traditions, we find that its way of pursuing economic ends persists in the customary manner. This may be particularly well observed in the political organizations of shepherds combined with agriculturists.

Among the Kaffcho, in Abyssinia, household utensils and furniture, clothes, ornaments, weapons, and implements are produced, partly at home, for home consumption (or as a subsidiary source of income), partly by trained professional craftsmen. At home, the men, or their wives, make skin sacks, wooden articles, such as bedsteads, stools, boxes, bowls, and walking-sticks, prepare the fibres of the banana tree and twist it into string and rope or make mats and baskets. The work of house-building is done by the owner, with the assistance of his servants and neighbours, except for the doors and the gates of the yard, which are made by craftsmen. Crafts practised by specially trained workers are those of the smith (a term which includes both the blacksmith and the worker in silver, who also mines and smelts the metal and works in wood, making doors, &c.). Other recognized crafts are those of the tanner (who also makes shields and saddles), the weaver, who combines with it that of sewing or tailoring, and the making of pots, which is done by the wives of the tanners.

The handicraft is usually practised in some part of the dwelling-house. Only the smiths work in special houses serving exclusively as workshops. Rope-makers, tanners, weavers, and women potters usually work in the open air, in the courtyards of their farmsteads. In these businesses no outside paid labour is employed, the only assistance being provided by the members of the household. In Kaffa, neighbours usually assist each other as an act of friendship, to be repaid, later on, by a meal. This may be called 'solicited work' (*Bittarbeit*). Forced labour also occurs. If the work exacted from their own dependents is insufficient for their purpose, it has been the custom, since 1897, to engage Gala or Ometos from Dauro as daily labourers for clearing the ground or felling trees. The wages paid consist of a bar of salt for one week's or two weeks' work.

The craftsmen work partly to order and partly to make stock for sale at the markets. The smiths alone, when working as carpenters, do so at their customers' houses. The various craftsmen possess a number of special tools. Wood-carving is practised as a subsidiary trade at home. The making of household utensils, clothing, and ornaments of, or containing, fibre, leaves, grass, straw, and glass beads (plaiting) is done at home among the Kafficho by the women of all classes, the wives of the nobles and the rich providing for their own household needs, and the wives of the peasants and the poor making articles for sale. The same applies to the making of rope, string, and thread, and to spinning. The preparation of leather and the making of leather goods (rugs, straps, purses, and horse-collars) is one of the handicrafts practised professionally. Fur caps are made by the Mancho alone from the skin of the Buressa monkey. Pots are made on the wheel by the tanners' wives as a trade, and for the market. Professional weavers weave cotton yarn on the loom, buying it in the market but dyeing it themselves. Cotton yarn, dyed yellow, dark blue, red, and green is imported to Kaffa from India through Abyssinia and bought by the weavers at the markets (see Bieber, p. 701 et seq.).

§ 7. The pottery made by the Akikuyu, of British East Africa, is, both in form and in style of decoration, very similar to certain prehistoric English vessels. The material used is a mixture of blue clay and fine sand. The pottery-making is usually carried on quite close to the spot where the raw material is found. The work is done exclusively by the women of a few families who live in the vicinity. The finished products are often carried a long distance for sale at the markets. Whenever a death occurs the owner's pots are broken. If we take into account the breakages of the fragile vessels in daily use we see that there must be a considerable consumption of pots.

Among the same people the smiths make all iron utensils. If any one wants an iron article he does not simply order it of the smith and pay for it or arrange to pay afterwards, but he must follow a certain routine. In the first place the customer calls on the smith in the early morning and gives him a small present. If, for instance, he wants a spear, the matter is thoroughly discussed, particularly the quantity of crude iron and charcoal to be handed over by the customer to the smith. This material he must procure by barter either direct from the iron-founder at his home, or in the market. The day on which the smith is to begin work is then settled. The customer next orders his wives to brew beer. On the appointed day, taking the iron, charcoal, and beer, he proceeds, accompanied by his wives, to the smith, in order to hand over to him all that he requires for the work. The smith starts work at once, a boy blows the bellows and the customer looks on. From time to time they refresh themselves with a drink. The customer is present so that the smith may not be able to complain of having received only slag or other useless material to work on. There is a fixed tariff for the payment of the smith according to the article made. For the making of a spear, for instance, the fee is a good goat (cf. Routledge, pp. 87, 97 et seq.).

§ 8. Among the West-African Kpelle the most important crafts are wood-carving and plaiting. The technical processes are taught in the schools of the secret societies, where they are strictly reserved to the initiated. This recalls the medieval guilds. The smithy is always to be found at the entrance to the village. It is a shed supported by stout posts, roofed with palm fronds and the leaves of trees and surrounded by a wall about one metre in height. The local inhabitants work in common on its construction. When it is ready, a hen is killed and the blood poured out as a libation, some of the bones being hung in the smithy. The smithy, in common with the 'palaver house', is used for meetings. The smith is called upon to act as marriage agent and to settle disputes between families. He is always a member of the secret society, in which he occupies a special position. Most villages, though not all, possess a smithy. This craft is to some extent carried on as an itinerant trade, the smith working at each customer's house as required. The payment to the smith is made in kind, either in produce of the field or in other articles of value. He receives no recompense for work done under the orders of the chief; in particular, he has to make and repair military weapons gratis; but he is freed from military service. The southern Kpelle obtain iron, mostly in the form of the iron bars used as currency, from the Kissi and the Gbande (Westermann, pp. 33 et seq.).

§ 9. In the peripheric regions of Europe and Asia remains of the primitive practice and organization of handicrafts are still to be found; for instance among the Georgians in the Caucasus.

Many things are still home-made, not only various wooden vessels but also clay pots, bowls, jugs, &c. But at the same time a certain regional and sexual specialization has come about. The Georgians living in the mountains make fur caps and overcoats. The women make cotton girdles, cloth, and felt articles, and also weave carpets. Pots, however, are made at home, but only in villages where suitable clay is available. Weavers, tailors, and carpenters are much engaged in itinerant job work, and skilled women are employed in baking by the more well-to-do families. Carpenters and masons go out on jobbing tours to construct the better buildings, but the poorer villagers themselves construct all their own buildings of wattle and daub. Work of this kind is usually voluntary, neighbours assisting each other (Gogitschayschwili, pp. 35 et seq., 61 et seq.).

§ 10. In the case of the West-African Pangwe it is not possible to speak of handicraft in the sense of carrying on a trade. On the other hand, specialization in home work has already developed. The simplest arts, such as agriculture, fishing, and the setting of traps, are known to every one; but, on the other hand, the making of a simple appliance for carrying a child, consisting merely of two strips of leather sewn together, is already a special craft; while the craftsman who makes wooden spoons cannot make any other wooden article such as a spurtle. A stool-maker can only make stools, a maker of bows can only cut bows, and the one who makes the men's carrying baskets can make nothing else, and so on. As there are often only one or two people in a village who understand a certain handicraft, the inhabitants have to purchase the common articles not made by them, in other parts of the country; and it may happen that long distances must be covered in order to procure a stool, a bow, or the like (cf. Tessmann ['13], p. 329 et seq.).

Among the Banyankole both men and women were engaged in making pottery, and in every family there was at least one man or woman who made pots. For this reason comparatively few came on the market. While their pottery was inferior as compared to that of their neighbours, the carpenters from Ankole were superior to the others, although they did not depart from the traditional shapes of vessels. They were men of the serf class, whose ancestors had learned the art and handed it down to their children. The smiths, like the carpenters, also belonged to the serf class, but they did not attain to the skill of the carpenters in their work. They formed a single class, for the metal was extracted by the same men who worked it. Carpentry and smith's work both involved much ritual and numerous tabus (Roscoe ['23/a], pp. 103 et seq.).

§ 11. Among inferior hunting tribes and those still in the stage of hoe-culture, such as the inhabitants of the Andaman Islands, the Semang, and the Philippine Negritos, races undoubtedly very similar both in physical type and in culture, technical knowledge is not yet sufficiently advanced to form a social barrier, not even where individuals or families devote themselves to some special form of activity which finds its expression in home industry. As these technical processes are comparatively simple little or no magical ritual is connected with them. The ceremonial observances of these peoples are limited either to the obtaining of their food, or to the critical periods of life, or to the symbolism of names or of ornaments or, finally, to the phenomena of nature. In particular, certain things in the external world are also credited with magical powers; such are red ochre, plants or trees remarkable by reason of their fragrance or other striking characteristics, beeswax, fire, or the flesh of certain animals. On the other hand, the various technical processes of the handicrafts practised by them—such as the knotting of nets, the plaiting of baskets, and the making of mats and pots—are almost free from superstitious accessories (Brown ['22], pp. 179 et seq., 407 et seq., 443 et seq.).

The feeling that the object made has a life of its own and may exercise a decisive influence on human life has led to its being considered as a natural product and even, in some of the places where totemistic ideas prevail, being credited with playing a peculiar symbolic part. In one family on Yap, for instance, the rope made from coco-nut fibre is considered as the totem ancestor from which this family derives its descent. The followers of this totem may not hang food-baskets on a rope of coco-nut fibre, for that, they affirm, would be incest (Müller, p. 218).

In the New Hebrides certain handicrafts were only practised by particular families in which the skill was hereditary. There was no right to the sole practice of a lay handicraft, and the native was himself able to make all he required for his ordinary use. Any one could build a simple form of house, plait a basket, carve a club, or make a wooden arrow. The products of such work, however, can as a rule be recognized as made by amateurs; they are not equal in finish to the products of specialists. The good old pieces are, as a rule, the work of experts as, likewise, are all articles which can be dispensed with in daily life, such as certain pots, feather money, shell beads, ceremonial mats, dancing-masks, &c. In addition to technical skill, a knowledge of magical expedients was considered necessary for the completion of the handiwork. Songs and ceremonies were supposed to aid the successful conclusion of the task; and without them there was no blessing on the work (Speiser, pp. 255, 257). It is clear that this conception was based on the recognition of the fact that certain individuals and families really produced better results than could be obtained by amateurs. This fact was, however, not explained by the natives on the ground that technical skill had been acquired early and the art practised for many years, but success was ascribed to certain incidental accompaniments of the work. The so-called 'magic' is, therefore, attributable to the erroneous assumption of causal connexions.

The fact of the handicraft being limited to single families often resulted in its loss when the family died out, as we know to have happened with boat-building in the Torres Islands, weaving in Ureparapara, and pottery-making in Santo. The knowledge of their handicraft is no small source of gain for the family, but it is never sufficient to permit of the workman living on the proceeds of his work alone. The handing down of skilled knowledge from the parents to the children is not so much a question of systematic training as of watching and imitating on the part of the child. But it was also possible to be initiated into the secrets by a teacher who had to be paid, more especially in the case of magical arts. In the execution of more considerable undertakings, such as the building of houses and boats, the professional expert does not carry out the work himself but only selects the material and superintends the construction of the whole, lending a hand at most on the finer parts of the work. The other men taking part in the building operations have had no previous technical training. The magical processes by which the expert secures the presence of *mana* are considered to be his special secret. The belief in such special arts is so deeply ingrained in the minds of the people that those not in possession of the secrets make no attempt to practise special handicrafts. Pottery, for instance, is limited to a few villages which possess the secret, while no one in the next village makes any attempt to copy the pots.

§ **12.** In earlier times the principal articles made by workers in wood were milk vessels, pails for drawing water, and meat dishes. Another set of men made canoes, which were used on the Upper Nile and Lake Albert Nyanza. Recent times have developed a third class of carpenters who construct chairs, benches, and bedsteads. The makers of vessels for holding milk or water used to produce them in large quantities and sell their wares for cowry shells, with which they bought goats, thus investing their capital in live-stock. They thus often possessed large herds of goats. Magical ceremonies were also necessary in this case, for instance, in felling trees to obtain wood and so on. The king had a special carpenter who made the large royal drums and also his milk-pots and meat-dishes. The built canoes were made in the first instance by the Basoga and the dug-outs by the Bakitara. Bark cloth and also hides were prepared by special craftsmen; these, likewise, were subject to certain tabus (cf. Roscoe ['23/b], pp. 217 et seq.).

§ 13. Wallace states that in the Konde country, on the Nyasa–Tanganyika plateau, only a few families smelt iron, the reason being that only these families possessed the necessary 'medicine', which consisted, in part, of crocodile's gall. In both processes of smelting and forging, the influence of the spirits is believed to play an important part. For example, the Kinga smith laid a piece of dark rock on the iron when he heated it during the forging, while under the smithy fire there was a charm made of five different kinds of leaves. The fact that a process so complicated as the smelting and working of iron, in which the work is not always successful, depends on a further series of factors, apart from the mere manual work of the craftsman, must lead those who do not comprehend all the links in the chain of causal connexion, and yet feel the need of explaining occasional failures, to tread the mystic path of so-called magical processes. Every one makes for himself all he requires except metal utensils. Pots are obtained from the Wakisi. The Wabundugulu assert that they were the first to bring fire and iron to the Konde country and that the aboriginal inhabitants, the Habirema, used to consume their food-stuffs uncooked (Fülleborn, pp. 170, 183, 302).

Blacksmith's work appears to have been known among the Pangwe from ancient times. The smith does not occupy an exceptional position in their society: he is not despised nor yet does he enjoy any special privileges. His skill is, however, recognized, and he is more highly esteemed than other craftsmen.

The smith, like the woodcarver, only plies his trade as a secondary occupation and only when there is a demand for it; he never manufactures any stock. He thus only works to order, and is paid for his work, not for the finished articles. Every customer has to bring the iron necessary for the article required. As payment the smith receives, e.g. in the case of spear-money, 10 per cent. of its value. If, e.g., the blacksmith was making spear-money on order, he received 10 per cent. of the spear-money's value. The smithy is in the community house, where most of the men's work is done, and, when the smith has work to do, a T-shaped trench is dug in the floor on the spot where a sleeping-bench stands. Above this is hung a pair of bellows with its nozzle. Special huts are seldom used.

The smith's work requires the use of special medicines and magical charms. Cock's feathers, and the flowers, leaves, and stalks of certain plants are buried under the anvil. These plants are climbers which are supposed to have the property of causing the particles of iron when forged to adhere together as closely as the fruit, leaves, and stalks of the plants in question. The cock belongs to the cult of good things, or fire, and its feathers are, therefore, the most important component of the charm. To increase the effectiveness the cock is killed and its flesh cooked with the leaves of *acanthaceae* and similar plants and eaten by the smith. The plants mentioned have strong and pliant stems: it is hoped that the iron, and in particular the spear-money, may be similarly firm and ductile. In a newly-built smithy no iron ore may be smelted at first, but only wrought iron.

The extraction of the iron is now only carried on in the south of the Pangwe territory, and the work is done by the Fang and a few Ntum families. The Bulu buy the iron from the Ntum, while the Jaunde and Bene obtain it from the Etun. In extracting the iron the assistance of medicines and the strict observance of rules of abstinence are also necessary. The smelting of the iron ore is carried out under the guidance and control of a medicine man, and other persons can only acquire the skill necessary for smelting iron by purchasing a charm from him. This charm costs five sheep, five fowls, and five pieces of brass wire (equivalent to about £6). It consists of a bundle tied up in leaves containing parts of the brain and pieces of the skull of an ancestor and also fern leaves and fragments of bark. The skull and the brains, as

K

the seat of knowledge, are supposed to secure the success of the
smelting process; the bark is supposed to cause the ball of iron
to lie compactly and firmly in the smelting trench, like a tree
standing alone without roots, and the fern leaves, as they are
closely coiled together when young, are expected similarly to
close up the particles of the iron. These tedious minutiae prevent
the smelting business from attaining a greater extension. The
whole process of iron working is mainly under the influence of the
fire cult; but it is also intimately connected with the worship of
ancestors, who are believed to do all in their power to promote its
success (Tessmann ['13], pp. 204, 224, 234 et seq.).

§ 14. The artisans of Kitara in Central Africa all belong to the
agricultural tribes or serfs (*Bahera*), who live in bondage to the
shepherd nobility (*Bahuma*). The best craftsmen are the smiths
and the potters. The first handling of the iron, i.e. the quarrying
and smelting, is undertaken by the Bajugusi. It is bought from
them by the pig-iron workers (*omusami*), who work up the crude
iron into pieces of various sizes, which are again bought from
them by the actual smiths (*mwesi*), who make of it knives, spears,
hoes, and other useful articles. The extraction as well as the
smelting and working-up of the iron are accompanied by much
magical ritual, observation of omens, tabus, and sacrifices. The
first smelting of the iron is undertaken by a master worker who
is responsible, among other things, for the correct application of
the magic medicine, as well as for the abstinences and correct
diet of his comrades and helpers. The pig-iron workers, when they
go to search for suitable stones for hammer and anvil, have to
observe the usual tabus and perform certain sacrifices. The smith,
again, can only make the hammer properly if helped by two other
smiths and in the presence of his parents, while observing at the
same time a further series of precautions.

The same precautions and restrictions apply to the making of
pottery, beginning with the extraction of the potter's clay and
lasting until the pot is made. Both men and women make pottery,
but the better kind of vessels used by the king and the more wealthy
chiefs are made by men. The king has his own potters, who belong
to a special clan, whose sons follow in their fathers' footsteps.
A potter who made vessels for general use always attached himself
to some chief. He prepared a pot and brought it to the chief as
a sign that he wished to serve him. He then settled on the chief's

estate, and gave him one out of every set of pots he made. The shepherds chiefly required milk-pots (Roscoe ['23/b], pp. 103 et seq., 217 et seq.).

A peculiar organization exists among the goldsmiths of the Ashanti, who make the well-known gold weights. These gold-smiths form a kind of brotherhood, in which each may consider his comrade's wife as his own. In earlier times they were a respected caste. Only they and their wives were allowed to wear gold ornaments, otherwise reserved for the kings, greater chiefs, and their wives. In the Bekwi district all the goldsmiths attribute their origin to one *Fusu-Kwebi*, whom they regard as the ancestor of their caste. Two pairs of bellows and a few weights which he is supposed to have used are still preserved. Even persons who do not belong to the caste often apply to him for an oracle. The goldsmith's art is handed down in certain families from father to son. If there is no son, the sister's son inherits; when there is a son, he shares with his cousin. The inheritance consists of the gold weights and the stock-in-trade of the father or the maternal uncle (Rattray ['23], p. 301).

§ 15. In former times the Trobriand Islands were an important centre of industrial activity, wooden bowls being made in Bwoy-talu, pan-boxes in some village of Kuboma, flat-lidded baskets with three divisions in Luya, and ebony pan-boxes in the village of Kavataria. These articles were traded for pots, turtle-shell ear-rings, nose sticks, red ochre, pumice-stone, and obsidian from the Amphlett Islands (Malinowski, p. 287). The inhabitants of Bwoy-talu are despised as pariahs, and at the same time dreaded as the most dangerous magicians, although, or rather because, they are the most skilful and industrious craftsmen on the island. They belong to several sub-clans, all having their origin in the neighbour-hood of the village near which, according to tradition, the original magician arose from the earth in the form of a crab. They eat the flesh of the bush pig and they catch and eat the stingaree, both of which are strictly forbidden to, and, indeed, abhorred by, the other inhabitants of Northern Boyowa. For this reason, these people are considered as unclean by the others and, in former times, had to crouch lower and more abjectly before the chiefs than any one else. No man or woman would marry or indulge in a love affair with any member of the Bwoytalu. Yet it is recognized that these people are by far the cleverest in wood-carving, especially in the working-out of the wonderful round dishes, in making plaited fibre-work, and in cutting combs. They make all these articles in large quantities for export, and have no competitors in any other village. The artisan villages above mentioned carry on fishing, but every village has its own fishing-grounds and also its own methods of fishing. Otherwise these people differ from each other in many respects. The district possesses no paramount chief, and even in war, the villagers used not to fight on the same side.

Some of the villages in the interior, already mentioned, are also remarkable, like Kitawa, for their well-cultivated yam gardens. They differ from the others in having a number of special customs, particularly in connexion with the funeral ceremonies. There is a lively exchange of products between these artisan villages of the interior and the agricultural districts of Kiriwina, the fishing villages of the west and the sailing and trading communities of the north. The craftsmen, though considered as pariahs, are nevertheless allowed to take their wares for sale to other localities. When they have many articles on hand, they go to other places and ask for yams, coco-nuts, fish, and betel-nut or any kind of ornaments, such as tortoise-shell ear-rings and discs of spondylus shell. This leads to exchange and bargaining. People often go to the artisan villages to make purchases. People of higher rank first make a present and wait for the return present. The inhabitants of the villages in the interior, in particular those in which yams and taro are plentiful, have their special partners in the villages on the lagoon, where fishing is done. When fresh food is brought home, each one brings his surplus to his partner and places the objects in front of the latter's house. This gift must be repaid by a corresponding counter gift (Malinowski ['22], pp. 67, 69, 187, 189,).

§ 16. Spieth, in writing of the Ewe of West Africa, says that in the earliest times handicrafts were distributed among single families. In Matse, every quarter of a town had its special calling: some men were smiths, others were hunters, and others farmers. The weaving of mats appears to be a comparatively new calling, yet weaving seems to have been long known to these people. The smiths were subdivided into those who made swords, hoes, rings, and chains, while others only made brass objects, and still others made ornaments. After the Ashanti war, many of these families became extinct, and those who survived took to plaiting mats with a view to earning more. Not all members of a smith family are

necessarily smiths; only one here and there will be found practising the craft. Smiths are highly respected. Any one requiring
an iron implement has to go and work in the smith's fields, while
the smith is working for him. Payment is thus made by exchange
of services rendered. When a smith wishes to build a smithy,
everybody helps him with the building ('solicited work'). The
smith's tongs are credited with magical powers, even enabling
them to kill people. These tongs are used to make marks on a path
so that evil magicians who step on them may die. Not only so, but
any one who breaks an agreement will die if he walks on such marks.
In former times, the smiths in the Matse towns were entitled to
catch fowls belonging to any resident, which they cooked and ate
in the smithy. The owners made no objection, regarding this as an
annual contribution levied by the smiths, whose anger was greatly
dreaded. They feared that the smith might, if provoked, fall ill
and be unable to practise his craft. Thus the rest of the population
felt themselves dependent on the smith's handicraft. The smiths
no longer catch other people's fowls, but buy them and cook them
in front of the smithy. The art of forging iron, which was mined
by the smiths themselves, had long been known in the country
(Spieth, pp. 56, 90–2, 762, 776).

Among the Ewe people pottery-making as well as spinning and
soap-boiling are exclusively practised by the women in their own
homes. Clay is first dug in damp places and rubbed in a stone
mortar with a stick until it is finely powdered. Nothing containing
salt is allowed on the place where the potter's clay is obtained.
While at work, the woman is neither allowed to eat anything nor
to drink water, and she must also be sexually pure. If these rules
are broken it is believed that the pots will break. To give the
finished pots a glaze they are painted with the bark of a tree,
ground to powder and boiled. In soap-boiling a certain ritual has
also to be observed. As long as the decoction is on the fire, no one
must take a brand from it, or roast anything on the fire (Spieth,
pp. 780–2).

§ 17. In the ancient Greek states not only were extensive home
industries carried on in the country, but handicrafts had reached
full development in the towns. In general they were held in that
degree of estimation which we have already noticed in the case of
various primitive peoples: 'While elsewhere barbarians as well as
Greeks and above all the Lacedaemonians look down with disdain

on the craftsmen, craftsmen are least despised in Corinth' (Hero-
dotos, ii. 167). In the smaller towns, it is true, home work continued
to exist alongside of handicraft, but in the large towns, owing to the
steady increase in the number of slaves, industries on a large scale
were regularly developed in later times.

§ 18. To sum up, primitive handicraft at first takes the form of
home industries, but the various kinds of activity very soon became
specialized. Indeed, it is obvious that, from the very beginning,
this would result from the special dexterity of some individuals,
combined with special contrivances or expedients which do not
become the common property of the rest as a matter of course but
are confined, for the main part, to near relatives. (In ancient Peru,
the tools were buried with the man who had used them during his
life.) Thus the practice of a 'handicraft' becomes the secret of
a family or a clan. With this is usually connected a lack of a comprehensive view of the causal connexions leading to a successful
completion of the work. Thus arises a mystical strain, in the
form of precautionary measures or attitudes which we are accustomed to describe as magical. The more these things are thought
about, the more numerous are the superstitions connected with
omens and the heed paid to incidental matters, especially in the
case of peoples possessing a richer technique and consequently
better able to visualize the conditions governing success. These
magical expedients are kept secret within the family or the guild.

A handicraft in the sense of a 'trade', as the means of earning all
necessary food-stuffs, only occurs by way of exception among
primitive peoples. It is chiefly found in cases where, during certain
seasons, nature either forbids, or greatly limits, the obtaining of
food-stuffs with the aid of inherited technical skill (cf. Barton,
p. 424). It was not until men gathered in large numbers at the
courts of kings or local chiefs or in towns that individuals or
families entirely abandoned the personal provision of food-stuffs,
for we must not forget that, even where the practice of handicraft is
strongly developed, it is usually practised by the wife or the husband alone, and that, side by side with this, either the man goes
hunting or fishing, or the wife tills the vegetable patch.

Primitive handicrafts are usually carried on without assistance.
At most, members of the family or neighbours do unskilled 'voluntary work' as, for instance, in the building of canoes or of houses.

The esteem in which handicraft is held is also a result of historical development. In general, it may be said that in places where the handicraft has become an emergency expedient for people to acquire food-stuffs by means of exchanging their products, the artisan-communities become degraded. This is especially the case if the resources of their district are scanty or at least so during a certain season of the year. In such cases they depend on exchange with their commercial friends. If the latter have abundance of food they take advantages of the need of the others to reduce them either to servitude or at least to a lower position. In other cases, on the contrary, the secret and incomprehensible completion of his work by the craftsman has led to his gaining a reputation for beneficent magic, which places him in a particularly respected position. Elsewhere, the relationship of the craftsmen to the subject agriculturists reduced the former to servitude. On the whole, the dependent position of the craftsman predominated, since, naturally, he is unable to acquire any dexterity in the handling of weapons and is unused to fighting.

The circumstance that primitive handicraft is not primarily dependent on profit permits of entire devotion to the work. This is the reason for the perfect finish of hand-made articles, which often excite our astonishment and which have been made with the most primitive implements. It is due to the specialization mentioned above that we see the infinite variety of form characteristic of all hand-made products.

IV

WAGES

§ 1. Wages as a return. § 2. Return services. § 3. Board as payment. § 4. Special payment for special services. § 5. Credit. § 6. Services without wage.

§ 1. The word wages can be taken to mean any kind of return whether for services rendered or for the completed results of work done to order.

Payment plays a large part in the mental attitude of primitive peoples, which is entirely based on mutual 'give and take', even although purely economic values are not always repaid by others of the same nature, for it not seldom happens that the repayment is also determined by social value. It is only in more highly-developed communities, consisting of a ruling and a subject class, that a change in this respect takes place. Under the despotism of a conquering aristocracy, the demand for unpaid service becomes insistent. In particular, great families possessing slaves form small self-governed communities in which wages, as payment for services rendered, no longer have any meaning. On the other hand, the importance of wages is minimized where finished products are exchanged on the market for money or for things to which a traditional value attaches. In this case, we have to do with 'price'.

The business relations of primitive people being predominantly based on exchange, payment in kind occupies the principal place, taking the form of food or of articles locally held in high estimation.

§ 2. As regards the mental attitude of uncivilized races, which is entirely based on the mutual nature of services rendered, as exemplified in Australia, in the South Seas, and also in Africa and America, the remark made by Crévaux (pp. 262, 404) is to the point: namely, that in these cases there is no feeling for presents. If the natives (the Guiana Indians of South America) are given a knife, they ask: 'What do you want for it?'. In the same way, if the Uaupes Indians give evidence of their hospitality by offering cassava or smoked fish, they demand some sort of payment in return for it. Even when the return service need not follow at once, it is expected that it will do so in the course of time (Roth ['24], pp. 633 et seq.).

It may be said that unskilled help usually given by neighbours is repaid with gifts of food, or the helpers are invited to a feast. For the work of specialists, a special fee consisting of special objects of value is given, perhaps in addition to the ordinary wage. The nature and the extent of the payments is governed by custom. In this case it is not a question of exact economic return values. The services rendered are estimated in a conventional way. The counter-gift is a matter of honour, which does not involve any bargaining. On the other hand, the payer is more respected if he gives freely, for all services are rendered publicly; at any rate they speedily become known to the community in general. The payment, rather, is given and expected as a return service, not only from an economic point of view, but also to maintain a certain equilibrium in the relationship between the two individuals. The entire social and ethical life in primitive civilizations is based on such repayment with, as far as possible, return services and deeds of equivalent value. In this case, it is a question of the kind of value attached to things and of the possibility of comparing different values.

On the Trobriand Islands a man receives gifts of field-produce from the brothers of his wife at harvest-time. These gifts are so considerable that they amount to the greater part of one man's share. They are an essential element of the social obligations in the life of these people. A boy tills the garden for his mother. When his sisters grow up and marry, he works for them. The recipient of the gifts has, from time to time, to make return payments in such articles of value as bracelets or a pig. If he asks his wife's relations to work for him, he recompenses them with meals. This remuneration does not represent a full economic equivalent. Full equality of value is particularly lacking in the case of gifts or services rendered to the paramount chief. The tributes given by vassal village communities are usually repaid mostly by small counter-gifts (Malinowski ['22], pp. 177 et seq.). The fact that services between relations are incompletely remunerated is accounted for by the strict matriarchal law, according to which the woman remains a member of her family of origin to which her children belong and by which she is supported, on the ground that she helps, through her children, in the maintenance and increase of her tribal group. The man takes part in these gifts, and in his turn makes presents to the woman and to the children. Thus, by reciprocal services of different kinds, a socio-spiritual balance is arrived at. This cannot be understood even with the aid of exact economic reasoning. The contributions to the chief are treated on the analogy of the obligations to the brothers-in-law, and in reality on the basis of the relationship of the paramount chief to the tributary villages. For the paramount chief has wives from all the villages dependent on him, and the inhabitants of these villages have to provide for these women, their sisters. This system of recompense, built up on the principle of 'like for like', has, in this case, been converted in the interest of the ruler into a one-sided system of greater services, although the old form is still preserved.

§ 3. In order to make clear the peculiar character of the recompense, as it appears among many primitive peoples, another example from the Trobriand Islands may be given in detail. If a chief wants to build a canoe, he does not do it himself but hires a specialist whom he remunerates. The payment consists in the first place of a present of food, on account. Besides this, the specialist, as long as he is at work, must be well fed and, moreover, receives special delicacies, such as coco-nuts, betel-nuts, pork, fish, and fruits of different kinds. If he works in his own home, the food-stuffs and delicacies are carried to him at frequent intervals. The future owner of the canoe inspects the progress of the work from time to time. When the canoe is ready, a feast and ceremonial distribution of dishes takes place, at which the builder receives a further special gift, consisting of several hundred baskets of yams, one or two pigs, bunches of betel-nuts, a large number of coco-nuts, and, in addition, a large stone blade, a girdle of red shell discs, and some smaller shell armlets. Similar payments are made on a smaller scale in the case of other work, as, for instance, the felling of trees for the canoe, when those taking part in the work are fed while it continues, and rewarded with a special feast when it is finished (Malinowski ['22], pp. 162 et seq.).

§ 4. The remuneration of specialists presents a comparatively simple picture. Besides the craftsmen, of whom an example has been given above, the witch-doctor is of special importance. Indeed, it is often difficult to draw the line of demarcation between craftsman and witch-doctor, most arts being mixed up with complicated ceremonial and sometimes with magic, while the actual witchcraft is accompanied by many mechanical operations. This is no less true of the tilling of the fields, during which the master acting as head gardener gives various hints, some of which are of real practical importance, while others are only magical hocus-pocus; and this also applies to the maleficent sorcerer who knows the properties of poisons.

Sexual services are also regularly remunerated where sexual matriarchal customs prevail, for example, on the Trobriand Islands and in many other places. Even between married couples, a few betel-nuts, some tobacco, one or two turtle-shell rings or spondylus discs, and the like, may be given. Further, certain privileges and titles are paid for in a special way. If the nephew, for instance, wishes to acquire a knowledge of the magical art, or the title to a garden plot from his maternal uncle, he has to make certain payments to him. The young man is not considered to be in possession of the art in question nor may he use the title to the land until the last instalment has been paid (Malinowski ['22], pp. 185 et seq.). In particular, the knowledge of dances and songs is acquired in this way. In this case the village wishing to perform the dance and song must purchase the right to do so, which is done by the ceremonial presentation of food-stuffs and valuables. This completed, the dance is taught to the applicants. An adequate payment must also be paid for the hire of a canoe when lent by the owner for a certain time.

The usual objects locally esteemed valuable are used to recompense the work of craftsmen. Among the East-African Masai the smith is paid two goats and an ox for a spear; a large cattle bell for a sword; a goat for an axe or ten arrow heads; for other things he is paid in milk. If the customer has supplied the iron wire, the payment is only half of the amounts named above (Merker, p. 113).

Among the Kafficho or Gonga of Abyssinia a number of handicrafts are practised as home industries, others, however, for payment. The latter include the extraction and working of iron and the carpentry work performed by the same craftsmen; further, the crafts of tanner (who is also a shield-maker and saddler) and those of the weavers and the women engaged in pottery.

The transit dues demanded by chiefs from trading caravans passing through their territory, for instance in East Africa (Paulitschke, ii. 293) and also in Loango (Pechuël-Lösche, pp. 209 et seq.) are characteristic.

§ 5. Sometimes payment is not made immediately. The inhabitant of a village in the interior of the Trobriand Islands, where yams and taro are plentiful, has partners in a village on the lagoon, where much fishing is done but garden produce is scarce. At harvest-time the people from the interior make their appearance, bringing large quantities of vegetable food, and each of them lays down his share in front of his friend's house. This is an invitation which cannot be refused to repay the gift by its fixed equivalent in fish. As soon as the weather permits, the fishermen put to sea in their canoes. The inlanders, who have been informed of this, then appear on the coast, awaiting the fishermen. The total haul of fish is taken direct from the canoes and carried to the inland village. It is worthy of note that the ceremonial distribution of food in the villages of the interior must be carried out in fish, whereas, in the coast settlements, nothing but agricultural produce is allowed for this purpose. It is not merely a question of satisfying hunger, for it often happens that large quantities of these provisions go bad before reaching their destination. A similar ceremonial exchange takes place with the artisan villages, but only by people of rank: others simply bargain and barter. Their products, such as arm-shells, are exchanged for food-stuffs.

§ 6. In the West-African kingdoms which are much exposed to alien influences from the north and east, contributions and taxes are no longer paid with counter-gifts. In this case it is purely a question of one-sided contributions or services, particularly in the case of strangers who have settled in the country, or of passing travellers who are obliged to make presents (Westermann, p. 96).

In the stratified and thoroughly organized political communities of West and East Africa, slaves are usually available to perform personal services, while the products of handicraft are purchased ready-made at the markets.

V

BARTER

§ 1. The earlier view that primitive tribes lived without trade in private domestic economy must be described as incorrect. It may be said, on the contrary, that even among the lowest tribes, consisting of hunters, trappers, and collectors, such as the Kubus, the Veddas, and the pygmies of Central Africa, &c., barter is regularly carried on. In the mountains of New Guinea, when the Papuan tribes first came in contact with Europeans, return presents were quite spontaneously made for what was given to them, as I was able to ascertain by personal experience. The idea of requital, like that of remuneration, appears to be one of the original reactions of mankind. When applied to wrong inflicted, the result is the blood feud, and when applied to gifts, the reaction takes the form of exchange or the development of trade.

Primitive trading where it is not desired to make money but always to obtain direct the goods required, appears at first sight to lack the pursuit of commercial profit in our sense. But it must not be forgotten that this trading is, in many ways, restricted by tradition, and that the endeavour to obtain greater commercial profit is frequently made, not in an indirect way by means of money or other medium of exchange, but directly, by obtaining possession of things for which there is a demand.

§ 2. In the case of ceremonial presents, however, which play a very important part in many societies, no attempt is made to make them economically useful, as, for instance, on the Trobriand Islands, where baskets of yams are exchanged during funeral ceremonies for small polished blades. These exchange transactions constitute social ties in this society (Malinowski ['22], p. 175). Such an exchange of presents, as a traditional friendly transaction, also occurs on the occasion of the ancestor festivals (op. cit., p. 184). It resembles the procedure on the occasion of a marriage on Buin (Solomon Islands), when the parties exchange the same quantity of the same kind of shell-money, so that, in an economic sense, no transaction at all takes place (Thurnwald ['12], iii. 12 et seq.).

The acquisition of knowledge, such as that of magic or of dancing (almost universal in the Melanesian regions of the South Sea), is on a somewhat different footing (for examples see Malinowski, pp. 185 et seq.).

§ 3. Ceremonial bartering is distinguished from lay trading, for instance, on the Trobriand Islands, where, in particular, the process of barter conducted with the artisan population is looked on with contempt (Malinowski ['22], pp. 189 et seq.). In ceremonial distributions and exchanges, it is considered undignified to show any interest in the gift, which is thrown down by the giver, and not always picked up by the other party himself, but by one of his followers.

With regard to ancient Switzerland see Schenk ['12], pp. 330 et seq. and 349.

§ 4. Life among hunting and women-collector tribes is generally conducted, despite occasional friction, in a comparatively peaceful and friendly manner (a circumstance specially emphasized by Wheeler ['10], pp. 8, 29, 66 et seq., 72 et seq.). Among the Australians the national festivals formed a special occasion for the organization of exchange transactions. There were also trading expeditions for which the Australian hunters, owing to their nomadic mode of life, had a special predilection.

In primitive trading there is a special preference for certain articles of which the mutual relations have already been determined by tradition. Thus, among the Ovambo of South-West Africa, grain is often bartered for meat. People who have a large household and do not raise sufficient produce in their own gardens organize a kind of auction (*ohasida*). Every purchaser has to bring a quantity of grain corresponding to each of the various joints of meat and also to the skin and the stomach (Tönjes, p. 85).

§ 5. The journeys of the semi-Arabian Swahili were accompanied by great preparations, all kinds of omens being observed and oracles consulted before starting. The organizer of such an expedition began by going to a merchant to borrow goods, but as a rule he did not obtain them unless he could induce a man of repute to stand surety for him. If he was personally known, he might obtain goods on credit for his undertaking without such surety, and, in this case, a promissory note had to be drawn up in a court of law. The value of the goods was estimated in cash. An expedition of this kind usually took from one to two years. The principal wares were cloth, brass wire, shells, glass beads, and sugar. After the leader had ceremoniously taken leave of his family, the caravan started out, accompanied by a special guide acquainted with the route. In the interior, the principal business was the purchase of ivory, rubber, and the like. The transactions were concluded by a handshake. The carriers were fed on millet and cassava flour which they carried with them in goat-skin bags. On the return journey, the leader sent messengers on ahead and was given a festive welcome by his own people. This was followed by the settling of accounts with the merchant, which often gave rise to a quarrel. This older form of trading expedition ceased to pay in later times, for the natives in Unyanyembe and Manyema demanded more return presents and the Negroes in Nguu and Uhehe became more sophisticated. Conditions changed owing to the coming of Europeans. The former traders had to take to farming, for they could neither find sureties nor get credit from the merchants (Velten, pp. 284 et seq.).

§ 6. In communities with a strict system of economic distribution, we frequently find a monopoly of external trade in the hands of the distributing authority.

The description of the old West-African kingdoms in which the king as banker lent gold to his vassal 'counts' (chiefs) is noteworthy (Bowdich [1819], p. 295). See also Kuiper ['21].

In accordance with the monopoly of external trade prevailing in the West-African states, in many of them in the seventeenth century, the kings did not permit white men to trade with their people until they themselves and their court officials had received presents. In Benin, trade with white men was conducted through the agency of a few state councillors and merchants who alone were allowed to come to the Europeans. The warriors were specially forbidden to trade with white men, or to visit the European stores, the latter prohibition applying also to women. Such visits, in general, were only allowed to persons who had received express permission from the king. Markets were, moreover, held in different places every three or four days. Quarrels occurring on these occasions were settled by the nobles, for the local judges had no great authority (Dapper [1671], pp. 484, 487 et seq.)

A phenomenon to be noted is the attitude adopted towards proceedings injurious to the common weal, which arise from the development of trade in archaic states, such as the hoarding of grain. In the Pahlavi texts of the ancient Persians (West ['82], p. 174) various kinds of buying-up and holding-back of grain in order to obtain higher prices are condemned in the severest terms. Moral rules are also laid down regarding buying and selling, especially in the case of cattle. These are so many indications that, on the one hand, in this archaic society not only was money already in use but that also the spirit of profit-making—in contrast with the non-profit transactions in primitive society—had already gained ground, while, on the other, the moral condemnation proves that the new proceedings were not recognized as legitimate by the upper stratum of society.

VI

TRADE

§ **1.** The application of the principles observed in hunting to the obtaining of goods found outside the limits of the district, led to certain forms of exchange which appear to us later on as trade. In many cases regular expeditions are made for the above purpose by almost all the full-grown male members of the group. The knowledge that some useful object is to be found in a certain place may possibly be attributed to the fact that the group in question once lived permanently or temporarily at the place in question, or, perhaps, branched off as a daughter-group from one living there, or gained such knowledge by marrying women from those parts. In the arrangements for these expeditions, which often bear the character of foreign trade, the principle of collectivity makes its appearance.

The Central-Australian Dieri every year, in July or August, make an expedition to the south to obtain the red ochre used by them for painting their bodies. This is valued both as a charm and as a marketable commodity. Such an expedition is always regarded as a dangerous business. The seventy or eighty men selected to take part in it are all carefully armed and accompanied by a trusted guide. The distance to the spot where the stuff is found is about 500 km. (half the distance across Germany). When they pass beyond the limits of their own territory the party set a watch every night. When they come back great festivities are held in their honour. The Dieri also dispatch expeditions every year to the distant Herbert River territory in north Queensland, to obtain supplies of *pitcheri*. Their neighbours, the Yantruwunta, organize similar enterprises for fetching red ochre and sandstone slabs, for crushing grass-seed, from the Flinders Hills, 800 km. distant. In both cases it may be necessary to fight for the articles wanted, if the local people offer resistance

L

to their removal (Howitt, pp. 710 et seq.). The success of such expeditions is also dependent on whether the places whence the raw products are obtained have come into the power of an influential tribe.

The principle of recompense and of give and take is, without doubt, deeply embedded in human nature. If a foreign party arrives and finds the place to be exploited already occupied the only possibilities are (1) that the enterprise is permitted unconditionally, (2) that resistance is offered, and (3) that this resistance is overcome by the fulfilment of certain conditions. Such conditions may be of various kinds. The Aranda have to obtain a general permission from the groups in whose territory the stones they require for axes or hoes are to be found (Spencer and Gillen, p. 590). In another case a certain compensation has to be offered, thus, for instance, Billi-Billert, the headman of a local group of the Wurunjerri (in the neighbourhood of Melbourne), while strictly observing friendly behaviour, only allowed other groups to carry off stones on payment of compensation in the form of skin bags (Howitt, pp. 311–12).

§ 2. The group trading described above logically involves the requirement that the articles obtained collectively should be distributed among the individuals. For users or consumers must always be individual persons. The distribution takes place absolutely in accordance with the principle on which game killed is distributed. The Dieri chief, Jalina Piramurana, distributed the presents he had received from neighbouring groups, namely, pouches, skins, ochre, and so on, to his people so as to give no occasion for jealousy (Roth ['97], pp. 132, 134), this being the ultimate motive which impels the individual to share his surplus with others. When, on the occasion of the festivities for the young men's initiation, the head of the group offering hospitality received gifts from the strangers present, it was always considered his duty to distribute this 'catch' among the members of his group (Howitt, pp. 119, 305 et seq.). This participation of the members of the association in gains which may be said to resemble the results of a hunt is quite characteristic of the life of hunters and trappers, even when their women are collectors or hoe agriculturists.

A matter of peculiar importance for the circulation of goods is the distribution, not only of portions of the dishes but also of valuables, at feasts in the Melanesian and also in the Polynesian area of the South Sea, as also in many other places. Thus, for instance, the feast on initiation into the secret society (*sukwe*) on the Banks Islands is followed by such a ceremonial distribution of portions of food and shell-money. The distribution begins by the maternal uncle, as initiator, distributing at a certain stage of the festival half strings of his nephew's shell-money, whereupon a certain cake is eaten, songs chanted, and so on. It is not until the following day that the real distribution of shell-money by the nephew takes place. He uses not only his own savings but also contributions from his relatives and friends, and often distributes as much as forty strings in accordance with a certain procedure. On the other hand the maternal uncle gets back half a string from every one present and he again in his turn presents a whole string to the donor. This is followed by a distribution of food. It is generally considered that in the confusion of give and take the initiator ends by having to meet the deficit (Rivers ['14], i. 66 et seq.). The essential point of the procedure is the display of super-abundance or the appearance of super-abundance, with a view to increased social consideration.

§ 3. Among several tribes in the stage of hoe culture, collective trading journeys have assumed great importance, and secured a special position in the cultural life of the tribe by reason of the ceremonial inextricably connected with these enterprises. The annual barter journeys of the Motu people of Eastern New Guinea to the river mouths in the Gulf of Papua, when the south-east monsoon breaks, may count as trading expeditions of this kind (cf. Seligman ['10], p. 96 et seq.).

§ 4. A peculiar form of trading expedition is practised in the T.obriand Islands, to the east of New Guinea. The arrangements for building the canoes and the journey itself are undertaken, as in the case of the Motu, with many ceremonial preparations initiated by the ruling families, careful regard being paid to all sorts of dangerous influences and hostile powers. But in this case there is no question of bartering useful commodities such as pots and sago; the main point of the trade is the exchange of arm-shells and necklaces. However, these are not really regarded as ornaments but as articles fetching a fancy price. Moreover, the object of these transactions is not that any given article should come into the possession of the buyer, for the articles are said never to remain longer than a year in the possession of the person acquiring them, and he is then expected to pass them on to a third party. In addition to this, it is strictly laid down which neighbours are to receive the arm-shells and which necklaces, for, on the islands concerned in this trade game (*kula*), the arm-shells move counter-clockwise and the necklaces clockwise (Malinowski ['22], p. 83). The *kula* trade is only conducted among certain partners and in such a way that the number and importance of the *kula* friends increases with the rank of the man. While common people have only a few partners, great chiefs often have relations with several hundred. The *kula* friendships are generally inherited. The possession of the objects used in the *kula* ensures for a man the respect of his fellows: they are shown to neighbours who are told from whom and how they were got, and to whom they will be given later. They form the principal theme of tribal gossip. As these articles constantly change hands, very many of them pass through a man's hands in the course of his life. One piece takes from two to ten years to go the round. The articles exchanged always are spoken of as presents, and the counter gift must never be mentioned. Haggling is not allowed, but in general it is considered good form only to give good objects in return for good objects. If the man in question has no suitable piece at his disposal he can settle with his partner temporarily by means of an intermediate gift.

Still other presents and wares are taken for purposes of barter on these ceremonial trading journeys: a secondary trade is conducted side by side with the *kula* game which is bound up with the strictest ceremonial and, where it is played, governs all the allied activities, canoe-building and trade (in the usual sense) being subsidiary to it. On these trading journeys the secondary exchange is extended to yams, betel-nuts and coco-nuts, for which the less fruitful districts exchange the products of craftsmanship, such as red shell discs or turtle-shell rings. While, for instance, pots are brought on the market from the Amphlett Islands, and wooden dishes of different sizes and degrees of finish from other places, other villages produce armlets of plaited fern fibre, wooden combs, lime pots, or axe-heads.

Other barter transactions, also of a ceremonial kind, must be distinguished from this commercial trade, such transactions being conducted on certain occasions not only by these people with their fondness for trading, but also by many other primitive peoples. Thus, in case of a death, a number of gifts must be

balanced in strict equivalence by return gifts between the relations
of the dead person and the brothers of the widow. In the same
way a similar exchange of presents takes place when canoes are
consecrated, or when a garden is hired, or, on the occasion of visits,
even among friends.

Trading between the inhabitants of the coast and the people of
the interior has also been confined to ceremonial channels. In
this case the people in the interior exchange yams and taro for
the fish provided by the coast people. Here also the group trading
is localized to two individual partners. Often so much is given
that the surplus is left to rot. Trade here involves no one-sided
exploitation, nor does one party attempt to impose on the other.

§ 5. The so-called silent trade may be regarded as a variety of
primitive group-trading. This form of trade is known to us from
ancient times, and consists in objects being laid down at a central
spot by a person who then withdraws, whereupon, in accordance
with traditional agreements or notified by certain signals, the other
parties to the transaction appear, carry off the goods, and, after
a certain time, lay down at the place agreed upon the counter gifts,
which they have in readiness for the purpose, and of which the
nature has been fixed by tradition, and in their turn withdraw.
If the first donors consider the counter gifts insufficient, they leave
them lying in order to be changed or added to, as required;
otherwise they take them away. Such conventional forms obviously
presuppose a certain mutual understanding and are found to be
necessary with timid peoples who feel themselves inferior. The
Singhalese carried on this form of trading with the Veddas as late
as the middle of the nineteenth century. At present the Veddas
are visited by pedlars of Singhalese origin, who bring them European wares to exchange for honey and dried meat; but even these
traders have to remain at a considerable distance from the villages
(Seligman ['11], pp. 33, 39 et seq.).

Silent trading is reported from various parts of the world, e.g.
in the *Chronicle of Unknown Men in Eastern Regions*, supposedly
written by a Novgorod merchant about 1500. According to him
the people in question lived in the Altai Mountains. The traveller,
who visited one of their towns on business, exchanged his wares
for things which were spread out in front of every door, and of
which he was allowed to take a quantity corresponding to the value
of his own wares. If he took something without leaving an

equivalent, he was deprived of what he had taken. The same author mentions the existence of silent barter in many other places and among various peoples. He says that such trading was carried on in the past to the west of Gibraltar, and also in Africa between the Moors and the Negroes. He reports that in the East this kind of exchange was in use, even among the Chinese; and it was also found in Sumatra and Timor. It appears that in West Africa silent trading was the usual practice between alien tribes. Herodotus relates that the Carthaginians, on their journeys beyond the Pillars of Hercules, had dealings with the natives of the West-African coast by means of silent trading. In later times the Muhammadans of Morocco conducted their commerce with the people of Ghana in the same way. The Gola people in earlier times acted as middlemen between the Kpelle and the coast tribes. The Gola had their fields tilled by the agricultural Kpelle, many of whom were living among them as slaves. A few decades ago the pressure exercised by the Gola was so severe that they completely dominated the trade between the interior and the coast, and vice versa, so that the Kpelle coming from the north were forbidden to travel through the Gola country. The exchange of goods was effected by the Kpelle laying down their wares at a spot previously agreed on, where the Gola took them over, leaving in return articles of corresponding value. This silent trading was always conducted at a distance from the villages, and the memory of this usage survives in the Kpelle word for market, *dowo* (bush) (cf. Westermann, pp. 21, 27).

§ 6. Among the Pangwe of West Africa trade is carried on in a peculiar and peaceable way by means of presents, exchanged during friendly visits (Tessmann ['13], pp. 209 et seq.). A start is made by friendly visits among families of the same clan as well as among those of different clans who are on a footing of hospitality with each other. On these occasions the younger people in particular pay visits for one day, or for some weeks, or even months, even if this involves a week's march. Any sort of connexion, even a slight acquaintance, is a sufficient excuse for an unannounced visit. It is only complete strangers who cannot count upon hospitality. When visitors arrive in the village they first go to the meeting-house, where they are greeted in the following way. Each of the local inhabitants sits down on the knees of the guests and is embraced by the latter in this position. After the ceremony has been carried out by all the hosts, both men and women, with all the guests, a fowl (in Jaunde even a goat) is killed, while stories, questions, and reports pass from mouth to mouth. During the rest of his stay the guest helps his host in the garden and the wives of the guest who have accompanied him help the hostess in the house and in the fields, as if they belonged to the family. After a month or so the host leaves the guest alone in the village and goes in search of presents which he has to make to him, and which are often worth several hundred marks in German money. He usually selects things which his friend does not possess at home and cannot get easily for himself: for example crude iron, if the host lives in the neighbourhood of a foundry, European goods if he has connexions with a store. Advantage is taken of this opportunity to acquire various articles of daily use and also luxuries, for the host is expected to present as many different articles as possible. The guest then makes his way home with what he has obtained; but the host goes with him in order to pay an immediate return visit, and to remain in his host's village for weeks or months until he in his turn has received presents. On this occasion it is considered proper, not only to return the value of the articles received but, if possible, to give even more. Some time after, both parties again repair to the first village, and in this way the exchange of visits and of presents is several times repeated. It is, however, not in every case obligatory for the visit to be returned at once, it may be delayed for a month or even longer. Hospitality and the giving of presents are made of service to trade.

In view of this form of trade the holding of markets, which is otherwise very widespread among the Negroes of tropical Africa, is not usual among the Pangwe. Locally forged iron, in the form of small axe-heads tied together in fan-shaped bunches, was used as currency. At the present day it usually takes the form of the spear-head, varying in value according to size and simplicity or richness of design (Tessmann ['13], p. 1,212).

Among the Kpelle also (Westermann, pp. 36 et seq.) the essence of barter is an exchange of presents. In view of the prominent part played by the chiefs, trade appears to be virtually monopolized by them. The stranger, whether European or native, enters the village as the guest of the chief, makes him a present, and receives from him a corresponding return present either in the form of goods or in that of food and accommodation. Each party knows

what sort of things will be acceptable to the other. The visits of
the guests are not always accidental, but often really business
journeys, but the exchange of goods is conducted under the guise
of the exchange of presents. The chief is always anxious for the
arrival of the visitor, for frequent intercourse with the outside
world tends to increase, not only his wealth, but also his reputation
in the neighbourhood. Moreover, the other inhabitants also profit
by such visits, since food has to be purchased for the traveller's
carriers and various much-desired articles can be acquired by
exchange. Indeed, in their prayers they often make a request for
many strangers to arrive and bring good things, a custom quoted by
Dapper (1685, p. 412): 'The king invokes the souls of his father and
mother and asks them if they cannot bring it about that more
whites should arrive with articles for trade.' There are, moreover,
no markets in the southern Kpelle country, but only among the
Gbande and Gbunde. The wholesale trade in kola, cattle, horses,
and slaves is in the hands of the Mandingo.

The exchange of presents is due to a variety of causes. It is
often suggested by differences in natural surroundings, such as
the contrast between the mountains and the coast lands. Thus
the hill tribes provide the Makeo people on the southern coast of
New Guinea with feather ornaments, stone axe-heads, and clubs,
while the latter reciprocate with shell ornaments and fish. With
other tribes, long-standing, friendly relationships are strengthened
by means of frequent intermarriage, as is the case between the
Makeo and the Roro peoples (Seligman ['10], pp. 204 et seq., 313).

The contact between tribes resulting from migrations has led
in many cases to hostilities of a more or less permanent character,
but also sometimes to the establishment of friendly trade relations.
This is the case in New Guinea and also in the adjacent islands.
The relations between the tribes of the coast and those of the
interior are characteristic. In any case these relations must not be
regarded as entirely hostile nor as undisturbedly friendly. In all
relations, however friendly, there is a not inconsiderable under-
current of mistrust. In many cases the friendship is started and
maintained by the exchange of women and at the same time of
presents; the inland tribes of southern New Guinea, as we have
seen, supply those on the coast with feather ornaments and stone
implements, while the latter, having access to the sea, can obtain
shells and salt. Small parties often undertake long journeys in

order to procure ornaments, more especially those required for festivities (Williamson ['12], pp. 210 et seq., 233).

§ 7. Among the Masai herdsmen in East Africa the principle of barter is cattle for cattle. A fat ox for slaughter is paid for a small cow. When cattle were still abundant in the country, before the rinderpest made its appearance, and donkeys scarce, a donkey was bartered for two small cows. Conditions have changed since then, and the price of a donkey is now five goats. A fat goat or a sheep can be bought for a male calf two or three months old. In dealings with caravans, iron, brass, and copper wire serve more especially for barter as well as cattle, also glass beads and, in recent times, gaily coloured cloths. The demand for the individual articles of exchange varies very much. At times the supply of some things so far exceeds the demand that they are either not accepted at all or only at a rate much below their usual value. In the same way the value of other things rises out of all proportion, owing to the increased demand. Every transaction, whether barter or sale, is preceded by a lengthy discussion. As a sign of agreement the seller spits on the object in question. The exchange is completed on the spot, credit is only allowed to trust-worthy acquaintances. In the case of cattle, the risk attached to the object purchased is not transferred to the purchaser until the day after the sale, but in other cases it is transferred at once. With regard to presents, properly so called, a return present is obligatory. The non-acceptance of a present is regarded as a serious affront. In making the present the giver always spits on it when offering it (Merker, pp. 204 et seq.). Among the Kpelle, salt, iron rods, kola, male and female slaves, and cattle serve as standards of value. A slave is considered as equal in value to one head of cattle, Three hundred packets of salt (consisting of five sacks each weighing 56 English pounds) are the equivalent of a male slave, Three hundred and fifty packets must be paid for a female slave as the offspring to be expected is taken into account, just as is done in the case of the wife. One hundred iron rods, notched at both ends, are the equivalent of a male slave or one head of cattle, while 120 rods are paid for a female slave, and so on in proportion (Westermann, pp. 36 et seq.).

§ 8. A peculiar form of marketing has been developed among the Masai, where, at intervals varying from three to six days, the kraal of a family (since the time of the great epidemic about twenty years ago, several families usually live together in one kraal) is visited by a caravan of old women, accompanied by a few old men, who offer their stocks of maize, bananas, sweet potatoes, &c., for sale. These peddling caravans often come from a distance of four and five days' march, and remain for some days in the kraal before starting on the return journey.

The Wandorobo (south-eastern neighbours of the Masai, who turned to a predatory life, although formerly herdsmen akin to the Masai) devote themselves particularly to preparing the skins of the animals killed in the chase. If a number of skins have accumulated of which they cannot themselves make use, some old men start out, with the women and children, laden with the skins and with packages of desert salt, and make their way to the neighbouring districts, either to sell their wares at the regular markets or to peddle them among the cultivators. On these occasions the Wandorobo also endeavour to dispose of the flesh of the big game they have killed, elephant, rhinoceros, or beasts of prey. They obtain vegetable food-stuffs in exchange (Merker, pp. 30, 225).

Among the Swahili the organization of expeditions to the interior occupies an important position. They are doubtless strongly influenced in this respect by the Arabs, and both money and credit play an important part in their commercial undertakings. If any one meets a single person on the road it is considered a bad omen, but if he meets two men when starting out he hopes for good luck, and so forth. The obtaining of barter goods on credit from the coast traders and the taking leave of the family are accompanied by many ceremonies. The caravan is preceded by a drummer and the bearer of the *kome* (a staff, or a small flag, used as a protective charm). In former times the Wanyamwezi used to bring cattle, goats, ivory, hippopotamus teeth, and ostriches from the interior. In the case of larger transactions, especially in ivory, it was customary, when the full amount could not be paid at once, to pay at least something on account (Velten, pp. 286 et seq.).

§ 9. Even among a hoe-agricultural population we occasionally find individual groups of settlements specializing in certain handicrafts or in trade. This is carried so far that the population in question is, to a large extent, under the necessity of obtaining food-stuffs from others by barter. It appears, for instance, that on

the island of Tubetube the manufacture of pots and shell ornaments has assumed such dimensions that these things are traded
far and wide in the neighbourhood, while the inhabitants themselves obtain all other articles of daily use, including food-stuffs,
by trading. At the present time many of the Koita-Motu villages
are neglecting their cultivation, while devoting themselves to trade,
and living on imported food-stuffs (Seligman ['10], pp. 92, 526
et seq.). Even if this is an exceptional case, it is still a remarkable
fact that such a widespread and one-sided concentration of
activities should occur in places where hoe-agriculture, fishing,
or hunting and trapping are the usual means of livelihood.

§ 10. Another way of establishing connexion with shy and remote
tribes unaccustomed to trade is journeys taken by individual
traders after communications have been opened with these remote
districts. Thus we hear of Singhalese merchants visiting the
Veddas in Ceylon (Seligman ['11], p. 94), and Malay and Chinese
traders travelling up the rivers in the forest regions of Borneo in
fully laden boats, with a crew of only two or three men, before
the advent of European governments. These would remain for
months in the villages in order to trade in iron, cloth, tobacco, &c.
They were, it is true, often robbed and even murdered by the
Sea Dyaks, but were never attacked by the Kayans or Kenyahs.
The trader places himself under the protection of a local chief,
and can then feel that his life and property are safe (Hose and
McDougall, p. 202). The villages of the Kubus in Sumatra are
also visited by traders, whose boats often unite to form whole
flotillas. They have thus developed the habit of agreeing upon
certain halting places, such as, for example, the junction of the
Sungei-Danku and the Lekoh rivers. These occasional meetings
of buyers and sellers, being repeated from time to time, give rise
to the conditions necessary for the establishment of markets.

§ 11. In the lowlands of the Cameroons, markets are held in
the neighbourhood of certain villages, to which people come
from the direction of Nguti, and also from Mbinjon, Ossing,
Mamfe, and the Keaka districts. The markets are not held in the
villages, but outside on an open space shaded by low trees
(Staschewski, p. 38). One thus gains the impression that this
kind of market is derived from an earlier custom of silent trading.

In the market places of the Bali people everything required
by the Bali for their daily life is for sale, with the exception of

ivory and slaves: locally made baskets, mats, hoes, and pots;
sheep, pigs, goats, redwood, pipes, tobacco, fibre pouches, war
caps, knives, daggers, spears, &c. Ivory and slaves are only traded
at night or, if by day, then in remote places or behind closed
doors, as the people are reluctant to expose these commodities to
public view owing to their great value (Zintgraff, pp. 218, 219).

§ 12. Among the tribes of north-eastern Africa three kinds of
trade must be distinguished: (1) small trade among the residents,
(2) trade with the Arabs and Arab half-castes through the agency
of individual itinerant traders and, finally, (3) the caravan trade.
The caravan trade adheres to old customs and also to old routes,
the caravans, as a rule, making for the ancient traditional market
places (Paulitschke, i. 295 et seq.).

In Loango trading expeditions are usually organized by the
coast people, who conduct their caravans far into the interior and
back. The principal difficulty in these undertakings is the transit
journey through the numerous small sovereign states. It is usually
necessary to negotiate before entering the next 'kingdom'.[1] The
leader hurries on ahead and arranges the amount of the contribution; in his capacity of messenger his person is inviolable. By
threatening to turn aside and seek his luck elsewhere, he manages
to secure advantages for himself, for, if the traders are subjected
to too much pressure, the chief runs the risk of their seeking other
routes and of his thus losing the advantages of the transit trade.
The caravan leader usually makes it a special condition that his
caravan should not have to meet a funeral or a dead leopard, for
that would bring ill luck to the undertaking. A great chief sends
his staff bearer, or a messenger, who walks in front of the row of
carriers beating an iron double bell and conducts them safely to
the next district. In many cases, however, a 'kingdom' buys up
all the wares of the caravan in order to trade independently with
these goods. Districts which lie on much frequented routes or
convenient passes are naturally able to exact a more oppressive
rate of duty than others. Watchmen are often posted at the
entrance to their territory. Stationed at old fords are people in
whose family the office of guide is hereditary. The paths followed
are usually traditional, but trading caravans are not supposed to
move by night. They often endeavour to get through by following

---

[1] Really 'district' under a sub-chief (*kongozovo*). See Dennett, *At the
Back of the Black Man's Mind*, pp. 30-2.

by-roads in order to avoid the tax. If on a path or in a village
without a firebrand or a torch, they may be held to ransom.
A messenger or an urgent errand is allowed to pass, but he must
make his presence known by clearing his throat and call out
gently in a chanting voice, in order that he may inform those
who are awake without disturbing the sleepers. There are also
some chiefs who endeavour to entice caravans into their territory
and, on their own account, send envoys into the interior as a kind
of trade agents. This is done in order that the messengers may
observe, not only the movements of the caravans, but also those of
the people in other districts and may establish relations with the
latter (Pechuël-Lösche, p. 221 et seq.). These envoys, in token
of their office, carry staves, knives, switches of honour, iron bells,
and even presents.

The Banyangi traders of the Cameroons may serve as a living
example of energy in a trading people. About the end of 1900
and the beginning of 1901, Banyangi traders came with rubber
from Bakum as far as Ndian in the Rio del Rey district. When
the trade was transferred thence to Nsanakang, they came to the
latter place and exchanged their rubber for other goods. Three
weeks later they reappeared and brought rubber, ivory, and bark
string. With this string they indicated the length of other tusks
which they had not brought with them, as the chief of the Abokam
had made difficulties about the transit through his territory. The
salt which is bought and resold by the people in Mamfe and
Tinto is also an important article of trade. The Keaka people, in
whose territory salt wells occur, boil the brine in pots or troughs
until the water has evaporated, and then pack the salt in palm-leaf
bags and dry it in the sun. In this form it has become a unit and
standard of value with which woven bags, mats, smoked meat, and
spears (large and small) are purchased. The Banyangi bordering
on the grass country visit it with salt, palm oil, and beads, and
buy young pigs, goats, dogs, and spears. In return, the inhabitants
of the grass lands now come to the Banyangi in order to trade.
In former times they did not know the way to Tinto and Mampe,
or were afraid of being attacked and sold as slaves (Staschewski,
pp. 37 et seq.).

§ 13. Among the Ewe, trade, especially in connexion with the
establishment of markets, has developed to a considerable extent, but most of the Ewe are agriculturists and do not engage in

commerce. We must, therefore, in this case, distinguish a professional trader class. The main business is the sale of local products in exchange for European goods of all sorts. Formerly, in the 'eighties and 'nineties of the nineteenth century and even later, the slave trade was conducted in secret, in order to obtain spirits, powder, and guns (Spieth, p. 410).

Just as when several small tribes settle side by side, one of them will gain possession of the trade owing to some special circumstance, such as unfavourable soil or a feeling of superiority with regard to its neighbours, so, in like manner, a trader caste becomes prominent in stratified and organically composed societies. For instance, among the Oromó (Galla) of North-East Africa, where the members of this caste cannot be called to account or punished except by their fellow-members, they make their appearance in person at the principal market-places, while sending their servants or other representatives from the *Mandaras* to the smaller places where business is transacted. Aliens who have not been adopted into a Galla tribe are reckoned as belonging to the trader caste (Paulitschke, i. 313).

The Baziba chiefs of Central Africa were enabled to become rich without difficulty, as each of them maintained a staff of elephant hunters who, without receiving pay, had to hand over all the ivory they secured. The Warasura had some means of extorting ivory from the natives in Unyoro and selling it elsewhere (Stuhlmann, p. 619). It often happens that chiefs who belong to an upper stratum monopolize the trade. The case of the Malay *Djenang* indicates how such privileges come into existence (Hagen, pp. 119, 218).

VII

THE MARKET

§ 1. The market and trade. § 2. Meeting-places as markets. § 3. Festivals as markets. § 4. Tribal families and markets—religious connexion. § 5. Market restrictions. § 6. Spread of market business. § 7. Preservation of order in markets. § 8. Markets in early history of Europe.

§ 1. The importance of the market, and of trade, in early times and for peoples lacking in technical skill, is usually under-estimated.

Meeting places where goods were exchanged and markets were held may rightly be considered to have originated very early. In this matter, people would naturally be attracted to districts where some special commodity was to be had, as, for instance, salt. But festivals also offered an opportunity for exchange which was furthered by religious and magical ceremonies. If we take into consideration the acquisitive impulses, sometimes increased by special circumstances, and the universal mistrust of strangers, we shall understand the restrictions which often accompanied exchange and which led in some cases to silent trading, and in others to armed markets. But these forms cannot be regarded as the original forms of trading or marketing. We must recognize in them certain special forms determined by particular conditions. On the other hand, certain traditions were firmly established at an early date which preserved the peace of the market, by introducing restrictions as to the goods or the amounts to be exchanged.

Markets are not found everywhere; their absence, while indicating a certain isolation and a tendency to seclusion, is not associated with any particular economic development, any more than such can be inferred from their presence.

Among hoe-agriculturists, and in cases where the woman plays an active part, we often find women as the principal visitors to the weekly markets.

Such markets, which take place every few days and where petty trade is done, must be distinguished from the fairs, for which large expeditions by water or land were often organized. In the case of the more advanced of the primitive peoples, the market is often held on an inhabited site. It is, therefore, incorrect to jump, as is often done, to the conclusion that the archaic town originated only in fortified places, and to contrast it with the modern town which grew up round a market. There is no doubt that the origin of archaic towns is also attributable to markets.

§ 2. It has been repeatedly pointed out that the camps of the Australian natives are often visited by members of alien groups and tribes. An occasion for this is provided by the festivals connected with the celebration of maturity. It is also accompanied by an exchange of presents. The visitors bring with them the hand-made products in which they specialize, and raw materials, the latter often in large quantities. The proceedings begin by making presents to the chief who is acting as host and to old personal friends with whom business relations have been established. Thus, on these occasions, there is developed a real process of marketing between two or more groups, the wares being exchanged either singly or collectively for foreign products intended either for personal use or to be traded to a third party. The women also take part in this business. They trade bags, baskets, nets, and digging-sticks, while the men as a rule deal chiefly in weapons, tools, and ornaments (Howitt, pp. 119, 305 et seq., 714). This market trading is especially developed in the South-Eastern Territories and North-West Queensland. Such markets are held in the South-East Territories and are quite distinct from ordinary neighbourly meetings. The trade messenger is inviolable. In certain places markets are held from time to time, as, for instance, in Kopperanama on Cooper's Creek. In Queensland, markets are often held on the initiative of individual chiefs, agreements being come to through messengers as to the kind of market, the time, and the class of goods; but it also happens that individuals take to the road in order to do business either on their own account or for others (a sort of pedlary). These trade relations and markets naturally further the exchange not only of material objects but also of idioms, songs, and dances as well as of ideas, customs, and domestic arrangements (Roth ['97], pp. 132, 134; Knabenhans ['19], p. 100 et seq.).

§ 3. The existence of markets is also reported among the Papuans in the interior of Dutch New Guinea; in this case they are for the sale of pigs and are followed by festivities and a ceremonial meal. Worthy of note in this connexion, on the one hand, is the strongly developed commercial spirit of the Papuans, possessed in a greater degree by the tribes of the interior than by the coast people. This is shown by the existence of a currency token in the form of a small *Cypraea* shell called *Tingale*. On the other hand, lively intercourse over great distances takes place in the interior, and is not even checked by mountains 10,000 feet high. Visits are even paid to alien tribes whose language is not understood (Wirz ['24], pp. 120 et seq.).

In the New Hebrides (Oceania) periodical meetings are held at which pigs and other valuables are exchanged. Usually, but not invariably, these meetings take place in connexion with sacrificial feasts, as pigs often have to change hands when any particular man is not in a position to supply his quota. These meetings are in any case festive occasions, something like rural market-days in Europe, when people appear in their best clothes, meet old acquaintances, make new ones, and form new business connexions. It is, so to say, part of the native's civic duty to be present at these meetings, and in a populous district they take place about every three days. Nearly every man is directly or indirectly interested in the business done, so that he would not willingly miss such a meeting. These meetings are, therefore, the breeding-places of all intrigues, plots, and quarrels, not to mention the friction generated during the bargaining.

These feasts could not be held without such stock exchanges, because no one possesses the whole number of sacrificial animals required; the candidate for the secret society has to get some of them back from his debtors and borrow the rest from others. The transfer of the pigs from hand to hand takes place before the actual sacrifice, but does not form part of the ceremony. In East Santo these markets are conducted in accordance with a fixed traditional rite. The place is carefully cleaned and decorated with flowers and leaves, and various rites are enacted, to represent the borrowing and giving back of the pigs. The transactions have been discussed and prepared beforehand, what takes place now is the public and solemn declaration of the change of ownership made. The speeches and posturings which accompany the ceremony express the idea of renunciation or transfer of rights. If a man wishes at once to lend the pig which has been given back to him to a third party, three men take part in the ceremony: the original debtor, the proprietor, and the new debtor. In this way, a pig can often change hands, being passed on from village to village until the day of its slaughter at a sacrificial feast. The proceedings become more complicated when the liabilities incurred by a man now dead have to be discharged. The debts of the deceased must be taken over by his heirs, i.e. by his nearest relatives in the clan: his brothers and the children of his sister. It is worthy of note that in these ceremonies there is never a question of sale but only of exchange. When, at the present day, pigs are bought for money it is not necessary that the transaction should be conducted publicly. Buying with money is thus an element in a foreign civilization unknown to the old customs. At these stock exchanges it is mainly a question of exchanging pigs for mats. The festivities and ceremonies above mentioned are often connected with the *suque* club, for the right of entry into this society is bought by sacrificing pigs. Where money mats are in use they are piled up on the spot in long bundles and carefully counted and carried away by the recipient. They are often rearranged and divided every time they change hands. The natives dance round them as they dance round the pigs. Transactions are confirmed by the ceremonies mentioned ('contract in fact') just as if they had been certified in writing. They have the form of law, unless some influential man chooses to ignore them (Speiser, pp. 277–8, 407 et seq.).

When the kingdom of Kitara in Central Africa was at the height of its power, it possessed two important centres of the salt trade, of which only Kibero on Lake Albert remains in its possession. In this village there is an open shed serving as a market-place, where a brisk trade is carried on. People come from all parts of the country to buy salt, and bring, in exchange, beans, potatoes, plantains, peas, and other foods, cooking and water-pots, animals, firewood, and all sorts of things needed for clothing, domestic purposes, and building (Roscoe ['23/b], p. 234).

§ 4. In the Chaga country, almost every market-place is still connected with one or more clans who let it be clearly understood that they were the first founders and owners of these places. In the case of many markets it can still be ascertained that they were shifted when the clan migrated to another dwelling-place. After the power of the chiefs had arisen, the clans continued to perform religious duties in connexion with the market. The market must be regularly visited on market days. If any occurrence should prevent the holding of the market on one or more days, business cannot be resumed until the market place has been purified. This expiation ceremony must be carried out by the ceremonial elders of the clans concerned, each of them being accompanied by an old woman. For this purpose a ewe is sacrificed in the centre of the market-place, to the accompaniment of expiatory prayers to the ancestors who established the market. The whole market-place is then sprinkled with the blood of the animal, the contents of the stomach, and the expiatory water. The old women exchange field products which they have brought with them. It is only after this that the market can be visited without danger. The animal for sacrifice has to be provided by one of the clans connected with the market. These clans, no doubt, originally collected the market toll. In one of the clans the office of tasting is hereditary. The taster (*mosuhura*) was bound to appear in good time on every market-day. The bartering could not begin until he had collected the toll. He took one handful from the market-basket of every woman. In return, every woman had the right of cuffing him once. He then carried away the tribute with the assistance of his wife. A well-attended market provided considerable returns. The tribute was only levied on field-produce, bananas, and salt. Milk and butter were free. This would appear to point to the fact that field-produce and salt were the first articles to appear at this market, while the animal products did not make their appearance till later. This market tax had presumably a magico-religious meaning, for dangers which might possibly assail the goods were averted by arranging for the collection of the tax by the clan conducting the market through the agency of the taster. Thus, the women said on one occasion, when a taster declined to accept this office, that they could not visit the market any more as they did not dare to cook the untasted market-produce for their children. This office of taster had nothing to do with the market police. The protection of the market, along with many other clan rights, has been transferred to the paramount chief, and, at the present time, life is as secure under his authority as under that of the taster. The wives of the chief and the district headman are responsible for honest dealing on the part of all and provide a speedy expiation for all breaches of rule. In former times, the market-place was considered as desecrated if blood was spilt on it, not only in a quarrel but even by accident. Every injury occurring on the market-place and involving the shedding of blood necessitated immediate expiation. From that moment, no woman was allowed to leave the market-place and no goods might be touched; they had to be cleansed before they could be carried away and used for food. At the very least, a goat had to be sacrificed at once. A more extensive and more serious expiation was necessary if a woman bore a child or had a miscarriage on the market-place. In that case a milch animal was necessary. In addition to this, the homestead of the chief had to be purified by means of the sacrificial blood of a milch cow. All the women in the country were thus sprinkled, district by district, (Gutmann, pp. 425 et seq.).

§ 5. Passarge, writing of the upper Benue (Adamawa, Central Sudan), describes a scene on that river (p. 360), where the Munchi had brought skins and meat for sale, while the Jukum appeared at the appointed place, on the opposite bank, with fish and grain, only the men being present. Every man (see illustration, Passarge, p. 353) stood prepared for battle, with bow and arrow in his left hand and the knife in his right, in front of his treasures. In every canoe sat a Jukum ready to push off. Trading in these parts usually ends in bloodshed. When the war alarm sounds, the Munchi rush into the bush and the Jukum escapes in his canoe, while arrows and curses fly to and fro. The combatants then go home, leaving a few dead on each side. Probably this custom should be regarded rather as the result of strained relations than as a survival from the earliest times.

In East Africa markets play a conspicuous part, although they have not spread everywhere to the same extent. In some places they appear to be totally lacking, as in Eastern Ruanda. Markets are probably an old institution which has been kept up in the north and west of Ruanda, but disappeared in the eastern provinces after they had been conquered by the Batutsi, because the commodities were frequently confiscated on account of arrears of taxation. In Nduga two markets for hoes have been recorded, and others which were much frequented by smiths. In Nyundo markets for the sale of food have been held daily from early times. The people used to meet early in the morning and separate again between 11 o'clock and noon. In the western district of Ruanda, the markets are met every three or four hours' march. In Njundo goods are exchanged through the agency of middlemen, who receive a commission. In order to avoid the market charges, agreements are often made on the roads in the neighbourhood, so that small subsidiary markets have come into existence at the crossroads (Czekanowski, pp. 64 et seq.; Kandt, p. 294).

In the Abyssinian territories, the Baza had no market-places at all and avoided all intercourse with alien traders. They maintained relations only in the north with the Barea, from whom they bought honey and grain. They visited the market of Mogelo, which was frequented by other alien traders. This market was held every morning outside the village, on an open space surrounded by a fence, which was treated by everybody as neutral ground. The market of Mogelo was frequented until the village was burnt and laid waste in 1861 by Sadiq's troops (Munzinger ['83], pp. 119 et seq.).

§ 6. In the northern Kpelle country there are no markets, but they are found among the Gbande and Gbunde. Here, owing to the Islamic influence of the Mandingo, a market is held every week. The market-place is within the settlement, or at a certain spot between two villages. The goods offered for sale are of different kinds: palm oil, raw and cleaned cotton, brass buttons, which are worn instead of beads, dried fish, crabs, red pepper, kola nuts, salt, iron bars, palm-nuts, sweet potatoes, bananas, rice, beans, tomatoes, gourd bottles, tobacco, cloth, butter, mats, cowrie shells, &c. The Liberian Government some years ago attempted the forcible introduction of markets in the south, but in so abrupt and tactless a manner that the people resented the innovation, and the plan was a failure (Westermann, pp. 36 et seq.).

Among the Kafficho and Gonga, in the interior of North-East Africa, all the petty trading is carried on at the markets. It includes grain, coffee, beer, cattle, and various food-stuffs as well as manufactured articles. The traders from Kaffa, especially those from the districts adjoining the northern and eastern frontiers, go to the markets of Jimma-Kaka, Konta, and Dauro. The wares they bring with them do not as a rule amount to more than a head load per man. They mostly bring grain, chickens, and sheep, which are sold in small quantities or singly. There are special fair grounds for wholesale trading which are also visited by alien merchants. In these places, every foreign trader was permitted to build a dwelling house for himself and a store for his stock in trade. These traders also possessed small plots of ground which they had either purchased from the owners or had had allocated to them by the ruler. The fair ground of Gonga was divided into quarters, each of which was assigned to traders from one district. In other cases, the whole ground was destined only for traders coming from one particular place, as, for instance, one for those from Jimma-Kaka, others for those from Gera, and those from Gudru. The alien traders were forbidden to stay in the town or in other sections of Kaka. These foreigners, moreover, could not leave the place of the fair without the permission of the ruler. During their absence their house on the fair ground was closed or guarded by a servant or a slave. The merchants residing at the fair had no further charges to pay except tolls and tithe. They had, however, to make presents to the ruler out of all the goods brought by them to Kaka. The trade was carried out in accordance with certain traditional usages. In the case of larger transactions the presence of sureties or witnesses was customary. Barter was not customary in the case of wholesale transactions (Bieber, pp. 425 et seq.; cf. also Joyce).

Among the Akikuyu the exchange of their home products on the markets forms an important part of their daily life. Markets are held at different places, which in populous districts are often not more than three or four kilometers distant from each other. The markets are usually held on open spaces and on rising ground. But such places are not selected in the immediate neighbourhood of a village but rather placed so that they can be easily reached from different districts. Markets are usually held every four days, and the dates are so arranged that they do not clash with similar meetings in the neighbourhood, so that any one can visit the various markets one after the other. The paths leading to a large market place are usually crowded from nine o'clock in the morning with men, women, and children, all hurrying to the same point and carrying their wares with them. A troop of women may be seen approaching from the wooded districts in the west and carrying firewood, while, from the other side, another company approaches with grain and other articles for barter. By evening, the loads have been exchanged. Herdsmen bring cattle for sale, young people ornaments or beer, others iron, and yet others charcoal, &c. The market is at its height between eleven and one o'clock. Between 4,000 and 5,000 people meet at the great markets. Market supervisors act as police and allow no weapons to be brought to the market or to its vicinity. About four o'clock the crowd begins to disperse, and the deserted market-place presents a forlorn appearance, strewn with scraps and rubbish, while the visitors endeavour to reach their homes before sunset. In 1903, European money had not yet made its appearance, and glass beads were the measure of value and the medium of exchange. By 1910 the use of money had become general and coins were only refused in outlying places (Routledge, p. 105).

Many of the markets held by the Galla tribes in East Africa are very old and much frequented. Caravans often visit them from long distances. In Somaliland and the 'Afar country, real market-places were seldom met with inland; the ports on the coast serving as trading centres, though there are no regularly visited markets on the coast between Rās-Alula and Makdishu. In the interior of the Danākil country, at Aussa, and on the boundary toward the Galla country there are five standing markets of the 'Afar, where, however, business is only done when the durra harvest has been reaped. In Somaliland markets are held at points on the frontier of Gallaland. In any case, political conditions often made penetration to distant places impossible. The markets in the Galla districts south of Schoa, and in the town of Harar, are developed to an unusual degree. In the last-named place, market usages of the Arabs prevail, side by side with those of Somaliland and Gallaland. Among the Somalis and the 'Afar, the markets are seasonal or annual, while those of the Galla are held weekly, principally during the dry season. All the large Galla tribes and several of the smaller ones possess a market-place of the first kind mentioned and subordinate ones at various points in the country. In the Lega-Galla region, there are five important market-places, where business does not begin until about 10 a.m. and finishes comparatively soon, because the traders wish to reach their homes on the same day. In the neighbourhood of Harar, the business of the market begins at some places in the afternoon. The traders there group themselves according to sex, and this leads to a grouping by classes of goods, since women and men offer different commodities for sale. The wares should be paid for and removed at once by the purchaser. In spite of this, however, debts are occasionally contracted (Paulitschke, i. 312 et seq.). Breaches of the market rules only entail minor punishments.

§ 7. In Loango, on the west coast of Africa, special regulations are in force for the preservation of order on the market. Violence either to buyers or to sellers on the market-place is strictly prohibited, as is also the capture of a fugitive slave or a hostage in the crowd. Erections of various kinds symbolize this 'truce of God'—mounds fenced in with stakes, memorial posts, and structures of poles intertwined with branches of the large-leaved, spreading figtree known as *nzāndu*, the market itself being called *lizāndu* (plural, *māzandu*). Not far from the market-place heaps of earth may be seen, with the butts of guns projecting from them. No arms of any sort, and not even a bush-knife may be brought to a market. An armed man is compelled to avoid the market or pay a heavy fine to the market-masters. If he sets the latter's authority at defiance he can be seized and his gun taken from him, which is then buried for three-quarters of its length, after the lock has been destroyed. The market-masters usually take immediate cognizance of theft, cheating, quarrels, or cases of assault; they also act as arbitrators in case of disputes, pacify excited parties, and remove intoxicated persons. This intervention is, however, seldom necessary, as all those present (often amounting to many hundred or, indeed, occasionally several thousand persons of every age and rank) are in the habit of keeping order and dealing honestly, a matter favourably remarked even by the earliest authorities. A market-place of which the peace has been rudely disturbed is occasionally closed for a considerable time or, under given circumstances, even moved to another site (Pechuël-Lösche, pp. 231 et seq.).

In the coast districts of East Africa also, markets have attained considerable importance. Food-stuffs of various kinds—tobacco, mats, cloth, butcher's meat, and fish—are the principal articles at these markets. Stuhlmann (p. 64) reports that the Arab Governor appointed by Emin Pasha had set up a kind of market-police who were charged with preserving the peace in the market and seeing 'that the purchasers obtained their proper measure'. At that time, strings of red and white beads were used as currency.

§ 8. The fact that trade and, doubtless, also markets are a very ancient feature in the past history of Europe is indicated by the prehistoric finds. Not only the region of the middle Rhine during the earlier Bronze Age, but also the Danube Valley during the later Bronze Age (c. 200–150 B.C.) and at the beginning of the Hallstadt Period (c. 100 B.C.) were important trading centres. While in earlier times the Rhine valley was the principal focus of the eastern trade, Switzerland and Italy subsequently came to the front. At the beginning of our era, some of the Thuringian tribes were engaged in active commerce with the Romans (Schumacher, p. 209; Varges, Dopsch, i ['18], p. 274; ii ['20], pp. 441 et seq.). Not only did the Romans extend their commercial operations as far as north Germany, but a considerable amount of trade undoubtedly existed within the Germanic area. The cattle trade with Italy at the end of the fifth century A.D. must have attained notable proportions. The trade of ancient Germany was carried on exclusively by barter, but Roman coins were probably used at an early time for special purposes, in the same way as we find among primitive peoples that foreign money or similar tokens of value are apt to be speedily taken into use for their own trade. The existence of markets is natural under these circumstances. The introduction and spread of Christianity helped to maintain and develop the old intercourse with the Roman Empire. According to Dopsch (ii. 446 et seq.) the migration of the Teutonic peoples not only had no restrictive effect on trade, but even created new connexions. The commercial relations actually existing at that period find their characteristic expression in the national laws of the early Middle Ages. The Bavarian law makes a distinction between two classes of foreigners: those who passed through the country on religious errands, and those who came on business: pilgrims and commercial travellers or tradesmen. The impediments to be met with in the public trade-routes and on by-ways and foot-paths are mentioned in detail. There are also detailed regulations regarding transactions in stolen goods, directions for taking charge of them, and also for storage and loans at interest. This applies not only to animals, but also to gold, silver, jewellery, and other commodities entrusted to others for custody or sale. Provision is made for the liability of the trustee when these things are lost, and for the payment of compensation; it is illegal to give away or sell an article of which the terms of ownership are in dispute. The juristic conditions presupposed by these legal provisions, which were extremely advanced for the time, must have been based on contemporary trade usages. These laws, having, as we see, their roots in commercial life, prove that we need not assume, as is done in one obsolete theory, that the economics of the period in question were of a purely private and domestic character exclusively dominated by the self-sustaining manors, but that many kinds of commercial transactions between other peoples were carried on, and extended not only to movables (bondsmen and cattle, &c.) but also to immovables.

The old theory gives prominence to the importance of the clerical landowners, who were the first to be granted the privilege of free transport for their produce and of exemption from tax for their sales at the market. This exemption was intended to supply the actual necessities of the religious institutions in question. Anything in excess of these was subject to taxation. It is, perhaps, only in this connexion that we can completely understand the canonical regulations prohibiting the clergy from trading for profit. But even in pre-Carlovingian times the large landowners, both clerical and lay, were accustomed to spend their surplus, not only on increased production but also on articles of luxury, such as jewellery and costly robes, as well as extending their landed property. It even happens that the income from farms is used for amassing such treasures (Dopsch, ii. 456 et seq.). All this leads to the conclusion that Carl Bücher's ['19] theory lacks foundation. It is not true that all economic activity was embodied only in the mansions producing everything required for themselves. In fact besides the large households of the barons and thanes trade and markets played a considerable role in the life of the people.

The importance of the large self-sufficing mansions in antiquity, too, for example in the case of Greece, was formerly often over-estimated (cf. Ed. Meyer, pp. 193 et seq.).

VIII

PURCHASE

§ 1. The purchase of goods among primitive people is conducted, as a rule, by barter. From a legal point of view it is pre-eminently a question of giving and receiving on the spot, though we may also speak of credit transactions even in the most primitive stages, as in the case of the so-called 'silent trading', the giver laying down an object in the confident expectation that, after a certain interval, the other party will put something of equal value in its place. In particular it is usual, when the return is not made immediately, to give the partner something on account. The object of this is to express in a symbolic manner readiness to perform a return service and to reassure the partner, so that he may not become suspicious but feel a certain momentary satisfaction and consider that he has received some immediate and tangible acknowledgement of his services. That is the psychological root of such a 'contract in kind'. It is necessary to understand clearly the way in which the idea of material recompense permeates the whole life of primitive peoples in order to apprehend the principles of primitive economics and economic relations. On the other hand, the origin of interest payable on account of deferred payment may be deduced from the payment on account, although the original form of payment on account by no means carries this implication.

The act of buying implies a set of traditional values, but we must, nevertheless, bear in mind that these values are not yet in 'money', as the term is applied by civilized peoples. In primitive values it is not only the intrinsic utility of the goods which has to be taken into account, but also many magical ideas, while, at the same time, the transactions are limited to members of certain ethnic groups or strata.

On the other hand, not all human property has been so 'economized' as to be a normal object of buying and selling. Thus, as a rule, it is only movable objects that are subject to sale and purchase, and of these only such as are not so intimately connected

with the life of the sept or tribe that the existence of the community
depends on them, as in the case of cattle. It frequently happens
that no important object can be bought or sold without the consent
of the senior of the sept or the father of the family.

§ 2. Peoples who are active in trade and have abundant means of
communication, such as the Ovambo, in South-west Africa, have
developed certain traditional forms of buying. The principal
measures of value and mediums of exchange used by the Ovakuanyama tribe are salt and tobacco. Salt is imported from the neighbouring tribes, the Aadonga and Aakuambi, and tobacco from the
north in the form of small round balls. Articles of clothing, as well
as different kinds of glass beads, are also used for this purpose.
Grain is very often obtained in exchange for meat, especially by
people who have large households and do not raise enough produce
in their own gardens. In this case a so-called *ohasida* is organized.

The animal intended for the purpose is slaughtered and cut up.
As meat is always much in demand there is no lack of salesmen.
One of these who has special knowledge of the business is entrusted
by the owner of the carcass with the sale of the meat. Every purchaser receives a piece of meat traditionally accepted as equivalent
to the amount of grain he has brought. The skin is utilized for
making women's dresses and the stomach is made into leather
aprons. Each of these pieces of leather costs a hoe. Bargains are
as a rule speedily brought to a conclusion. Important transactions
are conducted in a quiet and dignified manner, particularly when it
is a question of cattle. On such occasions it is not unusual to invite
friends who are supposed to help the purchaser in making a good
bargain. They are the persons who in case of any dispute arising,
may serve as witnesses. The business is never completed without
some bargaining. Every possible advantage is taken by the other
party of the need of the seller or the keenness of the buyer (Tönjes,
pp. 85 et seq.).

§ 3. Among the Masai, of East Africa, the seller spits on the
article as a sign that the deal has been concluded. (Spitting in this
case probably means a transfer of mental power.) The exchange
takes place on the spot; credit is only given to trustworthy acquaintances. The risk (chance of loss or damage) is transferred to
the purchaser on the day after the sale of cattle, in other cases at
once (Merker, p. 205).

§ 4. When dealing in cattle, their most important article of commerce, the Hereros used to give a guarantee against defects not obvious on inspection. This was, however, occasionally abused in a fraudulent way by spoiling and bringing back articles already purchased (Felix Meyer ['05], p. 74).

§ 5. Among the Swahili when trading with the Wanyamwezi, it is the custom to shake hands when buying or selling and to say 'the business is concluded, my friend' or (jocularly) 'it is dead'. It is customary to make a deposit before undertaking an important transaction (Velten, p. 291). Among the Swahili more complicated transactions are met with, even those in which the purchaser does not see the goods when concluding the deal. For instance, in buying slaves, if the slave has been incorrectly described and turns out to be less valuable than appeared from the description, the transaction is void. The same applies to business done with fraudulent intent. If, for example, the seller is beguiled by the offer of a higher price than is alleged to be current in the neighbouring town, while, in fact, it is lower, the dishonest buyer can be prosecuted and the sale declared void. Fruit that is still on the tree, such as mangoes, may not be definitely sold, and even the price may not be finally fixed until it is gathered. In the same way field-produce such as cassava, may not be sold before it is harvested. Both buyer and seller have a period of three days' grace before concluding the bargain, during which it can be cancelled if some defect is discovered, as, for instance, if the slave purchased turns out to be diseased. As a rule, a difference is made between a transaction which is concluded immediately (be'i maqt'aâ) and one with a reservation regarding defects and which can be cancelled within three days (be'i khiyari). The seller must not be under age, must be in full possession of his senses, and a free man, not a slave. A slave can neither buy nor sell without the consent of his master. Furthermore, it is not permitted to exchange silver for silver unless in giving change for a coin of a higher denomination, or in paying money for silver utensils or ornaments. On the other hand, silver may be bartered for gold, millet for rice or cassava, as these are things of different kinds and each has its own value (Velten, pp. 375 et seq.). The main features of these usages doubtless originate in the Muhammadan world.

§ 6. The negotiations which take place among peoples with well-developed economics in connexion with the so-called purchase of women for marriage are apt to be protracted. Among the

Wanyamwesi, of East Africa, the matrimonial agent had first to bring
some calico. Negotiations were then begun by him with the father
of the bride regarding the price to be paid, which, in Emin
Pasha's time, was about 20 doti of cloth both white and coloured,
in addition to 30 iron hoes and 5 goats; if the bride belonged to a
respectable family the price included several head of cattle and
some slaves. A small quantity of calico had, moreover, to be provided for the father's household. The purchase price had to be
paid in a lump sum and not in instalments (Stuhlmann, p. 80).

§ 7. The purchaser does not always obtain complete ownership
of the article purchased. Among the Abyssinian Bogos any one
selling a piece of land can take it back during the life of the purchaser for double the sale price. The right lapses on the death of
the buyer. If the seller subsequently quarrels with the purchaser
regarding the extent of the ground, the former is recognized by the
courts as the only expert having knowledge of the boundaries, and
is thus a witness in his own cause. If the second owner of the land
sells it to a third person and disputes arise, the second owner
appeals to the first one. If neighbours dispute regarding the
boundaries of a piece of land they appeal to the oldest residents.
If there are no witnesses the matter is decided under oath (Munzinger ['59], p. 69).

§ 8. Among the Kaffòcho or Gonga, in Abyssinia, all purchases
and sales were conducted for immediate payment in money, i.e.
Maria Theresa dollars, bars of salt, beads, or skeins of yarn.
Genuine barter only took place in trading food-stuffs. The purchase of horses and mules was only legally binding if they had been
entered in the market-book by the market judge or his writer, with
particulars of colour and age, the latter being determined by the
teeth. A surety accepted the responsibility for the accuracy of the
details given by the seller. A certificate was made out for the
buyer, attesting the regularity of the purchase and thus enabling
him to prove that he had obtained possession of the animal in a
legal manner. A fee had to be paid for the entry in the market-book
by both purchaser and seller, usually amounting to one Maria
Theresa dollar. The quantities bought and sold were fixed by
tradition and, in many cases, the prices also (Bieber, pp. 454 et seq.).

DISTRIBUTION OF GOODS AND WEALTH

§ 1. When there is a surplus of any commodity in small communities, the democratic demand arises that nobody should have and enjoy more than his neighbour, and that a man should surrender his surplus, or the neighbour may put in a claim for a better portion. But this does not prevent friction, and alleged unfair treatment is bitterly resented and sometimes even avenged by magical means.

On the other hand, a generous present causes a flow of further gifts. If any one wishes to obtain a special object by exchange, he must gain the favour of his *kula* partner by gifts of pigs, specially fine bananas, yams, or taro, the valuable large axe-heads or whalebone spoons. At the same time, overseas trading is by no means confined to the *kula* exchange; it is only that commodities standing in a *kula* relation to each other belong to the same social sphere. This system by no means excludes the accumulation of goods. We will, perhaps, not be wrong if we assume that, as regards *kula* exchange, we are dealing with a remnant of relations among a stratum of immigrants which have long been absorbed into other communities and which maintained the feeling of homogeneousness by regular presents, the nature of which is determined by convention. This may be corroborated by a number of similar usages. The Kai and other tribes of the central and eastern part of northern New Guinea pawn family jewels, such as boar tusks, strings of dog teeth, &c., for a pig, with the understanding that the partner has to return them when the pawner offers a pig to him. On account of that no haggling as to the jewels occurs, but the quality of the pigs, however, is considered carefully (cf. Keysser, p. 102; Thurnwald ['30], pp. 622, 624).

§ 2. Attention has been called to the peculiar circulation of valuable articles which do not come into the possession of the individual, but whose importance consists in their being given and received by certain persons between whom friendly relations are maintained in this way (Malinowski ['22], pp. 82 et seq.). These objects thus fulfil a certain socializing function. While, on the Trobriand Islands, the necklaces of red shell discs (*soulava*) are passed on from right to left on a certain fixed course between the islands by a limited number of men belonging to the *kula* society, the bracelets made from the white *tridacna* shell (*mwali*) change hands in the opposite direction. Each of these valuable articles encounters the complementary article in the course of its constant journeys and is exchanged for it. Every move in the proceedings of this *kula* exchange is ceremonially determined by tradition and accompanied by magical rites, which are also applied to the building of large canoes, to the long sea voyages which are occasionally undertaken, and to funeral ceremonies. The *kula* maintains friendly relations of a ceremonial kind, accompanied by secondary barter transactions, between members of different tribes. The articles in question, which are to be regarded primarily as ornaments, are carefully preserved in the house and only shown at great festivities; but the head chief lends them, on request, to relations, friends, or vassals, who are allowed the use of them. He himself only wears the ornaments on great occasions, unless he intends to dance himself. In a similar way precious beads, 'money' of the island of Palau (Caroline Islands; cf. Kubary ['95]) or the Rossel Island (cf. Armstrong, pp. 59 et seq., 76 et seq.), change hands only within the class of chiefs. The dowry or 'bridal wealth' in cattle among pastoral or semi-pastoral tribes of Africa circulates in a similar manner. The gift received for the daughter is generally reserved to help to get a bride for the son. In fact all the various kinds of treasure-valuables are symbols of social distinction and at the same time help to maintain traditional bonds among certain families. Therefore they cannot be regarded as 'money' in the purely economic sense of the word.

§ 3. Wealth assumes a particular aspect in the more primitive forms of civilization. The elevation of the individual and the display of power are achieved by the use of economic means other than those used by us. The conditions of life are different. Economic goods do not appear in the form of abstract values but as concrete objects of consumption or use; they are, therefore, related to many other sides of life besides the economic one, and are affected by the connexion of the object with supernatural powers and forces, in so far as these form the basis of the mental attitude of the people. This excludes the possibility of regarding economic possessions from a one-sided rationalistic point of view. We must not forget that even among us the purely rationalistic-economic conception of all things in life is the expression of one mental attitude among several others. The economic factor is, with us, by no means the only decisive one governing the behaviour of the individual.

The attitude towards economics among primitive peoples is, in the first instance, limited in an entirely irrational and uneconomic way by prejudice or by respect for certain forms of activity. Certain occupations, for instance, are limited to certain families or to one sex in a strictly traditional way. Moreover, the resources at the disposal of the tribe are not always completely utilized, as, for example, among the Manchus, where the cows are not milked and both steers and cows are only used as draught animals (Shirokogoroff, p. 130).

Among the Ashantis certain spirits are considered the real owners of the land (Rattray ['23], p. 218).

The rights of property in movables are often extraordinarily limited, although, at the first glance, it may seem correct to speak of individual property (Driberg, pp. 170 et seq.; Czaplicka, pp. 45, 57).

Firth (['25/a] pp. 357 et seq.) has recently pointed out that even such a simple occupation as catching birds among the Maoris of New Zealand cannot be accounted for merely as an endeavour to obtain food. Even if the obtaining of food is the primary motive, the desire to catch the greatest possible number of birds is influenced by other considerations as well. Various ceremonies are performed in connexion with bird-catching. Special trees and special kinds of bait are selected, and the snares are laid in a particular way. Here the Maori is helped by minute and extensive observation of natural life to utilize the weaknesses of animals and birds. All these occupations, however, are influenced, not only by notions based on practical experience, but by others, especially those connected with religious traditions. The traditional methods are the result of opinions, not only regarding the life and behaviour of animals but also regarding their relations to the world and mankind. Thus, the bird-catcher is compelled by his belief in tradition to devote an extraordinary amount of time to the careful collection of all feathers, even those which have been scattered, in order to bury them. In the virgin forest, when his food is scarce, he often throws away a bird as a sacrifice to Maru or Tane. Besides this, there is the competition in catching the birds and in plucking them before cooking, and above all, the craving to carry out all the traditional proceedings more correctly than one's neighbour and thus to win the recognition of others. This pursuit of distinction in the community is a factor which militates against rationalistic economy. Social considerations form a more powerful inducement than a purely economic point of view. The results of individual activity are delivered at the communal store-house, no separate payment being made for the work of each individual. The same procedure was followed with regard to bird-catching; the birds caught were displayed on the *marae*, the central open space of the village, and afterwards taken to the common store-house. In this case the owner of property is the community and the individual finds distinction in contributing as far as possible to the increase of wealth and thus enhancing the reputation of the community. It must not be forgotten that a number of other occupations, such as dances, the carving of decorations, the making of ornaments, and the polishing of weapons, are connected with those directed to economic ends. But all these occupations by no means originate in any kind of economic need, but are rather to be considered as an expression of energies aroused by a man's desire to distinguish himself by the excellence of his work. It is for social distinction that work is done, not for the acquisition of money or material goods, since these do not play the same intermediary role for acquiring reputation that they do in our society. On account of the absence of these intermediary means the personal ambition of the individual tends in other directions. The introduction of money, therefore, causes a lessening of emphasis on quality, for social distinction is now dependent on money rather than on the accomplishment of the work.

The relationship between the man and his work was in the olden times much more personal. Firth relates (p. 360), for example, how a man rose in the middle of the night for sheer love of work in order to polish his ceremonial club (*mere*.) Indeed, many were quite dejected when they had finished a piece of carving or other work of art, because they had enjoyed so much pleasure in shaping and finishing it. The motives leading to economic activity are thus of a complex kind and connected with the traditional culture and form of the society in which the individual, in accordance with the mental attitude and scale of values in his community, strives for distinction and recognition. This appears very clearly in the economic tendencies manifested by the more advanced hoe-cultivators, fishers, and craftsmen. (For the way in which fish are caught by the New Caledonians, see Lambert, pp. 211 et seq.; for food-stuffs, prohibited dishes, see Strehlow, pp. 1 et seq.)

Among the Kafirs in the eighteenth century any one who possessed less than he needed for his own support or that of his family could borrow from another, who had cattle to spare, a few cows for two, three, or more years, in consideration of which he had to give up half of the calves born. Such support was often given without the smallest advantage being agreed on for the lender (Schmidt, p. 123).

§ 4. All observation of primitive peoples teaches us that the social motive, the desire for an exceptional position in the group, has outweighed the economic motive. Indeed, it must not be forgotten that, even with us, energetic application to business is very often only the means to an end—that of attaining or maintaining social rank. The economy of primitive peoples is different from ours in that it is direct, while ours takes a roundabout course by means of money, capital, and credit. Accordingly, wealth has a different form among primitive peoples and adapts itself to the manner of living. In modern economy wealth in Africa is based on exactly the same abstract standard value (gold) as riches in Greenland: it is essentially represented by the possession of value expressible in terms of money. Among primitive peoples the values representing wealth may, according to the mode of life of the particular tribe, be either arm-rings or necklaces, sago or yams, bear skins, mats with fine red birds' feathers, iron lance-heads, or cocoa beans; they are thus purely qualitative and are 'values in kind'.

The second point in which wealth among primitive peoples differs from our wealth consists in the fact that the former finds its expression not so much in possession as in being given and taken, so as 'to be the cause of a large turnover'. The man who possesses anything is considered to a certain extent as the trustee of the community and also considers himself as such. *Noblesse oblige* is, in fact, the social norm which regulates behaviour (cf. Malinowski ['22], p. 97). Gain for the sake of profit in money values is, therefore, unknown.

The lack of purely economic points of view is everywhere visible in the life of primitive peoples. On various occasions, valuable food-stuffs and stocks of all kinds are destroyed, burned, or thrown away from motives connected with religion or witch-craft. This is particularly the case in funeral ceremonies. Thus, for instance, in many West-African countries (as in North-West Togo) immediately after the death of the king becomes known, not only is the market plundered by the natives but domestic animals, such as fowls, goats, or sheep, which are moving about in the open can be killed or taken away by anybody who wishes to do so. Indeed, it is even said that farms may be plundered. On the other hand, the dangerous crocodiles which live in the water-holes are considered sacred and may not be killed (Zech, p. 123). Wealth *is* wasted in this way. For instance, at the annual cere-monies for the dead among the Indians of South California large quantities of shell-money, baskets, and similar things are burned in honour of the deceased. Each family makes an offering for its own dead (Kroeber ['23], p. 303).

§ 5. The fact that many objects valued by primitive peoples are far from durable, e.g. stocks of food-stuffs, tends to prevent the accumulation of such objects on a large scale (cf. Knabenhans ['19], p. 107). A distinction must be drawn, however, between the hoard-ing of food-stuffs and delicacies and that of manufactured articles; the point of view with regard to these two classes of objects varies. In the case of food-stuffs the principal demand is that they shall be for the good of the entire community. This is not so easy to arrange in the case of tools, or vessels, such as pots or bowls, and even less in that of weapons. But the idea of personal property, and the joy of possession, attach above all to articles of luxury like glass beads, shell rings, bone necklaces, and the like. The posses-sion of wives is one source of wealth among hunters and collectors and also among most of the hoe-agriculturists. Wives are the oldest form of 'profitable capital' not only on account of their offspring and because the husband profits by having his food supplied, but also because of the women's skill in handicrafts. As a rule, how-ever, it is only men in a certain position, so-called 'chiefs', who are able to obtain such advantages on a large scale by the possession of several wives. Also the superiority of chiefs does not depend so much on accumulating possessions which can be inherited as such, as on personal advantages and the influence and respect acquired through the distribution of presents and the entertaining of guests.

Success is always supposed to depend on certain mystic relations with supernatural powers. Among the Ewe tribes in West Africa a hunter who is repeatedly successful in killing large game, such as the buffalo, is praised by his fellows. This praise induces others to obtain magic charms from him. The hunt and the preparations for it are often interwoven with numerous ceremonial usages. If the hunter discovers the spoor of an animal he makes passes in the air with a long, pointed stick, in the direction in which the animal was moving and then strikes its footprints with the stick. He believes that he can in this way charm it and catch it easily. If a hunter has killed a horse antelope and distributed all its flesh, he then, after five or eight days, with the assistance of his paternal uncles, erects a little house to the hunter's god, Adee, where he, under the direction of an old hunter, offers a piece of flesh from the neck of the dead animal, which has been kept for the purpose. At that time some broth is made with much ceremonial observance. The distribution of a large dead animal (buffalo, wild boar) is undertaken in a way rigidly prescribed by custom: the head belongs to the hunter's companions (age-mates); the jaw-bone of the animal, one hind leg, and the kidneys are given to the uncle on the father's side; the back of the neck is the share of the sister on the mother's side, and so on. The distribution of the various pieces is based on symbolic grounds, for, if the hunter meets with an accident while out hunting, his companions have to look for him. They precede the members of the hunter's family as if they were the head of his body. If the accident has proved fatal the senior uncle on the father's side makes a speech and begs that any debts left by the deceased may be remitted. In this way he must exert his mouth, and therefore receives the jaw-bone. The sisters get the meat from the neck because they have to bend their necks and bear the burden, namely, if the dead hunter has left a debt behind they must pay or serve as hostages until it has been wiped out (Spieth, pp. 387 et seq.).

§ 6. Among the tribes of Loango in West Central Africa the ground and everything of value contained in it belonged to the people of the whole district; nobody attempted to own land. On the contrary, an effort was made to get into connexion with men offering security and thus to obtain a favourable place in the group.

The produce of fields and trees, the profits of trade, domestic animals, and slaves form the property of the maternal family. Although there is no private ownership of land there is, however, a right to the produce of cultivation and to everything spontaneously produced by the earth: 'the man who tills the ground, holds the land'. Unplanted fruit trees may neither be removed nor damaged. If a piece of forest is cleared, all the oil palms remain untouched. An effort is made to conceal from the neighbours unusually rich crops of a durable kind, to get them home quietly and to make a profit out of them. This is done to avoid provoking envy and avarice and to give no opportunity for begging. It is dangerous to boast of success in farming or trading or of the increase in the number of a man's cattle (Pechuël-Lösche, pp. 205 et seq., 207.)

In the Loango countries, for instance, it is the custom that any one meeting a funeral procession may be robbed of half his portable possessions, or even more, by those taking part in it. The successful hunter who has killed a leopard (a beast sacred to royalty, while at the same time hated for its ravages among domestic animals) carries round his spoil amid the shouts of the villagers and is entitled to relieve those he meets of the half of their property, to enter any of the women's huts which may be open and help himself to anything he pleases. Trading caravans which, during the dry season, often come to the coast from far distant tribes in the interior, could formerly be held up by a community who would purchase their wares in order to sell them again at a profit. The caravan leaders could only escape this extortion by paying transit dues, which payment was often postponed until the return journey (Pechuël-Lösche, p. 220).

The villager is always in danger from the envy of his neighbours. It takes the form of bringing pressure to bear in order to induce him to give away his surplus and thus equalize their shares and his own. But this distribution is the source of the respect paid to the wealthier man, and personal distinction thus consists in sharing one's own surplus with others. Riches, therefore, do not represent permanent possession but a temporary power of disposal of commodities in which the individual permits the members of his group to share. It may be said that primitive wealth is not of an economic but of a social nature; the man who has, by whatever means, acquired more cattle, grain, or valuables of any kind than his neighbours has not done so in order to hoard his wealth for his own benefit, but that it may be used for the good of the other members of the community. This giving and distributing is by no means entirely due to altruism, but is chiefly actuated by two principal motives: first, the pressure exercised by the envy of the less fortunate, and, secondly, personal vanity which makes a virtue of necessity. This explains many collectivist phenomena among primitive peoples. On the other hand, any one compelled to make a distribution may attempt to secure something for himself by hiding part of his store.

§ 7. The researches of Malinowski on the Trobriand Islands have shown that there, for instance, food-stuffs are by no means valued in the first place for their utility or because they can be conveniently preserved for future use, but because they serve for the display of wealth in food which means, potentially, power, i.e., the possibility of laying claim to the reserves of others. The yam store-houses are so built that the quantities stored can be seen and estimated through the wide interstices between the beams. The bunches are so laid that the best specimens can be seen from without. Special kinds of yams, which are often more than six feet long and may weigh several pounds, are framed in wood, decorated with paint, and hung up outside the yam house. The right to this display of food is so highly valued that it is jealously claimed by chiefs of high rank and the people of lower rank have to close up their store-houses with coco-nut fronds in order not to give the appearance of wishing to compete with the chief. For the social position of the Trobriand islanders depends to a great extent on the display of wealth in yams. These stored-up yams are supposed to be kept as long as possible, and a special kind of magic, *vilamalya*, is performed for this purpose. It is said that the desire of the villagers to eat this surplus is thereby lessened, so that they are inclined rather to consume the wild fruits of the forest, or the mangoes and bread fruit of the village plantations. In this way, half the yams often rot away in the store-houses and have to be thrown away on the dung-heap behind the house, in order to make room for the new crop.

In the matter of handicraft activity, it can by no means be said that the inhabitants of the Trobriand Islands set to work under pressure of necessity or only for the purpose of gaining their living. Their activity may more truly be said to originate in tradition and in sheer enjoyment of their art, which is felt by themselves to be the result of magical inspiration. This is particularly the case among those who make objects of high value and do their work with understanding and real love. Rare forms and uncommon material in shells, wood, or stone are particularly valued. It is not the utility or the intrinsic rarity of an article (op. cit., pp. 172 et seq.) but the amount of work bestowed on it which should be regarded as the basis of the valuation. This kind of valuation has no aesthetic influence on the production of works of art, for the amount of work expended on them is apt to be disproportionate, and for this reason wooden drums or canoes are often overloaded with ornamentation.

§ 8. The attitude towards the possession of wealth is different among those people where movable property plays an important part in life. This can only take place when the clan association has been destroyed and replaced by stratification. This usually implies the associations of the restricted or the extended family or, at least, the distinction between free men and slaves consequent on the establishment of a powerful chieftainship. The chief who belongs to another ethnic stratum is, from the first, distinguished by the abundance of his possessions. This difference in possession is admitted and recognized by both sides. The wealth of pastoral peoples, such as the Beni-Amer, in the Egyptian Sudan, consists in herds of cattle (Munzinger ['83], p. 355), and is thus limited to certain concrete goods.

The Batutsi use certain symbolic terms to indicate the number of their cattle: when one of them says that he has 'one calf', this means a small herd of not more than ten, 'a small cow' means a herd of thirty to sixty cattle, 'one cow' means several herds. But if one of them says he has 'many cows' then he wishes you to understand that he is both influential and wealthy. The possession of cows dominates the whole life of the Batutsi (Czekanowski, p. 125; cf. Herskovits).

Even among archaic peoples, as, for instance, the ancient Persians, hoarded wealth took the form of horses, waggons, swords, silver and gold, and more especially that of cattle, tribute grain, and food-stuffs, the idea, however, everywhere persists that great lords and despots store up these things principally in order to play a brilliant part by means of a generous distribution (cf. Darmestetter, p. 273).

§ **9.** Punishments through the loss of property usually appear to take the form of its destruction. On the Oleai Islands, which belong to the West Carolines (South Seas), the following punishment is inflicted on the seducer in a case of adultery: as soon as the fact is discovered word is sent to the men on the neighbouring islands, most of whom immediately come to the island of the guilty man, burn down his house, cut down the coco-nut palms and bread-fruit trees, and smash his canoe, so that he is deprived of his means of livelihood (Born, p. 189).

OWNERSHIP AND PROPERTY

§ 1. Superficial observation would lead us to assume that under strongly developed communal economics, governed by the principle of distribution, it would be impossible to possess or accumulate objects of value. But it is most of all in advanced systems of communal economics, such as that in Samoa and in the Maori communities, that private property is found to exist and objects of value, such as mats, are hoarded. This right of private possession however, extends only to objects generally held in high estimation, and does not affect the elementary necessities of life; it may, to a certain extent, be compared to the way in which the crown jewels or cherished family heirlooms are preserved and treasured in Europe. The possession of these valuables confers personal respect and distinction and, in these stratified societies, it is limited to the chiefly caste.

Possessions thus conferring personal distinction are often considered in primitive societies to be so intimately associated with the individual that they are either buried with the corpse or destroyed.

Dapper [1671] (pp. 45 et seq.) relates how, as early as the second half of the seventeenth century, the inhabitants of Madagascar considered the possession of cattle as the most important matter in life, and next to it that of silver, which they valued more than gold. Glass beads were very highly prized, but strings of red shells were counted the most precious of all.

In the seventeenth century the wealth of the King of Benin (West Africa) consisted of jasper and carved coral, which he displayed on certain days. On these days he presented serfs and women to persons whose service he wished to reward, and assigned the government of various villages and towns to officials of his choice. Personal respect attached to rare stones and elaborate pieces of carved coral, for they were difficult to procure, and the artistic craftsmanship gave rise to a pleasurable feeling of enjoyment (Dapper, p. 492).

Among the Ashanti, of West Africa, the spirits are considered to be the real owners of the land, though the King of Ashanti in fact claimed all the land of his loosely constituted kingdom. But the power even of important personalities among these kings was limited by the hereditary councils and, even more, by the clan system, in conformity with which no man, woman, or child was considered as an individual but as a member of the clan (Rattray ['23], pp. 213 et seq., 224).

§ 2. Landed property, in the case of hunters and herdsmen and hoe-cultivators with sufficient space at their disposal, is the area from which the whole horde, clan, or settling community derives its means of livelihood and subsistence. A claim to the private ownership of special pieces of land within the district is generally not recognized. It has been pointed out, however, in another chapter, that the principal source of individual property in a non-stratified community is derived from labour, as the planting of a tree, vegetables, cereals, and so on, or the building of a house. Thus a certain kind of 'immovables' can be held by individuals.

§ 3. A horde of roving hunters, trappers, and collectors may well claim a common territory for the gaining of their livelihood, but individuals have no cause to attach great value to the exclusive ownership of a piece of ground. This also applies to nomadic herdsmen, but it is otherwise when the cultivation of soil is begun. Among less advanced hoe-cultivators there is generally such ample space available that, though land may often lie fallow for several years, good soil can always be found for the whole tribe to cultivate. But even here friction is apt to arise through opposing claims of the tribes and even of the families within the political union on account of traditional use of a certain piece of land.

A typical example of concrete existing conditions is found among the Bergdama (Vedder, pp. 78 et seq.). Any one wishing to lay out a garden at a water-hole discusses its locality with the head of the kraal. Any one who breaks up a piece of land and cultivates it is virtually its owner. If he goes away the land is claimed by the clan, the political unit. Any other member of the clan can now till this piece of ground if he has arranged the matter with the head of his kraal. Open springs and artificially opened water-holes are considered among the Dama as public property; but any one passing with a herd of cattle which he wishes to water is expected to inquire of the headman whether the supply of water is sufficient for the purpose. No payment is demanded for this (Vedder, p. 147).

The absence of free private ownership of the soil is, in general, applicable to the American Indians, who remained uninfluenced by the more advanced political and economic developments originating in agriculture combined with cattle-breeding, though in some regions a high order of hoe-cultivation was to be found. This even applies to the Nahua and Inca peoples with their complicated constitutions. Though the exclusive right of individual social groups, of gens, clan, local group, or family to certain areas was clearly recognized, and though in the highly organized administrative mechanism of the ancient Mexican and Peruvian states, certain dues and taxes on real estate were collected, yet the conception that real estate could be sold or otherwise transferred was entirely absent. Generally speaking, fields were allotted annually to each household of the group, which shows that all had an equal right to possess land. The boundaries of the land assigned to any one group were strictly laid down, and any attempt to alter them was threatened with capital punishment. In the socially graded communities of the Nahua and Inca peoples certain stretches of untilled ground were reserved for the ruling class, and the people were called upon to cultivate them when required. The whole of the agricultural work was supervised by expert officials (Wissler, pp. 183 et seq.). We may summarize by saying that the following principles are applicable to collectors and hunters as well as to herdsmen and hoe-cultivators: (1) ownership of the land by the sept or the family without the right of sale or transfer; (2) the special claim of the ruling class to the land either by lending it to people of lower rank or by reserving certain areas; (3) constant supervision of agricultural work by special functionaries. In modern times the influence of Europeans in the Caroline Islands and the misinterpretation of native institutions have led to occasional assertions that these include private property in land; but this circumstance must not be regarded as constituting an exception to the general rule that communal tenure of land is the established system for all primitive communities which have not yet reached the agricultural and ethnically graded state.

The conception of a common claim to the soil on the part of the entire sept can still be distinguished when private ownership of the soil has already gained a foothold. This is markedly shown in the method of proving ownership adopted by the Ewe tribes of West Africa. The man who claims the possession of a certain piece of land, though his right to it is doubted, places himself in front of a small mound of earth and repeats aloud the names of his ancestors, in the presence of the chiefs and other witnesses. Whole family trees are recited. He then, on the chiefs' invitation, throws some earth at his adversary and cries out, 'may this earth kill you' (Spieth, p. 114).

As land becomes private property principally through being cultivated, a separation between private landed property and common landed property (government land) makes its appearance in more highly developed societies as, for instance, in the Islamic East (division into private land = *mulk*, government land = *miri*, and mosque lands = *waqf* (*habu*)) and also in medieval Germany (cf. Thurnwald ['23], pp. 300 et seq.).

§ 4. In the first place a clan lays exclusive claim to the use of a certain area for hunting, setting traps, and collecting. Any interference is unhesitatingly treated as a breach of the political 'sovereign' rights and, as a rule, involves the killing of the trespasser, the clan being the highest political unit. In primitive societies the personal claim to spoil is of great importance. Whatever a man kills or traps is considered in the first instance as his personal property. However, it is accepted as obvious that the individual who has, as a rule, gone hunting or trapping in company with others and who always feels himself to be a component part of his little community (without which he cannot exist, being linked with it in regard to all the essentials of life) should share his spoils with his clansmen; they, in their turn, share with him on another occasion. The provision of food and lodging, of everything needed to support the existence of the individual members of the community, is treated as a communal matter. Among hunting tribes, who often have difficulty in obtaining food, the spoils are, as a matter of course, treated as common prey, as among the Eskimos, and it is considered a distinction, indeed a matter of rivalry, to succeed in bringing home a good and abundant provision (Nansen, p. 96). The man who succeeds in bringing home something to-day expects to receive from the other something to-morrow.

§ 5. The position is different with regard to movable property in daily use. Soergel (p. 147) at least is of opinion that in the most ancient palaeolithic times ownership in material, tools, and utensils did not relate so much to the things in themselves as to the skill required to make them. He considers it necessary to assume that the nomadic hunters of the later Stone Age made their tools *ad hoc* every time they settled in a fresh place, and that when they moved on they did not take these things with them. It is clear that they had no means of carrying them, and they could not burden themselves with things which were not, like their weapons, absolutely necessary.

We are now in a position to state that, with primitive peoples, the manufacture of such articles as a netted carrying bag, or a carved bone dagger, or the planting of a tree, in short the creative part of the work, is the source of the personal claim to its possession. Moreover, the point is not merely the claim made by the individual but rather the recognition of this claim by the other members of the community. We shall not be far wrong in associating this recognition of personal claims to objects with the acceptance of mystical or magical relations conceived to exist between the objects and their makers or owners. Indeed, tools are, in fact, prolongations and complements of the human organs. It was only in later times that work in our sense came to be regarded as the ownership of creative power.

Among the Bergdama skins are considered as private property, but only of the chief or the so-called food-master who receive them as their share from the booty of the other men. On the other hand, wooden platters and pots are considered as common clan property (Vedder, pp. 20, 30, 65). The Bergdama have only begun to keep goats within comparatively recent times. The flesh and milk of the goats may be partaken of by every one, but the owner of one or more milch goats can declare them tabu or forbidden by striking them with the stalk of a certain variety of nettle in the presence of the kraal. The milk may then be drunk by the owner only, or by one who entered the initiation school with him. The same restrictions apply to the flesh of the animal, which can be eaten by no one else, not even by his wife and children. If the animal is to be sold or given away he must first raise the tabu which he himself laid on it by striking it with a switch of the Foũ bush and spirting a mouthful of water over it (Vedder, pp. 36, 37).

Personal ownership of houses, utensils, tools, and food also existed among the peoples of the New World, though land was, as a rule, held by communal tenure. The possession of all movable property by the women—whether descent was reckoned in the female or the male line—is due to the fact that, among hoe-cultivators, the woman tills the soil and is concerned, in the first place, with the house and the hearth. We must also take into consideration the fact that the conception of the family is based on the grouping of the family property and the family relationship round the mother. In particular, her brother is her contemporary, and may be expected to survive when the elder generation, in the person of the father, dies out (Vinogradoff, p. 193). These circumstances explain the position of the maternal uncle in almost all primitive societies, without our being compelled to assume in every case a formally developed matriarchal system.

While in the case of most primitive peoples land is held in common, and none is owned by individuals, the claims of the individual in other departments are more strongly emphasized than among us, this being the case with regard to certain forms of non-material ownership. In the islands of the South Sea and the Malay Archipelago, and still more among the North-American Indians, the performance of certain rites, the singing of ceremonial chants, the practice of certain arts and even trades are the privileges of individuals who can openly sell, transfer, or bequeath them (Wissler, p. 184).

§ 6. The claim to private ownership of objects is expressed by various signs of prohibition (tabu signs) and marks of ownership, which are intended to distinguish these objects among others. A case of this kind was mentioned in the previous section, and we even find them among the less advanced of the primitive peoples. Game that has been killed is often left lying, to be fetched later on, and the hunter contents himself with placing some branches on it, as a tabu sign. Such signs are generally respected, and it is assumed that the thief who lays hands on such forbidden things will meet with an accident, as, for instance, among the Bergdama, who believe that his hand will be affected with gangrene and at last drop off (Vedder, p. 66). If a bees' nest is found in a hole in the earth or a hollow tree, the finder lays a stone in the opening or sticks a twig into the ground close by, to assert his prior right to the honey. These marks of ownership have been developed in various ways in later times.

§ 7. Possession in our legal sense requires, however, a distinction between the actual holding of a thing and the legal claim to it. Such a differentiation is unknown in the lives of the less advanced primitive races. But where the relations of debtor and creditor, pledges, deposits, sureties, and where, more especially, the recognition of mutual obligations have been developed, the differentiation between possession and property acquires importance, but it can only be completely carried out in cases where, as in archaic states, ownership has become a clearly defined term. Islam and the German medieval law presuppose this differentiation from the beginning.

§ 8. There are two main avenues leading towards individualization of property. The one refers to movable objects of personal use such as ornaments, weapons, utensils, &c., and is connected with the most ancient assertion of personal rights, which we find even among animals. These objects are handled as if they were part of a mysterious aura of the owner, and consequently are buried or cremated with him. Such customs are rather common among predatory tribes. These objects are thus treated not because of their economic function, but on account of religious or magic ideas associated with them. The above-mentioned objects increase in number with the progress of skill, become more and more secularized and are used as objects of barter, which goes on among the most primitive communities.

The other way to the individualization of property concerns objects of greater economic importance, such as cattle and land. Here we have to refer to certain events in the political and social history of the tribes involved. The main objects of economic value are the plants and animals of a certain district claimed by a number of related families settling together. The spoil of their hunting and trapping is divided among them and they protect each other against animals as well as against human enemies. These more or less temporary aggregations become more settled and accumulate tradition among agriculturists and herdsmen, though in a different manner. They are then called 'clans'. These clans may split into parts called 'septs'. Clan and sept remain generally the paramount economic units besides the family and the settlement. Although the economic pursuits of clan and sept are on a strictly democratic basis, the leadership in planting and harvesting among agricultural tribes is often conferred upon 'persons of knowledge', i.e. upon sorcerers. Among pastoral tribes the men leading the movements of the clan in search for other pastures acquire a supreme influence associated with the belief in their mystic superhuman power. In this way certain members of the clan, i.e. leaders, attain outstanding social and economic positions as individuals.

A new factor comes in by 'stratification' of one tribe by another, especially of agriculturists by cattle-breeders. A process of new valuation starts. The wealth of the superposing people is envied by the subjected ones, and symbols of it are cherished for the personal reputation and social distinction they carry within the community. Thus cows, slaves, shells, arm-rings, boar-tusks, glass beads, &c., depending on the particular situation, acquire prominent value, especially as magical qualities become associated with their possession.

But these objects later become more secularized and then they acquire an economic function, in that the possession of them in large quantities allows the leading families to attain a distinction and higher position than other members of the clan, who dispose of fewer symbols of wealth. The process of stratification was carried on by single families gaining influence over clans of agriculturists, subduing them to some form of dependence. Thus agricultural tenants and slaves render the services formerly provided by the clan, i.e. food supplies and protection against enemies. In fact the basis of the economic life undergoes a fundamental change.

These circumstances act as a selective process which pushes a few individuals into leading positions. The new unit which takes the place of the clan or sept is also a political organization and is of an aristocratic rather than a democratic nature. The new idea of social differentiation is supported by the symbols mentioned above. Within this upper stratum there then appears a rivalry for the possession of the greatest number of these symbols. This means the rise of plutocratic valuations which begin to supersede the aristocratic ones. Consequently among these leading individuals there is competition for the acquisition of these symbols, first because of their social value, secondly because of their economic importance. Family property in cattle and land, administered by the patriarch, becomes a feature of the new order. The gifts of the agriculturists are no longer returned, but are converted into tribute or taxes. The captives of war are not killed any more, but

o

instead are made to work for their captors. Consequently the 'labourer' does not dispose of the product of his toil as he did in the small homogeneous democratic communities. Leading families of chiefs, &c., are enabled to increase the number of symbols of wealth which can be employed for different purposes. One is for the maintenance of relations among themselves which replace to a certain degree the bonds of the former clan. Thus a rotation of these symbols as compensation for some special favour takes place, e.g. the donation of cows for a girl given in marriage, or of a boar-tusk ornament for a pig, &c. As the cows received for the daughter may be utilized for acquiring a wife for the son, and the boar-tusk must be returned for a pig provided by the original owner of the tusk, these circulating symbols fulfil a social function. When other people use these symbols they come to have an economic aspect, similar to the character of money. This, however, presupposes a certain individualization of property.

Another use of these symbols is the acquisition and hoarding of them to increase the power of the family. With these treasures, alliances with other clans, families, tribes, can be bought, captives of war acquired, slaves or women for working plantations, &c., be purchased. War becomes a means for acquiring wealth. Thus these symbols again become associated with political power. The symbols of value, however, help to bring into relation to them a number of objects not originally connected with them, such as food that is grown in certain, districts, or implements and utensils (pots or metal wares) manufactured exclusively by certain people. Thus they widen the possibilities of exchange. By the accumulation of these symbols the potentiality of economic values was discovered which open the way to a family capitalism. Especially did the automatic increase of the seed and the productive power of the animals kept by herdsmen suggest the idea of capital bearing revenues from an investment.

The idea of social distinction is also paralleled by actual differentiation within the society, in that the primary archaic states are composed of people of various origin and different kinds of skill, united under the domination of a leading family, in a smaller or larger domain.

XI

FEUDALISM

§ 1. When we speak of feudalism we are usually thinking of the Middle Ages in Europe. The feudal organization is consequently regarded as an institution belonging to a later period of history, but this view can only be accepted with considerable limitations. The conditions necessary for the rise of feudalism are provided in any case by a stratified society; its forms are alien to 'homogeneous' communities. Feudalism has, therefore, in reality nothing to do with the lowest forms of association. However, it is an institution which very soon makes its appearance in stratified communities. The fact that most transactions are in kind and that the upper stratum claims all the land or cattle, are the economic causes of feudalism, of which, however, various forms must be distinguished (cf. Hintze). The rise of feudalism is conditioned by political domination, and it makes its appearance when this domination is so far rationalized as to make economic exploitation possible. As stratification is a necessary condition for feudalism, it appears to be connected with aristocracy.

Nevertheless, convulsions in the traditional aristocracy are by no means necessarily followed by similar convulsions in the feudal system, so that the entire balance of the political union is not upset. The aristocratic feudal system may be replaced by the enfeoffment (vassalage) of officials. Yet the mutual relations of feudal lord and vassal are always based on a relationship of protection as opposed to one of allegiance. Indeed, in communities based on the enfeoffment of officials, the personal tie, whereby the weaker secures the protection of the stronger by means of gifts, is even more strongly marked. While the overlord is interested in having the largest possible number of retainers, not only for use in war but also in order to increase his income, the vassal finds in the overlord his champion against other rulers. The amount of contributions is not, as a rule, precisely fixed, but in any case 'the best' is demanded at an early stage and, later on, 'the first'. In the beginning the contributions are usually recompensed with return services, presents, or feasts, and, as both lord and protégé come off well under this system, there is no hostile feeling. Feelings of critical tension are first caused through rationalistic exploitation by the lord, or failure to carry out his obligation to protect. These feelings, however, under certain technical conditions, do not at once lead to a change in the system but, at most, to a change in the leading personalities of the ruling class. It is only when economic factors make their appearance, with the rise of trade and the increased use of money, the mobilization of landed property, and, finally, a change in the attitude of the individual to the community, that the whole system is doomed to perish. It must also be remarked that the feudal system is usually connected with two forms of dependence: that of a non-resident vassal and personal servitude at the residence of the overlord. For the feudal lord is in the habit of maintaining a court, and usually surrounds himself with a staff of personal servants and a number of retainers.

§ 2. Here is an indication of the beginning of feudalism. In those parts of the Trobriand Islands where great chiefs rule, such a chief is the overlord of the clan which is recognized as having the highest rank. The headmen of villages in his district are subject to him. A number of villages are tributary to this chief, and in part respect his authority. In time of war they are his allies and assemble in his village. Should he have need of men for any purpose, such as felling trees, building canoes or houses, he sends to the subordinate settlements for workmen. These subordinate villagers make their appearance on the occasion of all the greater festivals. It would, however, be incorrect to suppose that the tribute from the villages comes to the chief as a matter of course. He must be ready to pay for all contributions made and services rendered. It is a point of honour for him not to be niggardly with recompense. He provides himself with the necessary supplies for making this recompense in a peculiar way, by taking a wife from each of his subject villages. Her family has then to provide him with agricultural produce in accordance with Trobriand tradition; for it is the custom that a wife should be supported by her brother and her maternal relatives. As this woman is always a sister or a near relative of the headmen of the subject village, it usually ends in the whole community being called upon, in one way or another, to take part in the work. In former times the chief of the foremost clan (Omarakana) had no fewer than forty wives, through whom he received from one third to one half of all the crops produced in his district of Kiriwina. But even now, when he has only sixteen wives, he possesses large store-houses filled up to the roof with yams (Malinowski ['22], pp. 63 et seq.; cf. ['15] and ['21]).

§ 3. On the American continent we find widely differing forms of political union: agglomerations of clans united on a basis of equality, such as the Pueblo Indians and their neighbours, the Apache, the Ute, or the Navajo; or the Cherokee, the Creek, the Powhatan, but, more especially, the Iroquois League, the Pawnee, and the 'Council of the Seven Fires', the Dakota, and many others. The specialization of many clans, septs, or families which often occurs introduces a differentiating element into the agglomerations of co-ordinated clans (cf., for example, Radin, pp. 204 et seq.), but this differentiation has no significance in connexion with class distinctions, unless the specialization is expressly associated with varying values attached to the several professions and official positions. Among the Indians of North-West America this is not yet clearly perceptible, although we already meet with an aristo-cratic stratum and a class of bondmen. The existence of a regular protective, as opposed to a loyal, relationship, accompanied by regular contributions can, however, be definitely stated in the case of the three organized governments of the New World at the time of its discovery: namely, those of the Nahua, Inca, and Chibcha governments. The units of the whole system, of which all details are, however, not yet quite clear, were the family groups or septs. Every sept had a chief who had a seat in the council of the next higher group. The government was in the hands of a single sept who elected the prince, without regard to his relationship. In spite of many differences these are the basic features of all the govern-ments mentioned. The political organization in Mexico was, however, less strictly centralized than that of the Inca state (Wissler, p. 156).

§ 4. In order to obtain a clear idea of the Micronesian feudal system we may take the Island of Kusae, in the Caroline Islands, as an example. All the land belonged to the king, who gave it in fief to the titular chiefs. These latter distributed the land on

Uàlang through their subordinate chiefs (*metskùsuk*) to the people
(*met-šišik*) of their districts. It is, however, also affirmed that the
land was 'private property'. In any case it could only be a question
of limited private possession, as is usual in societies where land
cannot be disposed of. The right to the land was, however,
personally heritable. The mother's dowry in land was tilled by
the husband and his children, but passed only to her own children
in the event of her death. In accordance with this, the feudal dependence had not developed into a system of villeinage, for the people
(*met-šišik*) enjoyed extensive freedom to settle where they pleased.
The population of the various districts had to till the fields of the
subordinate chiefs and, under their supervision, that of the chief.
Part of the yield had to be delivered to the subordinate chief who
passed it on to the chief. In the same way, when large fishing
expeditions were organized, certain portions of the catch were
handed over to the chiefs. The amounts due to the titular chiefs
were not precisely defined, and the districts had merely to provide
food for the titular chief and his family. For this purpose the
subordinate chief had to send a canoe loaded with raw field-produce
and also cooked dishes every few days to Lölö, the island where
the titular chief resided. As every titular chief possessed several
tributary districts he was provided with fresh food-stuffs every
day. He demanded the best produce of every kind and the best
fish, and, in particular, coco-nuts, which were comparatively rare
on the islands. The titular chief even had his canoes and his
house built by his people. He selected the members of his large
domestic establishment, cooks, kawa-brewers, kawa-servers, food-
bearers, canoe-crews, teachers, and nurses, from among the inhabitants of his districts. The subordinate chiefs maintained their
courts in a similar way, but on a smaller scale.

At the season of fishing on the high seas, entire associations of
fishermen under a headman moved over to Lölö, the island where
the nobility resided. Whereas the regular deliveries of food-stuffs
were not recompensed in any way, it was otherwise with regard
to special services. The staff on permanent personal duty, who
lived with their wives and children at the chief's court, were
supported by him. Not only were the usual feasts given to
builders of canoes and houses and to the fishermen, in accordance
with custom, but, when their work was finished, these people were
rewarded with money and valuables. In particular, a recompense

is said to have been customary whenever a titular chief sent a messenger to demand special deliveries of food-stuffs from the subordinate chiefs (*metsùksuk*) of his districts, or when the villagers made him special presents.

On the occasion of the great competitions organized by the titular chiefs, the inhabitants of the district received special gifts from their lord. In these cases the titular chief first distributed his gifts to the subordinate chiefs, who then passed them on to the people, conforming to the rank of each person. It may be said that the nobility lived on their island of Lölö at the expense of the population of the large island of Uàlang (Sarfert, pp. 363 et seq.).

§ 5. In Samoa the land belonging to each tribe was held by the chiefs and princes as leaders of the tribes, and they bore titles to correspond. On the Tonga Islands this tribal property consisted for the most part of plantations, houses, and canoes, and the territorial prince (*tuitonga*) was considered to be the sole owner of the land. The subordinate chiefs derived their right to their land and their power (according to A. Radcliffe-Brown) from the prince, from whose family they were supposed to be descended and whom they regarded as their overlord. Authority once conferred by the prince could not, however, be revoked. The whole tribe had a claim to the land, but it was in the hands of their overlord, and was transferred after his death to his successor (Williamson ['24], ii. 229 et seq.). The princes and chiefs exercised extensive rights over the possessions of the people subordinate to them. With regard to Samoa, Pritchard expresses this forcibly, saying that 'among the Samoans a chief cannot steal'. They only say of him that he 'takes away' what he wishes from his people. His subjects merely feel flattered when this takes place. In particular they had to provide him with food-stuffs but, in return for this, he was expected to initiate and to take part in all the work of his community. The flow of tribute in the form of food-stuffs was often very irregular. The amount was not in any way defined. If a large quantity arrived, the head chief organized a feast. But, on the other hand, he had also to share what he received with his people and, in particular, to provide for his relatives, however distant, and for his guests. He had to make presents in return for the contributions received. This became an expensive business under given circumstances, and if the head chief was not rich he was helped by his tribe and his village.

Thus there existed between the paramount and subordinate chiefs and their people a system of exchange, in which the well-known Samoan mats, in particular, played a special part. For instance, a paramount chief paid his subjects for food-stuffs and other contributions or services, among other things, with mats, which were hoarded as valuables. On other occasions, as, for instance, a wedding, the paramount chief demanded large quantities of mats, which had to be provided by his subordinate chiefs who, in turn, collected them from the heads of village districts. In this way the mats circulated between the paramount chiefs and their people. Turner has called the heads of families the 'bankers' of the head chiefs (Williamson ['24], iii. 344 et seq.). The procedure on the Tonga Islands was similar. If the kind of presents to be offered to the prince (*tuitonga*) on the occasion of a sacrificial feast (*inaji*) was there more exactly defined, it was because the contributions for this feast had a certain sacramental character. For this was not a case of ordinary tribute, but of a religious ceremony, in which the prince apparently only fulfils the functions of high priest or representative of the god (op. cit. iii. 348 et seq.).

§ 6. We find cattle fiefs, for instance, in East Africa. The herds belonging to the Batutsi chiefs are driven away to distant pastures, and only the necessary milch cows kept in the vicinity of the settlements. These herds are entrusted to special Batutsi herdsmen, who tend them and receive in return the milk for the first two months, for the cow does not return to her owner's homestead until the calf is two months old. In addition, the herdsman receives a pot of beer valued at one hoe. He is responsible for the cows entrusted to him and must replace those lost, accidentally killed, or stolen. If drought prevails the herds of the Batutsi chiefs are often driven into the sweet-potato plantations of the peasants and cause great damage, which the owners are unable to prevent. In the herdsman aristocracy of Ruanda the agricultural labourers must always yield place to the cattle. The peasants were often driven out in this way. The hiring out of the cattle often involves complicated legal procedure, since a sub-tenancy is admissible (Czekanowski, pp. 143, 282). In a similar fashion we find among the Bakitara that the chiefs exercised a certain control over the herds of cattle in their districts (Roscoe ['23/b], pp. 176 et seq.).

A system with some resemblance to the feudal is also found among the Kikuyu of East Africa (Beech, pp. 46 et seq., 136 et seq.).

§ 7. Among the West-African Yoruba the land theoretically belongs to the king, but he only owns this land as the representative of his people. The king imposes limitations on the various tribal chiefs with regard to their landed possessions. The tribal land is the common property of the community, just like that of the septs, and the prince or chief is only the agent of the community. For this reason no land of any kind can be sold. Every town or village with a market is under a headman, whose office is hereditary. He again is dependent, through other chiefs, on the nobility, to whom, as well as to the king, the village has to pay tribute (Johnson, pp. 70 et seq., 90 et seq., and 95 et seq.). The feudal system is essentially based on the chiefs letting the land that must be tilled and obtaining revenue from this source (Dennett, pp. 195 et seq.).

§ 8. The mistake is often made of attributing the sentiment of resentment to the dependence which finds expression in the feudal system. Such an importation of sentiment into a completely different sphere of life and thought is, however, absolutely mistaken. Pechuël-Lösche (pp. 249 et seq.), writing of Loango, in West Africa, states that the relationship between lord and bondman is based not merely on law and habit but on genuine attachment. In earlier times, when the kingship was still in existence, the overlord was elected from among the ancient royal race, the caste of princes of the blood, said by tradition to have immigrated from the east, i.e. from among those persons who, without regard to their paternity, were the children of a princess. A prince or princess received a district from the king as birthright or fief; the recipient was then the district prince or lord of the land (i.e. district chief). He or she was next in rank to the king and was invested with the same rights in the district as the king. His power extended to all persons permanently or temporarily resident in the district; he was lord in temporal and in spiritual matters. These district princes and princesses are still named after their districts to the name of which is prefixed the honorific syllable *Ma*, as Malaungo, &c. Since the breaking up of the kingship, some of the princely families have become considerably impoverished and exercise hardly any political influence. At the same time members of princely families still enjoy a number of external distinctions, such as the right to wear ivory ornaments and fringed robes of a special kind, shoulder capes, plaited caps, and the like. They are also above the law and do not need to give evidence or make statements on oath. A prince has free choice among all the daughters in the country. A princess is the most favoured of all women, for through her alone can blood, rank, and property be inherited. As soon as she is of marriageable age she has a seat and a vote in political negotiations, and is the supreme judge in her district, with power of life and death. She has the right to nominate a man as her husband and to dismiss him again at will. Members of princely families only are buried on the hillock of Lubü. The view is held that the 'district lord' holds his lands in the last resort in fee from Nzambi, the creator of the Bafioti. The 'district lord' was always a prince, at least in earlier times. Next to him in rank, as councillors and administrators, are the headmen of villages and heads of families. The remaining freemen are the sons of free mothers and are publicly and ceremoniously recognized as members of the district while still infants. The whole body represents the district community. Their joys and sorrows are, however, shared by many other persons who were not born in the district or, if natives, have forfeited their freedom. Such are hostages, 'pawns', sureties, bondsmen, and, finally, slaves. To these must be added refugees from districts suffering from famine, pestilence, or war, and also debtors, wastrels, and tramps. The lonely man or the vagrant needing support or protection, both politically and socially, must become a member of some district and place himself under a master. Side by side with the princes and in spite of their caste privileges, trade and interchange with Europeans have tended to develop another class of persons whose influence is making itself felt. Most of the chiefs only rule over a district and a village, which form their mainstay. The district organization is represented by the individual chief in external affairs.

Quarrels about land seldom occur within the district organization. When necessary, the matter is discussed with the chief, who settles the question. A freeman who is 'poor', i.e. one who has no bondmen and cannot hire day labourers, will help in clearing a piece of land, but hoeing the ground or carrying water is the business of the women and slaves. Profits derived from work done in common are often administered by the chief or district head, who makes payments to the community and provides entertainment and presents out of such funds for guests and visiting traders and travellers. The district chief receives a contribution from the first of the season's crops, the amount of which is not specified; but about a basketful is brought in from each plantation. The cultivator is not allowed to enjoy the produce of his field before handing over the first-fruits. If his domain is large and fertile, the contributions are made in instalments, on demand, but in this case they cannot consist entirely of first-fruits. The district chief also receives the first-born of domestic animals. Any one who kills large game must sacrifice the head of every animal to the so-called animal-skull fetish, and also the hind leg which touches the ground in falling. Certain portions of all game and fish must be offered to the prince. The district chief also receives a substantial part of the fines collected. He raises contributions and tithes for roads, ferries, and bridges, even from trading caravans (Pechuël-Lösche, pp. 175 et seq., 186 et seq., 194 et seq., 203, 207, 218, 236 et seq., and 251 et seq.).

§ 9. As an example of the ancient oriental feudal system, we may take that of the Indian Empire in the third century B.C. The question of communications in itself made it impossible to rule the vast empire of Asoka (which included the greater part of India) otherwise than by means of a number of provincial administrations. A certain centralization was only rendered possible by a limited form of supervision and by the contributions made. In other matters each part of the country retained the customs, traditions, and laws peculiar to it (Mookerji, pp. 110 et seq.).

The protective as opposed to the loyal relationship is characteristic of personal relations in the bureaucratic states of the ancient East, particularly in Egypt (Thurnwald ['01], pp. 705 et seq.) and in Persia (de Morgan, pp. 579 et seq., cf. in particular Plut. *Alex.* 69; Thuc. ii. 97. 4). When the Persian king moved about among his Persian freemen, who formed the nobility, it was customary for him to make presents to them. In Tibet (Bell) and in the Far East (Sternberg, Amundsen) and, in particular, in Japan (Lange) similar conditions prevailed.

§ 10. The *Rectitudines singularum personarum*, drawn up in the tenth, eleventh, and twelfth centuries, defined the duties of two categories of persons in England at that time: the *thanes* and *geneats*, the lords and the peasants of the communities. The thanes are vassals dependent on the king. The thane must accompany the king on his warlike expeditions, help in the building of castles, and keep bridges in repair. While the first of these duties represented a personal demand on the thane, the second and third were considered as services rendered by the people subject to him. The thane, therefore, appears as a middleman between the king and the people. The thanes often began their career in the king's bodyguard, so that originally they might be classed as officials. This body of officials was usually, at first, augmented for the most part by recruits from the nobility. (This has also been the case elsewhere, for example, in the East.) These recruits are the younger sons of the lords, the real lords of the land, who take service at the king's court and later on are rewarded with village lordships. Such land usually became available in the king's wars waged against the independent nobles (Peake). Gradually in this way more and more land came into the hands of these vassals, a circumstance which naturally contributed enormously to the strengthening of the royal authority. In the army, at a later date, payment took the place of vassalage. The services rendered by the geneats, the peasants, varied in accordance with local custom. They had to make contributions in kind and perform various services, such as riding, transporting loads, mowing, reaping, and various other duties. Although these duties were not clearly defined, the number of days on which the services of the geneats could be claimed was fixed at an early date. The nature of these services, however, varied in different places and also according to the occupation of the individual and the amount of his possessions. A large proportion of the peasants were already in a position of marked dependence; they were tied to the land and had to work for their lord on certain days, although they were not slaves. Slaves were principally owned by the great lords (in particular the bishops and abbots). This old Saxon system was to some extent altered and rendered more complicated by the Norman Conquest, but the main principles continued to exist. In the *Song of Roland* there is clear evidence of this relationship of protection for loyal followers in the time of William the Conqueror, the relationship of the man to his master and of the master to God being defined— just as it was in ancient Egypt. This relationship was the origin of all responsibility and defined the duties of each, while providing the standard for justice (cf. Bacon, p. ix; as regards Ireland cf. P. W. Joyce, pp. 184 et seq., 491 et seq., and Maxwell, pp. 323 et seq.; for the Middle Ages in Germany cf. Hintze).

XII

FAMILY CAPITALISM

§ 1. Its nature and recognition. § 2. Illustration: the Banyankole of Central Africa.

§ **1.** Family capitalism was associated with the type described in Part II, chapter IX. The increase of cattle and the practice of entrusting them to subordinate herdsmen, who were paid with a certain number of the calves, suggested the idea of productive possessions and of interest on capital. Similar conceptions applied to the possession of a wife.

This possibility of increase distinguishes cattle-breeding from the hoarding of valuables by hoe-cultivators. In addition to this, there is the system of contributions brought into existence by the hiring out of the herds. We must assume that in agricultural societies the herdsmen's idea of productive capital which, in his case, took the form of live animals, was applied to the grain reserved for next year's sowing and the increase derived from it, and, finally, to an economic system which included both cattle and grain.

The preliminary condition necessary for the creation of private capital was the securing of independence by families in a larger community.

The protection afforded by the political authorities to independent families with regard to the disposal of their property implies the recognition of a certain distribution of property and of the traditional method of obtaining it.

§ **2.** The following description provides a typical example of the condition of property in a pastoral aristocracy.

Among pastoral peoples, such as the Banyankole of Central Africa, the land was never regarded by the herder aristocracy as part of their wealth, which was only reckoned according to the number of cows possessed by the pastoral chief. The land was, however, indirectly of value, as the cultivators living on a chief's estate could be called upon to work for him, and they supplied him with vegetables, grain, and beer (Roscoe ['23/a], p. 13). Among the Banyankole the land was divided into some sixteen districts ruled by important chiefs ('district lords') appointed by the prince (*mugabe*). These chiefs were called *bakungu* or *abamangi* and selected by each *mugabe* when he ascended the throne. If one of those so appointed died, the prince nominated his successor, who was, as a rule, but not necessarily, the heir of the deceased. These district lords were always members of the pastoral population and had under them, as serfs, the agricultural people who lived in their district, took charge of their sheep, goats, and dogs, and provided them with grain and beer during the periods when they, for one reason or another, could not drink milk, which otherwise formed their principal article of diet. The *mugabe* always gave each such chief (*mukungu*) a present of from one to three hundred cows, which became his private property and served to provide food for the chief and his household. Although such cows represented a 'present' to the individual and were regarded by him as such, the prince (*mugabe*) could take them away if he considered that he had grounds for doing so. No one was allowed to sell or exchange cows outside the tribe without the permission of the prince, who monopolized foreign trade in this way. It is said that there was once a time when men were free to dispose of the cows they possessed; but in later times the *mugabe* regarded himself as the owner of all the cows in the country. The herds of a *mukungu*, or district lord, could graze in any part of his district or, in common with all cattle-owners, he could send them to any other part of the country.

The authority of such a chief in his district was limited, for he had no control over the movements of the subordinate chiefs or those of other people who might settle in his district and pasture their cows there, for the whole country was open to all cattle-owners, who could settle where they liked and leave again when they chose. His only duties were to settle disputes between the various owners and herdsmen, to exercise a supervision over all the herds of cows belonging to the prince which were in his district, and to see to it that the men in charge of the cows treated them properly and did not get into difficulties with other herdsmen. There was no thought of animosity between the district lord and the subordinate chiefs in his district. On the other hand, the latter, who were quite independent, recognized him as a superior authority whenever any kind of difference occurred among them. It is only in recent times, under British administration, that one or two members of the agricultural class have been made district chiefs, a thing previously impossible.

The life of such a *mukungu* differed in no way from that of an ordinary cow-owner; he lived, surrounded by a number of his cows, in his kraal, while his other flocks moved about the country under the care of herdsmen. Besides the independent pastoral chiefs, there might also be living in the district various friends and relations of the *mukungu* on whom he himself had conferred chieftainships, and who then lived like the other *Bahuma* or pastoral people. These people brought a number of serfs with them, who tilled the soil and did other work, or else they found resident agriculturists who were ready to become their serfs. In addition, there were a number of chiefs called *bagalagwa*, who had formerly been in the service of the *mugabe* as pages. When they were too old for that position, the *mugabe* provided them with land, cows, and serfs. In the district, they were under the leadership of one of their own class and he, in difficult cases, appealed to the district chief who could refer a quarrel to the *mugabe*. The pastoral chiefs seldom lived in one place longer than two or three years, for it was considered necessary to move frequently in order to keep the animals free from sickness. The kraal was also abandoned when anybody died. These chiefs appointed men as herdsmen who were members of the pastoral race and who either possessed no cows or else not enough to support a wife and family. The cows entrusted to such an impoverished member of the pastoral race were considered by him as his own, and the feudal lord had no right to their milk, though he might ask to be supplied with some in case of need. The herdsman was also allowed to use the bull of his master and the salt provided for the latter's cows. His own return services consisted in looking after the herds. Such a herdsman could leave his lord without any further reason, if a young steer for meat or a cow-hide for clothing was denied him. In such a case, if no agreement was effected, the herdsman looked for a new master. Every cow-owner had attached to him a large number of serfs, from one to three hundred, as cultivators.

The *mugabe* distributed plots of land to his chiefs, which were cultivated by clients. Herds of cows were not allowed to trespass on these plots. These agricultural clients could leave their lord at any time; but they never attempted to set up their own settlements and live independently unless they had first obtained the direct permission and sanction of the prince, who only made over a plot of land to them as their private property for very special reasons. Besides providing their lords with corn and beer, they had to look after their dogs, goats, and sheep, and do building and other work (Roscoe ['23/a], pp. 14 et seq.).

XIII

WORK

§ 1. The place of work in primitive society. § 2. Impulses underlying work. § 3. Recompense for work. § 4. The origin of work. § 5. Communal work. § 6. Division of labour. § 7. Special processes. § 8. Organization of multiform work. § 9. Preferences as to forms of work. § 10. Methods of work: simpler forms. § 11. Craftmanship and artistic developments. § 12. The division of labour.

§ **1.** The position occupied by work in the lives of primitive peoples is different from that which it occupies in our own. It is not something that can be sold in the open market, but activity undertaken by the individual for himself or for others in order to bring about some direct result; but not, as a rule, with the object of gaining a livelihood. For this reason, the individual attacks his work from a point of view entirely different from ours. He performs it, as a rule, not under the pressure of any direct compulsion, such as the obligation of a contract or the control of a master, but of his own accord and according to his own inclination. But, even in this case, there is by no means an entire absence of compulsion, for, in all undertakings, connected with the direct search for food, the connexion between work and the desired result is clearly visible.

We cannot fail to observe that work is never limited to the unavoidable minimum, but exceeds the absolutely necessary amount owing to a natural or acquired functional urge to activity. This is particularly evident among the more advanced of the primitive peoples who have begun to devote systematic efforts to such work as the laying out of their gardens.

§ **2.** It is, for instance, reported (Malinowski) regarding the inhabitants of the Trobriand Islands that in an average year they grow about twice as much field-produce (yams) in their gardens as they can eat. In earlier times the surplus was allowed to rot, but it is now bought by Europeans for the people employed on their plantations. Work is by no means performed on the principle of doing as little as possible, but much time and great energy are often devoted to objects not strictly necessary. The neatness of a garden attracts the admiration of other people. The work is done in a spirit of emulation, although no part of the return may fall to the share of the gardener, who must hand it over to the husband of his sister (or mother) and his family. After the harvest an exhibition of the crops is held on the ground, which is visited and criticized by everybody. The importance attached to this display is shown by the fact that it was formerly even dangerous for any inferior to show better results than a chief. How far primitive work lies outside the sphere of strictly economic rationalism is shown by the way in which it is interwoven with magic. Magic arts accompany the progress and ensure the success of the work almost everywhere, in particular among primitive peoples in intermediate and superior stages. From one point of view nature is helped by performing magical ceremonies for the success of hunting or fishing, for the growth of plants, the increase of animals, and so on; from another, magic is considered necessary for the success of personal work, such as the building of a canoe or a house. Particularly among the more advanced of the primitive peoples, every fresh phase in the life of a cultivated plant is apt to be accompanied by magical ceremonies. These are not devoid of practical importance, for they exercise considerable influence in systematizing, arranging, and controlling the work. At the same time, however, the magical ceremonies entail a great deal of extra and seemingly unnecessary work. The magician is the expert to be consulted and the supervisor who dominates mentally both work and workmen.

The impulses governing the nature and direction of work are embedded in the traditions of the group to which the individual belongs. Tradition determines the economic needs and the impulses directed to satisfy them. If we imagine the ambition which gives rise to emulation, and the urge for personal recognition, we can obtain an idea of the impulses underlying the artefacts of the Stone Age and all works of art at any stage in the early development of mankind, things upon which an endless amount of time, patience, and attention was doubtless expended.

§ 3. It is for this reason also that work is rewarded on principles quite different from ours, i.e. 'in kind'. The principle is that assistance, as in the building of a house, should be repaid at the earliest opportunity, by the person helped placing his work at the disposal of his helper: 'solicited work'. The same holds true for hunting or fishing, and for the mutual support of one village by another in its gardening work. When a tree is felled and transported for the building of a canoe, the chief who is building the canoe provides refreshments for his people, consisting of roast pork, baked yams, green coco-nuts, sugar-cane, and betel-nuts. Magical rites are performed during the progress of the work. It is not the success of the work that is paid for, but the expenditure of strength. The extra efforts are recompensed by the arousing of particularly pleasing emotions (feasting, dancing).

§ 4. Even when payments or contributions are obligatory, it is customary to make small immediate recompenses (Thurnwald, ['12]) in order to avoid the impression that a service is rendered without a return service. For this reason, even menial work and professional work, which are based on the principle of the social division of labour, have not yet become subject to strictly economic calculations.

The view that menial work grew up in connexion with the utilizing of women is very probably correct. The oldest kind of work: laying out gardens, planting cuttings, and weeding was probably, in the beginning, women's work. Menial work by men in the ancient civilizations had its origin principally in the tilling of the soil and irrigation work on the banks of rivers, such as the Nile, the Euphrates, the Tigris, the Indus, the Ganges, and the Hoangho, which are subject to periodical floods.

Men as well as women usually prefer to work in company, whether in clearing a piece of virgin forest in order to lay out a plantation, or planting of cuttings in the clearing, or squatting in the men's house, where one man plaits armlets, another mends his stone axe, and a third cuts a lance or sharpens a bone dagger. In this case it is a question of individual work which each one does for himself, and equally so in hunting and fishing. Work done in company is without doubt the oldest form.

§ 5. Not only work like the above, but communal work, such as the felling or transporting of a tree and the building of houses and canoes, is one of the oldest components of human culture. The main object of communal work is to achieve results desired by all. It has also the advantage of stimulating to great efforts and thus guaranteeing a better quality of performance. The solidarity of the group, which is a necessary requirement for its existence, is strengthened by mutual aid and the exchange of services. This community work, in which the people of a village, relations by blood or marriage, members of a sept or totem comradeship, or even neighbouring settlements, assist each other, is based on the expectation of mutual help and the stimulus provided by special meals and the interruption of the work by dances, songs, and other festive performances.

§ 6. The division of labour is by no means the result of complicated economics, as one rationalistic theory will have it. It is principally due biologically to physiological differences in sex and age. The man's share is the roving and emotional life of the hunter and fighter, while for the woman's life a fixed abode and regular, even if not plentiful, food are essential. Thus, among the less advanced of the primitive peoples we frequently find the men hunting, trapping, and fighting, while the women, in addition to collecting, cultivate the soil. This has given superficial observers the impression that the whole burden of life rested on the shoulders of the female sex, but in reality the arrangement results from a natural division of occupation between the sexes. In particular, besides affording protection, the men have also always to do the clearing work which demands more muscular power.

Boys often cultivate their small plantations when only twelve years old, but they are not initiated into the secrets of magic until they have reached a more mature age. The mental direction of the work lies more or less in the hands of the old men.

§ 7. Nature, however, also provides for a certain free specialized division of labour. The local development of certain specialized processes is facilitated by the occurrence of stones or shells for axe blades, of elastic wood for making bows, of clay for pottery, by a situation on the sea-coast or a river-bank, favourable to trade, canoe-building, and communication, or by the presence of certain animals. Thus we get a local specialized division of labour, followed at an early age by an exchange of products, or barter.

§ 8. The organization of multiform work among the more advanced of the primitives, also, is more fully developed than would be apparent to a superficial observer. There are, however, considerable differences between the various tribes. Even in warlike expeditions, the part to be played by each individual is often minutely specified beforehand in order to render co-operation possible. In the making of large canoes and the building of houses and community halls, the linked-up work of persons differing socially and economically, as is the case in the communal existence of the more advanced primitives, is held together by one man, often under the direction of the great chiefs. For instance, special persons undertake the digging-out, the plaiting, the carving, and the ornamentation of the canoe, the plaiting and sewing of the sails, &c. The chief, however, appears as an employer supported by his community in order that they may undertake voyages in the canoe.

§ 9. Perhaps the attitude towards work of the less advanced primitives is distinguished from that of peoples of higher culture by the fact that monotonous, regular muscular action, such as that required in digging out a canoe, polishing a stone, or scraping a shell, is preferred to complicated manual dexterity which demands keener attention and sustained tension. That this is due not merely to training but also to natural constitution is indicated by the circumstance that, even when natives have grown up from youth in European surroundings, they cannot acquire a taste for operations requiring mental tension rather than mechanical activity. In particular, they lack, as a rule, the capacity for grasping the interplay of different arrangments, such as is necessary, for instance, in a European household. On the other hand, any one of them readily adapts himself to any special work assigned to him.

How far similar conditions apply to early historical primitives must be left an open question. But in this case we may certainly take into account the difference of mental constitution in individual tribes.

§ 10. Let us now examine from an economic point of view the manner in which man does his work. Attention has already been drawn to the difference in the activities of primitive peoples.

Wirz (['24], pp. 11 et seq.) writes as follows regarding the hill tribes in the interior of southern New Guinea: the natives only remain in their settlements at night and during the early hours of the morning. Before the sun has reached the zenith the village is deserted by old and young alike. The rest of the day is spent on the plantations, where there is something to be done almost all the year round. They do not return to the village until shortly before sunset, the women carrying on their backs net bags filled with sweet potatoes and leaves for the evening meal and that of the next morning.

In spite of an activity which is frequently assiduous, the work of primitive peoples lacks that concentration and discipline which seems to be only acquired through working with more delicate machinery. They are quite ready to make an effort when the work requires it, but they soon relax, and as they are not compelled to make any consecutive effort towards overcoming this tendency, they yield to the feeling of fatigue. Monotonous work, such as hacking out a canoe or a rudder from a whole log, is preferred to work which demands keen attention for a long time, or even the exercise of mental powers (according to my observations in the South Seas). These observations are in no way contradicted by reports from Africa, America, and other countries. Mental strain is hard for man in every society, but it depends upon the degree of effort. It may be said that mechanical work is always preferred to mental work and, further, that in making articles which are often very elaborately decorated, they are stimulated by the artistic impulse to creation, and also by the opposite feeling, that they are not compelled to complete the work within a given time, or to observe any other restrictions such as we should recognize. Moreover, primitive work never fails to take a comprehensive view of the whole process of production, whether in agricultural work or handicraft.

§ 11. In the higher stages of civilization, well-developed craftsmanship is connected with strong artistic development, but even in the lower cultures there is no lack of decoration on tools and implements. In stratified societies, however, the chiefs and leading classes seem to attach special importance to the impression made on their people by artistic objects which appeal to the popular taste. In this way they stimulated the development of artistic activity in the communal life. We know, for instance, that in the Maori civilization of New Zealand a great amount of time and work was devoted, in pre-European days, to the artistic decoration of houses, utensils, and implements. It may be said that artistic interests permeated their whole life. This decoration, of course, did not add to the usefulness of the objects; on the contrary, they were often rendered less useful, as was the case with certain stone axes. Such activities indicate a strenuous endeavour to change and develop in various ways the different technical expedients. The labour expended on making such show pieces, moreover, was out of all proportion to the increase in their usefulness and served exclusively to enhance the personal prestige both of the maker and of the destined owner. For the workman could not by any means secure an economic return for his vast expenditure of labour. Tools and utensils were certainly not ornamented and embellished for trade purposes. Thus, no economic value was taken into ac-

count in supererogatory work of this kind, or in the development
of special accomplishments and refinements. Such artistic achievements were not associated with any idea of profit (Firth ['26],
pp. 16 et seq.).

Though the above example may be taken as typical, yet differences are found to occur even in this case, when the practice of
handicraft assumes a professional character, and the work is thereby
subjected to other mental conditions. This also applies to field-
cultivation, in which the planting of roots and herbs and the
sowing of grain is the duty of the women, who are much less concerned with the cultivation of trees. Therefore, it is not by accident
that slaves should be required to dress like women (Hahl, p. 77).
The activity of the hunter or the herdsman cannot be characterized
as real work; consequently, when the standard of living improves,
they develop a tendency to live by robbery or by trade or, in certain
cases, to make trading forays (as, e.g., in the Sudan); or else
cultivation is assigned to alien women or prisoners of war. Even
the peculiar robber-trading practised by the pygmy hunters who
force their way into the plantations of the East-African agriculturists and leave game in exchange for what they take, may be
placed in the same category.

§ 12. The primary division of labour is that between the sexes.
A family specialization makes its appearance at an early stage in
the domain of handicraft. Nowhere, in uninfluenced primitive
societies, do we find labour associated with the idea of payment.
In these small communities, the individual who co-operates in the
building of a canoe or a house or the cultivation of a friend's field has
usually, as a member of the association, an interest in the results of
the work, for he may, perhaps, be able himself to make use of the
canoe. In stratified societies, also, a strong communal spirit
actuates the several associations which bear the burden of contributions as a whole. The slave, on the other hand, is glad to find
his place in the *familia*, for this is the only place where he can find
protection. Primitive society has no knowledge of paid work without a personal relation to the employer. The idea of *mana* is,
furthermore, apt to bring about the recognition of mental
superiority in the relationship of dependence, whether of a political
or economic nature, and to give it special sanctity.

It is due to such an attitude of mind that, even in the Middle
Ages, payment of work for strangers is something unheard of. It

was because they took money for services rendered, instead of being content with honour and recognition, that the minstrels were reckoned as little better than outcasts.

The only recompense known to primitive society is the payment of the magician (cf. for example Pechuël-Lösche, p. 371).

The result of the work falls to the share of the man who did it, as would naturally follow from the high degree of independence of the individual. This principle is also a decisive factor in preventing the full development of slavery in stratified communities. The first change in this respect occurs in archaic societies which adopt a systematic use of slave labour in domestic work, agriculture, and handicraft. Fresh problems thereupon force their way into prominence. Cf. Glotz.

A commercial treatment of labour does not make its appearance until contact is established with forms of economics based on personal property and connected with the circulation of symbols of economic value.

XIV

SLAVERY

§ **1.** The true definition of slavery is a state of things in which human beings are regarded as chattels. This state is conditional on property having reached a sufficient stage of development. Among primitive races, as already mentioned, the term property often has an entirely different significance from that which we attach to it. Slavery in the ultimate sense of the word, i.e. when human beings are regarded as chattels, can only take root where, at any rate, the existence of patriarchal group families has favoured the growth of definite family properties. It follows that the first persons to appear as slave owners are those to whom the other members of the community have conceded special rights and privileges, such as chiefs, or religious bodies and their rulers, the priests.

Dependence of a whole clan on another clan or sept, however, does not lead to slavery but to a state of tenancy or the like, which among consanguineous groups results in the subject-people also forming a group, which comes to be looked on as a serf-group.

If we confine the definition slave strictly to such persons as have been debased to the state of chattels, we must differentiate between this and the somewhat similar state of personal bondage, mostly of economic origin, such as bondage for debt. As the legal interpretation of this latter did not always permanently relegate the person involved to the status of a chattel it is best to designate such persons not as slaves but as bondmen and bondwomen.

A distinction must also be made not only between such slaves and bondmen but also between serfs and the lower grades of stratified societies. Theoretically it seems easy enough to classify each group according to its distinctive characteristics; slaves and bondmen defined above, serfs as a group liable to render homage or service; lower grades of a society or members of a low caste as restricted to the performance of certain despised labours or to a single social or economic service; but in reality it is often difficult to decide to what group subordinate persons belong. Moreover, we must take into consideration that these various forms of subordination have undergone many fluctuations in the course of time.

Slavery is subject to the same laws as other institutions resulting from man's social life. Given certain circumstances, particular practices will take root in a place and develop into a custom which spreads, in course of time, to tribes whose similar mode of life favours its adoption. Correspondingly, new configurations of social groups and changing ideas can subsequently destroy a custom, as has happened to the blood feud, atonement, sanctuary, matriarchy, and various marriage customs.

Moreover, slavery is not an institution dating from the earliest ages of mankind. The hunting, trapping, and plant-gathering tribes are ignorant of slavery, the conditions under which they live being unfavourable to the marked subordination of one class to another. It is obvious even on a superficial view, that the comparatively irregular life of these tribes would make the establishment of slavery impracticable, as a captive could soon escape. We may, therefore, infer that in general the hunting tribes of the Stone Age were ignorant of any form of slavery or bondage.

The still extant hunting tribes, such as the aboriginals of Australia, the Bushmen, African Pygmies, Tierra del Fuegans, Botokudas, Kubus, Veddas, natives of the Andaman Islands, Palaeo-Siberians, Eskimos, are usually backward and feeble or fugitive tribes, unable to assert their rights, either by force or by cunning, against more advanced people, in fact, the lower race often forms the reservoir from which the higher obtains its slaves. The very custom of silent trading practised by these lower peoples is a significant sign of their timidity and recognition of their own inferiority.

As we see, we must look for a different set of conditions, among them the necessity of hard and continuous labour, as having promoted the growth of slavery to a definite and recognized institution.

A small group of hunters cannot absorb more than a very limited number of new members, and those only gradually, if the yield of their hunting and other operations is to be sufficient for all. The case is different, however, among the herding, more especially among the agricultural, tribes.

Social and political evolution are also important factors in the development of slavery. In the homogeneous communities, for instance, the prominent members do not wield a decisive authority, even in gerontocratic oligarchies, such as those of the Australian aborigines, and the social organization of a consanguineous tribe prevents any individual from attaining a prominent position. The first assault on the ties of consanguinity binding group families together was given by the rise of chiefly families with their privileged claims to first choice of booty, cattle, and men. The achievement of independence by each family within the aristocratic group made possible the development of a family property, as a separate domain. Spoil taken in war was always private property, and, consequently, among raiding tribes, the possession of captives, mostly women and children, was a personal distinction, a token of particular ability. Such booty, since it reproduced itself and was also capable of labour, was economically advantageous to its possessor; for such a man would have a larger turn-over and be in a position to make richer presents, which, again, would increase his prestige. When the nobles had exhausted themselves in feuds and battles or when their authority had been undermined through the rise of a despot, the lower classes took the opportunity to follow the example of their superiors with regard to the acquisition of property, &c.

§ 2. A question of paramount importance is how, exactly, we should envisage the first stages of slavery. As a starting-point we must take the differences between individuals as well as between various tribes and kinship groups, which owing to constant inter-marriage developed certain special tendencies, so that we already find some kinship groups communally concerned in particular kinds of work of a very elementary technique. We also find certain grades of subordination and dominance, though these distinctions must not be regarded as clearly defined or invariable. The smaller the group, the more isolated is its mode of life, as is the case with the nomadic hunting-groups, both the lower and the more advanced (Kubus, Pygmies, Bushmen, Eskimos), and the less possible is it for any gradations of superiority or inferiority, either of an individual or a group, to become a settled institution.

In general we must regard slavery as having sprung from two distinct sources: the superiority (*a*) of one group to another, (*b*) of one person to the others. Where individuality is not strongly defined, group eminence resolves on personal lines.

Regarding (*a*), in general the superiority of one group to another, if it is to be permanent, results in a stratification of the peoples, marked by a system of tributes rendered and particular services due. Such a domination, however, can be made lasting only if it is based not alone on armed force, but also on moral, social, and intellectual superiority. Serfdom as, for instance, among some East-African tribes and the Micronesians, is always marked by a conspicuous differentiation in mode of life, occupation, and also with separate habitations. As the superior class often lays claim to the entire land, which is lent to the lower class, such a condition might be confused with a mild form of slavery; the principal difference, however, is that the salve is always a man without a community, 'without a soul', a chattel of his master without any rights whatever. These characteristics do not apply to serfdom, which at most might be called bondage and not slavery.

Regarding (*b*), the superiority of individuals depends on the individual in question. On the Andaman Islands, for instance, youths band themselves together under a great hunter (Radcliffe Brown ['22], p. 45), or during a feast, such as those on Tierra del Fuego, the people will group themselves spontaneously under the leadership of the master of the rites and ceremonies (see Koppers, p. 62). Such incidental gradations dependent on personal relationships are, however, very often negative in character, as among the Bergdama, where a blood feud can be commuted for a certain tribute from the spoils of the hunt. The commutation of a blood feud by expiation doubtless. originated the custom of personal bondage for obligations incurred. The primitive mode of thought, which is not disposed to indulge in subtle distinctions, regards a person as a complete entity responsible for an obligation, and, consequently, prepares the ground for slavery. This bondage, however, is entirely distinct from slavery, since, in fixing the bondage of a debtor, the principal factor is the economic value of the obligation incurred, and the obligation, as a rule, can at once be commuted for corresponding value. Neither is the bondman in the same undefined

situation as the slave, who not only runs the risk of losing his life
through his master's displeasure, but also that of being offered as
a human sacrifice should occasion offer. On the contrary, it is most
important to preserve the life of a bondman: firstly, in order that
he may live long enough to pay up his debt, and, secondly, because
he represents interest-bearing capital, and, where the principal
cannot be collected, his labour is equivalent to income on the
capital. In the course of time, however, certain characteristics
resembling real slavery were developed.

§ 3. We can get some idea of the lot of a prisoner of war among
people living in larger aggregations, and what part he took in agriculture, which was principally the women's province, when we
glance at the conditions formerly prevailing in North America. In
the first place, it is obvious that no one knew quite what to do with
those enemies who had survived the battle. Sometimes they were
killed outright, sometimes carried off to the captor's home, where
no one could think of any better use to put them than to torture
them horribly. Sometimes their fate underwent a complete revul-
sion, if, for instance, some woman intervened on the victim's behalf
and accepted him as her husband. Sometimes, also, prisoners were
adopted into the tribe. We can, therefore, conclude that no fixed
custom prevailed. The value of alien labour as an agricultural or
domestic asset had not yet been discovered, or at any rate the
discovery was neither recognized nor widely acted on. The
requisite conditions for the development of slavery are the existence
of stratified society and the importance of agriculture, and, above
all, the burden imposed by hard labour. It is possible though, for
society to consist of various classes without the inclusion of slavery,
was, for instance, in Micronesia. As, in this case, it was principally
women who cultivated the gardens, and the slave-owners were almost
always men, the demand for numerous slaves was not great, as it
was, for instance, among the Polynesians. It is characteristic of
slavery among the latter that it was connected with a sequence
of religious ideas. When we remember that, in ancient Sumeria,
the king and the temples were the chief slave-owners, we can at once
perceive the connexion with the traditions current among dominating strata that only chiefs and priests might own slaves. For the
best of the booty is always the portion of the chief. Moreover, the
pride of victory over a living enemy is at first so blended with an
unaccustomed sense of relief that the victory is regarded as due to

the help of supernatural forces (for example see the Maoris). It is only when overlordship reaches the rationalistic stage that slave labour is universally exploited; in the later age of the Babylonian and Egyptian civilizations we see that even private people were slave-owners.

Every institution once in being carries the seeds of continuity in itself and works out its own destiny. In a favourable soil it reaches its most luxuriant growth. This was especially the case in Africa because of the tension between different races and because of the wide divergence between the culture of the Arabs and that of the indigenous races.

The political constitution due to stratification, which took the form of despotism and exploited the belief in personal *mana* was favourable both to slavery and to father-right. Slavery does not attain its full stature under primitive conditions, but it attained its first real expansion under archaic [1] civilization, where it pervaded the entire social fabric. It is, however, precisely this that in the lapse of many generations awakened the forces which sowed the seeds of a moral reaction, only culminating in most countries within relatively recent times. We must distinguish, however, between the very diverse conditions under which the individual slave lives (with the feasibility of liberation or ascent into a higher social class, which always and everywhere can be managed) and the institution as such, which, with the attainment of a certain stage of mechanical, political, and social evolution, is reflected in certain trends of thought.

§ 4. The opportunity for slavery is provided by the capture of prisoners of war or by lapses into bondage for debt, and it is difficult to say which of these two was the decisive factor. Perhaps the state of personal bondage was originally in any case a limited one and did not involve the bondman's offspring, since they might be reckoned as part of the tribe.

In some places, prisoners of war can be ransomed by their relatives, as, for instance, among the Ovakuanyama and the Aandonga of south-western Africa, though should this not happen they remain in servitude for ever. This procedure is followed at the present time, not only with their enemies, but also with members

---

[1] This term is employed to designate a society in an aggregate state with ethno-social stratification enjoying private property based on family ownership, as, e.g., in the ancient Orient.

of their own tribe; for instance, when a person is a continual nuisance to his relatives, or if he has committed a crime for which they do not wish to kill him, they will sell him into slavery. It also happens that the chief of a tribe in commutation of a crime will demand from the law-breaker one of his female relatives as a slave, or insist that a murderer should offer his sister in expiation. It is regarded as a distinction to be the slave of a chief (see Krafft, p. 25).

Among hunting and gardening tribes the frequent small wars, mostly undertaken from a desire for revenge, seldom resulted in prisoners of war. Although prisoners of war were the mainstay of the slave trade in Africa during the last century, we must not forget that the moving spirits were foreigners living under entirely different conditions. This applies not only to the Europeans and Americans on the West Coast, but also to the Arabs on the East Coast.

§ 5. The second factor conducive to slavery is bondage for debt. This, again, may be the result of some breach of the law, particularly one which would be likely to start a blood feud, or, alternatively, it may be a case of freely chosen bondage, of a man offering himself as a personal pledge. This surrender of the right to dispose freely of one's own person is generally only intended to be a temporary one. When the obligation is not fully discharged the debtor does not regain his freedom, and servitude becomes a permanent state.

It is possible to lapse into bondage for debt even among the hunting and root-gathering tribes of the Bergdama. This is connected with the fact that a person accused of murder will try to buy himself off. This practice obtains since some of the Bergdamas have taken to keeping goats, and the price of freedom is generally from twenty to thirty animals. When the accused is a cultivator and devoid of any possessions, he has to try some other procedure; a murderer, for instance, would agree to surrender everything he takes in hunting for the next three years. There was, however, no question of personal bondage in such a case (Vedder, pp. 151 et seq.).

Among the Ila-speaking tribes of Northern Rhodesia a breach of the law is very often automatically followed by slavery, from which result the guilty person has to be released by a payment; this custom is called *buditazhi*. Here are several instances.

A women removed the bell from the collar of a dog and threw it away into the bush, upon which the owner seized the woman as a slave and sold her to another man who gave her to his sister. A woman visiting a woman friend was told to fetch what she liked from the friend's field; she went and fetched a cob of maize, but mistook the boundary and helped herself from a strange field, whose owner thereupon seized her as a slave. Subsequently he sold her to a Mambar trader who took her away with him. A man in one of the villages, hearing of her plight, advised her to throw ashes on his head and so escape from her master. She did so, and the man spoke with the Mambari who tried in vain to redeem her. The man in question, Salanga by name, later died and the woman fled in terror to Mono. Salanga's heirs had to pay three pieces of calico and a blanket to get her back.

Not only theft but also unimportant or even unintentional damage to person or property is sufficient to bring about the loss of liberty. For spitting on a man, for instance, or unintentionally breathing in his face, or otherwise defiling him, a person may be made a slave for life. This is also the case when a man knocks out another's tooth, either in serious or mock fighting. All these things are connected with superstitious beliefs. Moreover, failure to observe the traditional code of honour (*buditazhi*) entails slavery. If a man, for instance, takes a woman for his wife without having observed the customary rites or paid the bride-price to her relatives, and subsequently wishes to be rid of her, she has the right to claim him as her slave. He then becomes her property and that of her family, because he offended against *buditazhi*, the code of honour, &c. Or, should a man run away with the wife of another, the guilty man's mother or sister may be reduced to slavery should they not possess a slave with which to ransom themselves. Numbers of people are held in slavery for adultery. Generally the crime can be atoned for by a fine, but the injured husband has the right to enslave the seducer, or his sister or mother. However, as a rule, he does not exercise this right unless he has not received the due payment. The clan system often results in innocent persons paying the price of slavery for the deeds of their relatives, as has already been mentioned (see Smith and Dale, i. 401 et seq.).

It sometimes happens that a man will sell himself into slavery when he cannot pay the fine demanded of him. In such a case a man would go to some rich man and ask the latter to pay the fine for him, binding himself to serve his new creditor for a period commensurate with his debt, or till his relatives purchased his freedom. The new creditor generally took the opportunity of demanding high interest on the loan.

§ 6. There is another road to slavery; a man leaves his own village and goes to another, where he puts himself under the protection of the chief, offering to stay and work for him, for a time. It may happen that he gets entangled with the chief's wives, of which, when reported to him, the husband takes no notice for the time being. Later when trouble arises through the stranger's interfering with the wives of a visiting chief, he is fined, and, as he has nothing wherewith to pay and can get no help from his relations, whom he has disowned, the chief with whom he has taken refuge pays for him and thus becomes his creditor. When the offence is repeated, the chief again pays the fine and claims the man as his slave.

It occasionally happens, too, that a man finding himself alone and friendless will of his own accord embrace slavery; this applies also to women. The man or woman can always be ransomed from their master at any time by relations (Smith and Dale, i. 398 et seq.).

§ 7. In Loango such persons as have been cast out of the community on account of some offence and banished from hearth and home lose all rights, i.e. they are no longer part of the tribe and, though retaining their liberty, are despised and have lost for ever the support of their tribal associations. Consequently they must endeavour to induce some other tribe to receive them. This a man can do only by offering himself as a slave, which he is generally driven to do in the end by his desire for the society of his own kind. The outcast seeks refuge as the serf of a district or village chief. These are the only persons allowed to take slaves and legally represent them. The legal code in force here recognizes no other slave-owners. This, also, is nowadays the only way in which a person can be enslaved, except that the children of a slave-mother are slaves. Formerly, of course, when the slave trade was rife, when border wars were carried on, or the tribes of the interior incited to revolt in order to obtain these human wares for the Europeans, all captives were regarded as slaves, for business reasons. Even a few decades ago any solitary wanderer not belonging to the tribe was often treated as a slave, especially since it is concluded that such a man has been driven out by his people and lost his civil rights as the result of his own misdeeds (see Pechuël-Lösche, pp. 234 et seq.).

In Loango certain ceremonies mark the acceptance of serfs which, in fact, represent their adoption into the community, i.e. into the circle of kinship. A man who has signified his wish to become a serf kneels before his chosen overlord, breathes and spits on the soles of the latter's feet, puts his lord's foot on his neck and presses his face to the ground. Should the overlord decline to accept him he scatters dust over him with his foot, in which case the rejected person must leave the community before sunrise. If a virgin, however, desires him as her husband he remains in the community even if he has been rejected by the overlord. The community is thenceforward responsible for the serf it has accepted, except with regard to his debts, which as a serf he has no right to incur (see Pechuël-Lösche, p. 236).

§ 8. In Kpando (Togoland) a man who has incurred debts and cannot find any one to be security for him must hand over one of his children as a hostage until he has paid the debt. Only older children, boys or girls, are pawned, such as can already make themselves useful. The creditor employs these pawns in house-work or field-labour or as carriers, &c. He is responsible for their food, housing, and clothing. They receive no wages. This labour rendered does not reduce the sum of the original debt, which remains intact. Should the serf die he must be replaced by another. If the serf is a daughter her father's creditor can marry her or give her in marriage to his son. This, however, does not cancel the debt. Should another man wish to marry her, he must first pay off the whole of her father's debt in order to set her free, whereupon the son-in-law, of course, becomes the creditor of his father-in-law. On the day on which the debt is paid the child automatically becomes free and returns to its family. Even should a girl have been taken in marriage by the creditor she is still free to leave him at once, though, as is always the custom where the system of patriarchal marriage by sale prevails, the children belong to the man. On the return of a child from bondage a family feast is arranged in its honour and the father ceremonially thanks the child for the service rendered him. It is bathed and its head is shaved as a token that the debt has been paid in full. Debts, usually incurred on such occasions as feasts for the dead, are, as a rule, the original cause of such bondage (see Breitkopf, pp. 570 et seq.; see also Nieboer, p. 38).

§ 9. The practice of slave-trading marks the attainment of a certain economic level, not because of the fact that trading takes place, but because peoples on a lower economic level do not yet understand how to take full advantage of this human labour unit.

Among the Ila-speaking peoples slaves are obtained from two sources; they are either bought from slave-traders, or have been reduced to bondage in consequence of a crime committed either by themselves or by one of their kin. The Arabs and Mambari traders formerly carried on a brisk trade in slaves. In the course of inter-tribal wars prisoners were taken and kept as slaves. Although this source of supply is nowadays closed, the surviving slaves and their children are still held as slaves. Moreover, a secret trade in slaves still appears to exist. People going alone to fetch water or into the forest for wood are liable to be seized and dragged off to some distant place and sold as slaves. Slaves were formerly purchased with hoes. A boy fetched five or six hoes, a girl more, sometimes as many as ten or twelve. Other payments, however, were sometimes accepted, for instance, ten baskets of salt, five bunches of glass beads, and a hoe would be paid for a grown-up woman. While the negotiations were taking place the slave was generally sent for on some trifling errand in order to give the prospective buyer the opportunity of inspecting him. The boy was not told that he had been bought, but instead directed to accompany the visitor on his way and then return; he would be given no opportunity to say farewell to his relatives (see Smith and Dale, i. 398 et seq.).

The Swahili may be regarded as typical slave dealers. They were in the habit of raiding towns and villages wherever they could safely penetrate and carrying off the population, male and female alike, as slaves. The slaves were formerly brought to Zanzibar, then the centre of the slave-trade, whence they were shipped to the Arabian harbours. The Arabs engaged in this trade soon lost every feeling of humanity and came to regard the slaves only from the point of view of their own personal profit; consequently, the only thing they considered was to get the slaves to their destination in marketable condition, so as to ensure a sale at a good profit. On the African coast itself the slaves were employed in household work and on the clove plantations. In Arabia they cultivated the fields as well as doing housework. Household slaves were not badly treated, the women were often taken as concubines, and the men could even rise so far as to own slaves themselves and sometimes lived almost as free men, though always with the risk of being re-sold at their master's pleasure. As slaves became scarce near the coast the traders extended their operations towards the interior. In order to increase the profits slaves were generally loaded on the the way to their ultimate destination with ivory, horns, and food for the caravans. Ten or twelve were generally chained together in gangs by iron neck-rings and driven forward with whips of rhinoceros-hide. The raiders would kill the weak and those who fell ill on the way rather than let them go free. Stubborn slaves were loaded, over and above their burden, with heavy logs, to which they were bound at night (Roscoe ['21], pp. 9 et seq.; see also Velten, pp. 305 et seq.; Nieboer, pp. 396 et seq.). In the twelfth century the English sold their illegitimate children to the Irish. Moreover, the Breton laws gave a mother the right to sell her illegitimate offspring, though sometimes it was the father who sold them. Under pressure of extraordinary circumstances, such as destitution or felony, even legitimate children might be sold, especially daughters (see P. W. Joyce ['03], ii. 13).

§ 10. The existence of raiding expeditions, undertaken solely with the object of obtaining slaves for trading purposes, frequently gives a wrong impression of the economic conditions prevailing among such slave-raiding peoples, as the raiders, in many cases, are only the middle-men. The Arab slave-raiders and the powerful chiefs and sultans of West Africa belonged to this category, and often owed their high position to European gun-runners. Similar conditions probably also obtained in those archaic civilizations based on slavery which consequently developed the need for large numbers of slaves. During the eighth decade of the nineteenth century the Kalashi-speaking Bashgeli Kafirs of India, under the rule of Chitral, whose overlord was Aman-ul-Malk, were sold into slavery from time to time in order to increase the revenues of their overlord (see Leitner, p. 143).

§ 11. Among the Pawnees, prisoners of war were handed over to a women's organization composed of widows and unmarried girls, and controlled by a woman who wore a large shell on her breast as a token of her office. This involved a ceremony including torture of the prisoners and a public dance. For example, a Dakota found

on the field of battle by Pawnees, was carried off to their village
and handed over to the women by the chief. The prisoner was
bound to a post on the south side of the camp. After various pre-
liminaries, the women danced through the village to the place of
torture and lit a fire in front of him. This was the beginning of a
ceremony lasting four days during which the prisoner was un-
mercifully tortured. Finally, the little daughter of the chief was
brought to watch the torture. She shrieked and was carried off
weeping. At first her father scolded her, but in the end, as she
refused to be comforted, more and more people collected to
sympathize with her. The warriors and chiefs held a conclave and
decided to command the women to release the prisoner, who was
forthwith brought to the council house. The chief announced that
he had decided to accede to the wishes of his daughter. He bade
his daughter fetch water for the prisoner, and had his wounds
dressed. Finally, the prisoner was fed and clothed and sent back
to his tribe. Three years later he appeared with his people and
tried to conclude a peace treaty between the two tribes (Murie,
pp. 598 et seq.). This case clearly shows that nobody quite knew
what to do with a prisoner of war or how to put him to some
practical use.

§ 12. Stratified societies, where the men are hunters and trappers
and the women till the soil, have not necessarily discovered the
economic side of slave labour or how to make the best use of it.
All the same they recognize definite degrees of power, but regard
them as due to supernatural forces.

Although the inhabitants of the Micronesian islands of the
Pacific form a strictly graded society, we cannot recognize the
existence of slavery in the true sense of the word, in spite of the fact
that subordination to a noble class is recognized, and, indeed, the
sacred class of princes has reached a high stage of development.
It is rather a case of the relationship between nobles and serfs, of
land on loan, from the higher to the lower class (see Sarfert, pp. 361
et seq.). Similar conditions obtain on the island of Yap, although
here we find a group of decidedly inferior people, the Milingai, who
have their own separate settlements; nevertheless, we cannot regard
them as being more than a specially low grade of serfs (see Müller,
p. 249).

In the Polynesian islands, real slavery occasionally exists, though
subordination nearly always takes a group form, affecting entire

tribes and communities. Among the Maoris, as long as the member of a group which had lost its independence through being defeated in war remained with his group, he was, in common with the others, generally liable to tribute rather than personal service. Such a group having forfeited respect for its military prowess, was looked on as inferior. As a rule the women and most of the men were spared, only the most beautiful of the women being carried off by the conquerors. The rest of the tribe was under the obligation to furnish provisions on demand, as a token of their subjection; otherwise things continued as before. The conquerors even acknowledged the receipt of this tribute by reciprocating with special gifts. In order to prevent an undue increase in the population of a subject tribe the overlords were in the habit of requisitioning every attractive girl as soon as she attained puberty. Apart from this, individual prisoners of war who had not been eaten at the usual cannibal feast, were sometimes kept as slaves. Hence the opprobrious Maori epithet, 'Remnant of the feast!', or 'You weren't even worth roasting!' Such were generally well treated, well fed, and allowed a large measure of freedom in word and deed. Such a slave would not try to escape and rejoin his relatives, for they would certainly not accept him; he was regarded as a Jonah, a man marked by the gods, who otherwise would not have allowed him to be taken captive. As far as his own people were concerned he was dead or worse, and his presence among them would have been looked on as a living reproach. They feared him as an evil influence in their village, especially as it was believed that his presence would always ensure their defeat in war. The insult done to them through him could only be wiped out by the blood of his captors. Such slaves were partly compensated for the loss of their status as members of a tribe by automatically escaping from all restraint of tabu. A slave had no soul, his gods had forgotten him and, consequently, he was to all intents and purposes non-existent. Naturally he had to take care not to offend a chief's own personal tabu, as in this case he would have been executed, though the inevitable supernatural consequences of the transgression would be regarded as falling on the chief and not on the slave, since he was already non-existent as far as the higher powers were concerned. Such slaves, in consequence of their soullessness, their lack of any personal sacredness, were at liberty to perform many things forbidden their superiors, such as cooking, carrying burdens, and various menial duties advantageous to the tribe, with the result that such slaves were generally highly valued by their captors. The warrior, for instance, whose person was so sacred that it was defiled if he approached an oven, whose back was so sacrosanct that it must not be touched by any burden, had a good friend in such a man 'forgotten of the gods'. Moreover, it was looked on as ill-bred to treat an inferior badly. Occasionally a slave did work for another other than his master and received in return a gift, of which he generally offered his master a part who, however, seldom demanded it as his right. A slave was sometimes transferred from one master to another in return for some service rendered, the first owner surrendering any right to his slave's services. A strong bond of friendship and loyalty to the family generally grew up between master and slave. In spite of all this, it was impossible for a slave to be respected by the freemen. It was a continual source of humiliation to him that he was forbidden to approach the store-houses (where the sweet potatoes were kept), lest he should contaminate them with his presence; that he might not enter a burial ground or other forbidden place without previously removing all his clothing and leaving it outside. When he died no funeral rites were observed for him; he was simply buried in a trench without further ceremony. All this, however, was a small matter compared with the fact that he went in constant fear of his life in consequence of his lord's dislike or displeasure. He was also liable to be chosen as a sacrifice should some religious occasion demand a victim, such, for instance, as a chief's funeral feast. Moreover, should any stranger kill a slave, there was no one to avenge him.

A slave was often married off to some female slave whose offspring were likewise slaves, though the descendants were, as a rule, gradually absorbed into the tribe through intermarriage. A chief's household generally contained a larger or smaller number of female slaves or concubines who performed various menial duties. The poorer freemen of lower rank did not hesitate to marry slaves, and their children inherited their father's position in the tribe, though they were always liable to be reminded of their origin. A woman of high rank would sometimes choose a good-looking young male slave as a husband, should she wish to be the dominating element in the marriage, and among the Maoris a man who was adopted into his wife's family was subject to his wife's authority. Notwithstanding this, a man of forceful personality might become a prominent leader or even a war-chief notwithstanding the slave blood in his veins, though seldom treated with the same measure of respect as was granted to men of nobler birth (Tregear, pp. 153 et seq.).

§ 13. A curious kind of slavery exists among the Hababs, of Abyssinia (near the coast of the Red Sea), where many indigenous families are serfs. The conditions of this bondage, however, are not hard, as, should a serf be ill-treated, he is at liberty to seek another master, from whom he cannot be recovered. (In this case we see that we are dealing with 'serfs', who, nevertheless, stand in an individual relation to their masters.) According to Munzinger (['83] p. 155), this curious form of bondage is due to the frequent wars in which large numbers of captives were carried off. Moreover, poor people are in the habit of selling their children into slavery, as they are better off in bondage than they would be as free citizens.

Among the Beni-Amer (Abyssinia) a large part of the population consists of slaves. These have either been captured from enemy tribes or bought abroad; there are no other sources of slavery, as no Beni-Amer would ever think of selling his child, and he himself can never be deprived of his liberty. The slaves consist of two classes: those who have been bought and those born in the land (*wulud*). The newly-bought slave can be re-sold and does not as yet form part of the family. A native-born slave is a slave only in name, as is shown by the fact that he is allowed to intermarry with the lower class of freemen (*woreza*) and the children of such marriages are free, being the children of free mothers. In the district of Barka there is an indigenous tribe of serfs, known as Kishendoa ('slave-tribe'), who occupy their own camps, are entirely independent under their own chiefs and intermarry with the *woreza* at their pleasure. Native-born slaves (serfs) are allowed to live where they please, and the same laws of inheritance apply to them as to the free, though should they die without heirs their master is regarded as the rightful heir to their property. (This state of affairs may be regarded as being on the borderline between serfdom and slavery.)

In the case of the murder of a slave it is also of material importance whether the slave is a newly-bought one or native-born; if bought he is regarded as having been his master's chattel, and the case may be settled by repaying the latter his purchase price; if native-born, he belongs to the family, and his blood must be avenged by blood. If he has any relatives, they avenge him, if not, his master takes the responsibility. If this is not feasible, the matter is allowed to drop; the question of blood-money never arises. A case analogous to that of the above class is that of the serf-born dependants of the princely Tsasega family. These are still designated as 'slaves', but in reality they belong to the best families of the land; no one hesitates to intermarry with them and they often hold the highest offices (see Munzinger ['83], pp. 308 et seq.).

In Kita (French Sudan) the same differences obtain between slaves born in the household, those born in the land, and purchased prisoners of war. In general, only slaves belonging to the latter category are sold; and these are often forced to make long journeys under the strictest supervision. Even at home they are not nearly so well treated as the household slaves. As far as work is concerned, slaves and freemen are in the same inferior position to their over-lords. It is probable that the slave can change masters among the Kitas in the same way as is done among the Wolofs by injuring the child or the horse of the man whom he has chosen as a new master. We see that an act, a ceremony, inevitably creates his new situa-tion. The household slave (bondman), born in his master's house-hold, belongs to the family and may only be sold after continued misconduct on his part. He is allowed to own any property he may have acquired as the result of his labour in his spare time, and may even possess slaves himself. The principal disadvantage of such slavery as we find here is the slave's lack of any political rights. The lot of slaves in the king's household is more or less the same as elsewhere, except that they are not the individual property of the king but belong to the head of the reigning family. On the death of the chief, they are not necessarily inherited by the heirs of his body, but by his successor in office. Such slaves are so far from being treated as slaves that they may even have free persons in their service (see Steinmetz, pp. 168 et seq.; cf. also Spiess, pp. 98, 101; Wissmann, p. 158).

§ 14. The organized economic use of slavery is, as already indi-cated, the result of various factors, though it has obviously spread from certain central points to other tribes less economically developed. For slavery is an institution more suitable than any other for adoption, as it chiefly affects strangers and substitutes their labour for native labour. Consequently it can become an important factor in the domestic economy of even the smallest and least stationary community, e.g. in remoter parts of Africa.

As an example we may take the region of the middle Congo. Among the Boloki the number of slaves amounts to about 25 per cent. of the whole population. Of these, some are born slaves, others have become slaves through debt, a few have been taken prisoners in war, and many have sold themselves into slavery in order to pay debts which they have contracted through having committed adultery or lost a lawsuit. It is also customary to sell a man or a woman as a slave in order to pay the family debts. Sometimes a father gives his son as a pledge for a loan. The position of such a pledged servant or 'pawn' is somewhat higher than that of a slave, for he can be redeemed at any time and thus become a free man again. A pawn may not be sold or transferred to another party without the consent of the person who gave him as security. With the exception of the chiefs and headmen there are no absolutely independent men or women. They are all attached to headmen as relations, slaves, or pawns, or they may have surrendered themselves voluntarily to a chief. When, in consequence of a death, the family of a freeman becomes too weak to defend itself against possible attacks the head of the family selects an influential family to whom to attach himself, also transferring those relations dependent on him. Thenceforth he practically becomes a member of the family he has joined; he comes within the range of their interests, their quarrels are his quarrels and vice versa. His position is that of a freeman, and he is never treated as a slave. He improves his position by this connexion; if he, with his small following, had remained apart, one of the powerful families would soon have picked a quarrel with him and the result is easy to foresee—he and his people would have been enslaved. A slave is not allowed to anoint himself with camwood powder and oil. As a rule slaves are much better dressed than their masters, for the latter are very reluctant to make a display of their wealth. They are afraid they may be accused of practising sorcery for making other people's property disappear into their houses. A badly dressed man is also less exposed to the danger of being asked for a loan. It is only on festive occasions that they appear well dressed. The master is responsible for the actions of his slaves. The slaves are the property of their masters and can be sold or even killed by them.

They are, however, in general well treated, as the slave has the remedy in his own hands by breaking a witch-doctor's pot, which entails such a heavy fine on the master that he prefers to give up his slave. They receive everything necessary for subsistence, are married, and can look after their own affairs as members of the community. A slave can also own other slaves. A female slave is allowed to cultivate land belonging to the town of which her master is a native. The master takes great care that the right of his female slave in this respect is not infringed. She is not allowed to dispose of the land, but she may sell the field-produce (Weeks, pp. 112 et seq.). This is therefore a case of slavery in an already stratified society. See also Nieboer.

§ 15. Among the Swahili slavery had developed in various directions. A distinction was made in the first place between newly captured prisoners of war, persons pledged for debt, men enslaved for crime, and slaves born in the family. But there were also cases of the natives voluntarily offering themselves and even their families as slaves to the Arabs. The natives offering themselves as slaves were, however, not always fully aware of the consequences. A distinction was made between trained and untrained slaves, according to their capacity for domestic work. The unskilled slave, after being purchased, was provided with a new cloth, armed with a hoe, and taken to the plantation which was under the charge of the overseers. They showed the slave what part of the ground he had to work. He also received a small piece of land for his own use on which he could grow cassava, beans, and other vegetables. He was not compelled to give any part of this produce to his master, but when he sowed rice or millet, he usually offered his master the first-fruits. (The offering of the first-fruits is doubtless connected with the tasting by the senior member of the clan, as is customary, for instance, among the Bergdama and others.) Many of these slaves were allowed three days, others only two days, in the week for looking after their own work.

Many of the home-born slaves were taught handicrafts, such as the making of clothes and shoes, carpentry, and building in wood or stone. They were also employed to make purchases and conduct business transactions; they were generally allowed to keep for their own use the wages received from outsiders, but they would usually of their own accord give part of it to their master. The behaviour of slaves was quite definitely prescribed: they had to

obey the master's orders, always walk behind him when out of
doors, uncover the head on entering the house, never sit down on
a chair, come every morning and evening to greet him and wait
on him. They were not allowed to shake hands when greeting
him, nor enter the master's room without sufficient reason. The
slaves usually ate the same food as their masters, but not along
with them. In earlier times a slave could be recognized by his
dress: in particular, he was not allowed to wear a cap or sandals or
a shirt (*kanzu*) long enough to cover the feet. Slaves could be
pawned or borrowed, and likewise liberated.

§ **16.** In order to understand the character of such slavery as it
exists among many primitive tribes and recognize its distinguishing
traits, we will refer to the accounts given by Smith and Dale of
slavery as it actually exists among the Ba-Ila of Northen Rhodesia.
In general one may say that the existence of many slaves is quite
happy, though, however kind their master may be, the fact remains
that they are slaves and cannot dispose freely of their own persons.
They have no rights over their children, and are not entitled to
resent the word slave (*muzhike*) addressed to them. Even if a
female slave is married to her master or some other freeman she
remains a slave and her children are slaves. Her master has the
right to sell her children at his discretion. Should she be married
to another than her master she is obliged to till the latter's fields
as well as her husband's. She must be at the disposition of her
owner should he so desire, and her husband has no right over her.
A male slave is given one of his master's female slaves as a wife,
but she may at any time be taken away from him and sold. A man's
children by his female slave will be free and, if he has no other
children, a child of the slave wife can even 'eat' (inherit) his
father's name. Young slave girls are often 'lent' by the chief to
other men in return for presents.

A master is, in his own interest, concerned to protect his slave
against ill-treatment by other people. Although, on the one hand,
the slaves of a prominent man are well cared for, on the other, they
are entirely at his mercy. Should he beat or kill them it was—
under the old régime—no one else's business. Where bondage
for debt was concerned, the relatives might be inclined to resent
a slave's ill-treatment and especially his death, but the master
was in the position to reply: 'He or she was *my* slave, you might
have purchased his or her freedom, but you didn't.' If a slave

dies one or two cattle are sacrificed as the blood-offering (*luloa*), which the villagers eat in order to pacify the communal demigod. Notwithstanding the fact that they are in general well treated, some slaves are unsparingly worked in the fields. A slave can own no property; he may gain by trading or hunting, but anything he earns in this way can at any time be taken by his master. There have been cases of slaves who possessed more than their masters, but they are never free to dispose of their gains as they wish (Smith and Dale, i. 408 et seq.; concerning the West-African tribe of the Kpelle cf. Westermann, pp. 60, 80).

§ 17. A Muganda chief possessed, in addition to the retainers of his own clan, many slaves of both sexes, who all lived on his estate and were dependent on his table. The women were generally his concubines. Most of these slaves had been captured during raids on neighbouring tribes; some, however, had been bought, or were the offspring of slaves married to slaves. A female slave who bore the chief a child attained her freedom thereby. No formal declaration was made, but it was the understood rule. Peasants who could not or would not undertake some labour demanded of them by the chief, and were fined by the overseer for delay in executing it, pawned a wife or a child until they could pay the fine. The pawn remained with the creditor for such a period until he or she was redeemed. Sometimes they were not redeemed, but became slaves in name as well as in fact (Roscoe ['21], p. 93). The Mossi, of the western Sudan, made no distinction between bought slaves, prisoners of war, and native-born slaves (Mangin, p. 111). Slaves, as well as goats, salt, and cloth, are often used to buy wives, as, for instance, among the Wahenga, of Nyasaland (Sanderson, p. 132).

In Loango the position of a serf can be compared with that of a domestic animal. His master, or rather the community, has to support him and is in every way responsible for him; but he has neither property nor any right to his home. The lord of the community is at liberty to enter his hut whenever he chooses and appropriate his possessions. It is true that this very seldom happens, for, even allowing for the existence of brutality and covetousness, the feelings and the possessions of even the lowest are considerately spared as far as is consistent with the general welfare of the community. A serf is not despised, and moves freely among freemen and is no more burdened with work than they

are. He is supposed to devote three days of the four-day week
to his statutory labour, but he generally, like all serfs, works for
two days only. The rest of the time he can devote to his own
affairs. His children inherit the position of the mother. Though
the children of a serf-mother are according to matriarchal law
serfs, they are, so far as essentials are concerned, in a better
position than their parents; having been born in the community
and grown up in it they are intimately connected with it, and for
this reason descendants of serfs become free on the death of their
master's grandson; or, as others assert, the third generation is
born free (Pechuël-Lösche, pp. 197, 235 et seq.).

In conclusion, we find that life in common settlements, and
relationships established through intermarriage, knit the bonds so
close that, where no sense of economic advantage intervenes (as
happens where slavery has been introduced from outside and
paralysed the feeling of reciprocity), no socially separate class of
slaves can grow up. For the two principal factors are lacking, (1)
the incentive provided by personal property and acquisition of
economic influence to increase the burden of labour and throw it
on other shoulders, (2) marked racial differences between various
sections of the population arousing feelings of superiority in one
of them to the detriment of the others.

§ 18. Slavery in the real sense of the word, i.e. slaves possessing
no civil rights, existed in the early days of the Teutonic kingdoms.
In course of time this slavery was considerably affected by changes
which took place in the constitution of the tribes, one important
factor being the employment of such bondmen by the king and
the landed aristocracy in various capacities connected with the
then prevalent system of chivalry. On the other hand, many
bondmen became citizens of the towns, which, however, did not
affect the institution of slavery in itself (Hübner, pp. 83 et seq.),
for we must draw a sharp distinction between the altered conditions
of life within a class and an institution which continued to exist as
such. See also Dopsch ['18/20], ['21]; for England cf. Liebermann, pp. 690, 692, 693 et seq.

§ 19. The decisive factor in the development of slavery to its
fullest extent was the archaic system by which land was held
from overlords and which was closely connected with the feudal
system of the temples and the courts of the despots. We can
observe such preliminary stages at certain epochs of the early

archaic civilizations; in the northern kingdom of Egypt, for instance, in the Inca kingdom of Peru, in ancient China, &c. In all these places the members of the ruling class were endowed with *mana*, and possessed immense personal authority over the subject population who lacked it. Later on arose the organized exploitation of the subordinate classes for economic purposes, which served as the foundation for the archaic bureaucratic states.

Real slavery already existed in the Babylonian and pre-Babylonian society of the Sumerian Age. The slaves were distinguished both from proletarians and from patricians in being definitely regarded as chattels. The oldest sign for a slave (male) is a phallus combined with the sign for a mountain, and for a female slave the sign for a vulva (= woman) and that for mountain; which seems to indicate that both men and women slaves were derived from the hunter tribes inhabiting the mountain country to the east of Mesopotamia. We may infer from this that the principal slave material consisted of foreign captives taken in war. At the same time bondage for debt was in existence; as already mentioned, this is one of the oldest forms of slavery, though as a rule it affects only the internal affairs of a tribe. The slave was obliged to cut his hair and wear a badge indicating his condition. In the most ancient times nearly all slaves belonged to the king and the temples; private people as yet were not in the habit of having a large retinue of servants, they were generally content with a few female slaves. Male slaves were still scarce. The court slaves were a class apart; they were in the service of the ruler, and, consequently, often gained some measure of influence. The dependents of temples, most of whom were originally slaves presented to the god, also lived under signally favourable conditions. The laws relating to slaves were principally concerned with breaches of state laws, and with a master's right to demand compensation from the guilty party for the injury or death of his slave; this last came under the heading of damage to property. The treatment meted out to slaves was probably not at all bad, particularly of female slaves, who were often the concubines of their masters. The male slaves, too, were not only allowed to take wives from their own class but could also marry freewomen. Apparently a slave could also protest against his sale. On feast days, particularly at the new year, all class distinctions were laid aside. Attempts at insubordination or flight occurred at times, as might be expected. Slaves were not allowed to change their situation at will, but were inherited on the death of their master; they could also be given away as presents, or sold. The liberation of slaves mostly took place through adoption, which placed the slave in the relation of a dependent on his master until the latter's death, or through purchase, whereby the slave attained immediate freedom. This purchase was generally effected through the good offices of a friend, who borrowed the money from a third party. It was customary for a merchant trading in a foreign country to purchase such child slaves as he might find there; in such cases the merchant was subsequently compensated by the temple of his neighbourhood or by the king. A Babylonian slave, purchased in a foreign country, received his freedom on being brought back to his home, obviously because it was regarded as a disgrace to purchase a fellow-countryman abroad with the intention of keeping him as a slave. In Assyria many slaves managed to attain positions of importance. The numbers of the native slaves were supplemented by a continuous stream of foreign ones (Meissner, pp. 375 et seq.). See also Schneider, pp. 21, 36. Regarding Egypt, see Thurnwald ['o1], pp. 772 et seq. Regarding ancient classical times, see Ed. Meyer, pp. 79 et seq., and Sargent.

§ 20. The form of individual subjection existing among the Ba-Ila is, as already mentioned, not merely serfdom but real slavery, in spite of its various mitigations. A person who has been enslaved for a crime can, however, be redeemed at any time. This possibility, in accordance with all primitive conceptions of law, has no relation to the measure of the individual's guilt, but only to the external aspect of the act committed and its consequences. Moreover, the reconquest of liberty, like sanctuary, is regarded more as being an act of God than due to any personal merit or effort. A slave who is ill-treated beyond endurance by his master has one means of escape: to strew ashes on the head of another man to whom he wishes to transfer himself. This safety valve, like the right of sanctuary, which allows the first heat of a blood feud to subside, is a protection against the worst evils of slavery; and this ritual means of redress is no mean weapon in the hands of the slave. In Islamic countries the *notae datio* is a process of a similar nature.

Among the Ba-Ila a slave cannot purchase his own freedom, but through industry and zeal in his master's service he can attain a position of trust and influence and be called his master's friend (*mwenzhina shimatwangakwe*). He might for instance be sent to trade and gain slaves for his master; as they increased he would be regarded by them as their chief, and would be in a position to give orders to them (Smith and Dale, i. 411).

Where slavery rests on an economic basis the conditions are entirely different. Slavery here is firmly anchored in the legal constitution; the whole economic development proves this beyond dispute. The ceremonies which, as a rule, attend the liberation of a slave must be considered in connexion with the meaning of such a procedure according to primitive conceptions of law.

In the country of the Kunama (Abyssinia), the few slaves found there are definitely considered as chattels. Here, and also among the Barea and the Bazen, the native-born slave regains his complete freedom by leaving his master and going to another place. If a slave has reason to complain of his master he retires to another village, lives where and as he pleases, and marries free women, without incurring any blame or any disability. If a master in marrying off his slave acts as a father to him, he is by this act declaring his slave *ipso facto* free (Munzinger ['83], p. 484). The case, frequently observed, of slaves of princes and kings attaining such influence as to be superior to freemen is one of the first stages regularly marking the rise of organized rationalistic despotism, i.e. based not on magic but on the rationalistic use of power. It was the strength of his retinue and his personal bodyguard and the efficiency of his ministers which enabled the overlord to become more powerful than his rivals among the neighbouring noble familes.

§ 21. The disintegration of slavery as an institution has no relation to the primitive or the archaic constitutions. Each of the various peculiar institutions of primitive civilization worked out its own destiny, both with regard to its expansion and the term of its existence. The institution of slavery, owing its greatest power to the conjunction of agriculture, herding, and industry, which developed social stratification to its utmost limit and more or less canonized superiority, needed new points of view and new values to break it up. (See also Hobhouse, p. 299.)

As illustrating the disappearance of slavery under modern influences we may quote an example from Africa, the traditional home of slavery. At the same time we must not forget how far primitive economics, at least in its simplest state, is from being dependent on slavery.

§ 22. On the 16th of July 1906 the paramount chief, Lewanika, issued a proclamation to the Ba-Ila, declaring that all slaves held by him and his people were thenceforth to be free. Twelve days in the year devoted to certain obligatory labours as an equivalent for taxes were to be the sole exception. The people who were formerly slaves were, nevertheless, forbidden to leave their villages except in the following cases: (1) with their former master's permission; (2) in the event of marriage, should one party choose to live in the other's village; (3) in case of ill-treatment; (4) if the former slave were a foreigner and his people lived in another district of Lewanika's kingdom. Moreover, any one could purchase entire liberty at the cost of two English pounds (Smith and Dale, i. 411 et seq.). Compare also Roscoe ['21], p. 126.

XV

BONDMEN

§ 1. Bond service, stratification, and slavery. § 2. Bondmen agriculturists among pastoral people. § 3. Bondmen in ancient Samoan society. § 4. Bondmen as human sacrifices. § 5. Conditions in ancient Mexico and Central America. § 6. Among the Kpelle in West Africa. § 7. Among Abyssinian tribes.

§ 1. The term 'serfdom' is applied in different ways by specialists in research to the varied concrete phenomena presented by the social arrangements found in different forms of culture. In the cases available for examination in real life the distinction between bondservice and slavery is, in fact, often difficult to draw when social grading is not clearly defined. The difference between serfdom and slavery is, however, fairly generally recognized, for by serfdom is understood a much looser and less individually emphasized state of dependency of a whole stratum on a superior, aristocratic class. Such a relation of dependence is connected, as a rule, with the obligation to pay tribute or perform services, as, for instance, among the Greek Perioikoi or often, in former times, among the German peasants who were in different stages of dependency. The gradation of a society in strata of different rank is often connected with relations of dependency similar to that involved in serfdom. In this case also there are several intermediary stages between serfdom and the lower grades of freemen. Slavery is limited in theory to personal services for a certain master. Serfdom, too, is not free from personal relations to certain families, so that the line of demarcation between it and slavery is often blurred. It may be said, in general, that in the case of serfdom the obligation to render service in the form of contributions in kind or money occupies a prominent place, and that these services are legally limited. Where slavery is consistently carried out the whole person passes into the power of the master and is absorbed in his economic unit, becoming a machine for production which is used without any consideration for the individual, who has no legal rights. In practice, however, this extreme view is generally mitigated, as there is usually no authority able to carry out the principle to its ultimate consequences.

The difference between serfdom and slavery is also demonstrated by the fact that the serfs often represent a greater percentage of the population than the slaves.

Both serfdom and slavery have their origin largely in the capture of prisoners. Yet this is not always the case; serfdom, like social stratification itself, has other roots. When different ethnic, i.e. racial and cultural, groups have settled side by side and intermingled, certain traditional relations are likely to arise, expressed in the performance of mutual services and also in the estimation of the one group held by the other.

The system of *métayage*, or farming on shares, has probably developed in special historical circumstances, above all under the influence of long continued intermarriage. We can imagine that family specialization, mutual services rendered, and, in particular, the differentiation already apparent in the *métayage* system, of a section which was, or considered itself, socially superior contained the germ of a symbiosis which emphasized in a more acute form differences in values and also in the performance of services. It is probable that, historically, the pastoral peoples played a particularly important part in this respect. They also appear to have tried to domesticate man as they did their animals. It therefore appears that, given certain circumstances, it is not impossible that in peripheral regions certain milder forms of dependence should be regarded from a historical point of view, not as early developments, but merely as feebler imitations.

As a certain stratification of the population is a necessary condition for the rise of serfdom, so it is also a means for organizing the political life of the community among the more advanced primitives, as well as among civilized peoples. It presupposes in general the encounter of heterogeneous ethnic groups, in particular of pastoral peoples, with domiciled agriculturists.

Let us take a few concrete examples to illustrate the various forms of serfdom.

§ 2. The agricultural population of the lake region in Ankole (East Africa) are evidently descendants of an older stratum of inhabitants subordinated by immigrant hordes of a pastoral people. The latter made serfs of them and forced them to do work which they themselves could not carry out owing to various ceremonial customs connected with cattle. These agriculturists were not slaves, they could move about the country freely, leave one master and attach themselves to another of their own accord. They were, however, generally attached to certain districts, whence they had seldom cared to move, once they had settled down. They were distinguished by the wearing of goat- or calf-skins, the men attaching them to the right and the women to the left shoulder. Land was available in abundance, and a man who wished to cultivate a plot of ground only had to dig a little, or to pluck a few blades of grass, carry them home or fasten them to the roof of his house in order to establish his claim to the land. It was only in the case of disputes regarding claims to land that the man applied to the district chief, who belonged to the pastoral ruling class. The tilling of the fields was accompanied by various ceremonies. Harvest time was a season of rejoicing, during which marriages and dances were arranged. The peasant from time to time brought grain to his pastoral lord; there was no prescribed quantity, but he brought small contributions until he found that his stock was getting low. When this point was reached the peasant came for the last time with a large basketful, which was understood by the lord to be the last supply of the season (Roscoe ['23], pp. 94 et seq.). This is a case of a peaceable and friendly symbiosis of two races living under entirely different conditions. The inferior position of the serfs is not strongly insisted on. But there were also slaves who were bought and sold like goods. The children of slaves belonged to the owner. There were various grades of service: *muhuku*, a slave who had been bought and was employed for domestic purposes; *mwambale*, a servant in personal attendance on his master; *mwiru*, a peasant who was to a certain extent independent, although subject to his pastoral lord; *musumba*, a herdsman who milked cows and belonged to the pastoral class, but possessed no cattle of his own; *bagalagwa*, personal attendants on the prince (*mugabe*) who had received cows and land at the conclusion of their period of service; *banyiginya*, the highest class, men of noble birth who might be used by the *mugabe* as special messengers in confidential affairs (op. cit., pp. 77 et seq.).

Similar conditions prevailed among the Bakitara in Bunyoro, but in this case the dependence of the peasant population on the herdsmen appears to have been in many respects more marked. They were despised by the herdsmen, not so much on account of their poverty as of their manner of living, for in the eyes of a herdsman every one who ate vegetable food, tilled the soil, or practised a craft not connected with the care of the cows was

decidedly inferior. But even these serfs were not slaves or bound
to any particular chief, but could move about freely. It was
customary for a peasant who settled in the district of a new chief
to appear before him and inform him of his intention to serve him.
He was sure of a friendly reception from the chief, to whom every
serf meant another labourer and an increase in his wealth. These
serfs had to erect buildings for their master and perhaps also to
tend his flocks of goats and sheep, but also to provide an annual
contribution in grain and beer, though this was not regarded as
a compulsory tax but as a voluntary gift to the chief in return for
the land occupied. If a chief had appointed a serf to herd his goats
and sheep he rewarded his services with a few young animals out
of the flock. There were no limitations of any kind regarding the
amount of land that a peasant might work, and he might also
accumulate large herds of goats and sheep. At the same time, the
peasants were formerly never allowed to keep cows, and if they did so
they ran the risk of being plundered. It was only in recent years,
under European influence, that they could venture to acquire
cows, which were principally used for paying marriage fees. Not
only the peasants, but the artisans in Kitara (Bunyoro) belong to
the serf class. A few generations ago a king introduced a change
in their social relations by creating a new rank among the agricultural people: a man who showed special skill and had done the
king a special service was rewarded by being made a 'freeman'
(*munyoro*). This gave him the right to marry a woman from one
of the pastoral clans. In this way there arose an intermediate class
of well-to-do agriculturists occupying a superior position. The
consequence of these marriages was a certain deterioration of the
herdsmen, a growing laxity in the observance of the ritual connected with milk and the partial adoption of a vegetable diet.
The children of such unions could marry even into the higher
grades of the pastoral stratum. A distinction must be made
between the serf agriculturists and the real 'slaves', who were
captured in forays or fights, or purchased by wealthy people.
Domestic slaves were more highly valued than farm hands (Roscoe,
['23/b], pp. 9 et seq.).

§ 3. The structure of society in ancient Samoa was extraordinarily complicated, owing to the numerous grades of rank
and public offices. The social order was complicated, not only by
descent and possessions, but also by personal ability and special

family traditions. The next rank after the chiefs' caste (*ali'i*) was that of the *tulafale*, who possessed great authority in many districts. They were the advisers of the chiefs, and the official orators were usually selected from their ranks. Unpopular chiefs could be removed from office and banished by them. They formed a group of large landowners and consisted in some places of the leading families. Every chief had a *tulafale*, who was considered as his spokesman, and every settlement had its leading orator. The next in rank were the *fale-upolu*, who were also considerable landowners and had much influence. They provided the chiefs with food, for which they were paid. They are said by some to have formed the general body of the population. A lower class were called *tangata-nu'u* or 'men of the land'. They tilled the soil and fished in peace-time and bore arms in time of war. They attached themselves to the chiefs, and a chief's power and influence depended on the number of them that he had at his disposal. They were thus a kind of mercenary troop holding land. A still lower stratum was called *tangata-taua*. They were prisoners of war, whose position was described by some writers (Stair) as 'little, if anything, better than slavery'. They were exposed to contemptuous treatment at the hands of their masters, and they were probably descended from prisoners of war of lower rank. There was, however, no real domestic slavery, and domestic work was done by children and female relations. In the houses of the great chiefs there were also other assistants, in addition to the family connexions. These servants were called *angai*, and the office was hereditary in certain distinguished families. Only these aristocratic servants were allowed to eat from the dishes served to the highest chiefs, who otherwise rendered everything tabu. There were various offices of this kind, such as that of *songa*, or barber, who was also cupbearer, trumpeter (blowing a conch shell to announce the chief's approach), and messenger. He enjoyed a number of special privileges, being considered as a sort of jester or court fool. The *atamai-o-ali'i*, or 'spirit of wisdom of the chief', occupied the position of grand vizier and at the same time of herald. The *fa'atama* (father of the house) looked after the administration of the chief's household. The *salelelisi* (quick flier) played the part of court fool to a greater extent than was done by the *songa*. All *salelelisi* came from one particular village. Many of these chiefs' servants were descended from persons who had served the ancestors of the ruler in question, in this or some other capacity (Williamson ['24], ii. 366 et seq.).

§ 4. On Tahiti prisoners of war also formed a stratum that was disposed of arbitrarily. They were men who had been disarmed or wounded in the fight and had placed themselves under the protection of a chief. In particular they ran the risk of being slaughtered on some occasion as a human sacrifice (op. cit., ii. 392).

In the same way victims for human sacrifices were selected by the priests from the *nohoua* stratum on the Marquesas Islands. This stratum, which represented the common people, appears, however, to have been more numerous there. They had to till the soil, but they did not own the land nor were they warriors or house-builders (op. cit., ii. 399).

On the whole, it may be said of social arrangements in Central Polynesia that the population is usually divided into three castes, the aristocracy (chiefs), the middle stratum, and the common people. Priests and sorcerers do not usually belong to any special stratum but are found in all of them, although more frequently in the upper stratum. Only prisoners of war can be regarded as slaves, but they do not form a special stratum of the population. The different social strata have doubtless become more or less mixed in the course of time and, in particular, the lines of demarcation between one caste and the other have become very indistinct (op. cit., iii. 138).

§ 5. In ancient Mexico and Central America the aristocracy had beneath them at least two grades of freemen. Yet there also existed a class which must be described as that of slaves or serfs. In general, to be captured in war or to have committed a crime led to a position of personal dependence. In Mexico a family could engage to provide a master with one or more slaves for some years, these slaves being replaced by others at the end of the time agreed upon. At the same time individuals could be sold into permanent slavery. People suffering from great poverty could pledge themselves or their children. A famine lasting for two years during the reign of Montecuzoma compelled many families to take this step. It is stated, however, that a slave could not be sold without his own consent. If a female slave bore a child to a freeman it received the status of the father and was considered as freeborn. Slaves were in general well treated, but they were always liable to be sacrificed. They were under the protection of the god Tezcatlipoca, during whose annual festival complete licence reigned, as was the case in the Roman Saturnalia (Joyce ['14], pp. 132 et seq.).

§ 6. Among the Kpelle of West Africa the population is divided into three separate strata: (1) freemen (*wōlǫ* or *dǫi nālǫng*; the latter word means countryman, man born in the country, of a long resident family, feminine, *doi neni*, free-born woman). These freemen form the real Kpelle people, youths becoming full members through the puberty ceremonies of the *poro* league. They alone elect the supreme chief, and can, as a rule, attain positions of honour in the political community and in the secret societies. A freeman cannot be sold either by the supreme chief or by a private person, except for a serious crime, though the head of the sept can pledge a freeman. The children of free parents are counted as freemen, and also those of a freeman and a bondwoman or female slave, provided that a regular marriage has taken place. There is, however, a distinction between the children of a woman captured in war, who are always regarded as free, while the descendants of female slaves obtained by purchase are reckoned as slaves. If a freeman is taken prisoner in war he becomes a slave, but he can regain his position in his own tribe by paying the ransom demanded. Other slaves, too, can obtain their freedom by purchase. (2) Serfs. This includes (*a*) the children of slaves, in so far as they have been born and remain in the house of their parents' owner; (*b*) their descendants in subsequent generations; (*c*) persons who have become serfs of their own accord, or have been presented as children by their parents or guardian to a rich man, more especially to the king. Their descendants also remain serfs. A serf cannot be sold any more than a freeman, but he is at a disadvantage as compared to a slave, in that his freedom cannot be purchased and that his descendants remain serfs. It is, however, the custom to manumit serfs, or their descendants, as a reward for good conduct or for special services; yet there are also serfs whose families have been in this state for three generations. Individual serfs may succeed in becoming rich or in gaining positions of influence, for example, at the court of a supreme chief. The above facts make it clear that it is possible to rise from the serf stratum to that of the freeman, and that in this way the blood of alien captives is introduced into the old freeman stratum of the Kpelle tribe.

Somewhat similar to the serfs are the settlers (*ngwāya*), who, for some reason or other, mostly in order to escape the consequences of their crimes, have left their own tribal territory to seek refuge with an alien chief. Such chiefs usually assign them a dwelling-place and some land to cultivate, outside the village. They have to deliver part of the produce of their fields and of the chase to the supreme chief. Their descendants are automatically recognized as freemen. (3) Slaves (*duō*). This class mainly consists of captives not ransomed by their own people within the period allowed. A smaller number have become slaves owing to debt or in consequence of a serious offence. In buying slaves it is thought important that they should come from the most distant districts possible, as there is then less risk of their running away. Here too, when we remember that a slave can purchase his freedom, we perceive a way in which alien blood, even that of distant peoples, might effect an entry into the community of freemen in the Kpelle tribe. Along with this racial mixture the influx of captives brings with it the possibility of cultural influence and the transference not only of technical processes but also of religious and mythological conceptions. The lot of the slaves is not hard, but they rank below the serfs in social estimation and differ from them in that they can be sold or given away at their owner's discretion. Although their labour belongs to the master, yet he assigns both to slaves and to serfs a plot of land to cultivate for their own use, allows them to keep part of the wages earned by working for a third party, and thus provides them with the means of acquiring private capital (Westermann, pp. 80 et seq.). Thus these slaves must not be mistaken for bondmen. Although in this case the point of view of the powerful class is more emphasized by economic considerations, yet the weakening of the aristocratic idea renders possible a release from the fetters of the landless stratum, but instead of that the economic position becomes more decisive owing to the fact that a rise to the ranks of the free is possible on payment. The king's principal possessions are his wives, slaves, and serfs, whose productive power in agriculture, hunting, fishing, industrial work, and carrying loads (for payment) tends to the increase of his personal fortune (op. cit., p. 96). Slaves and serfs are given in marriage by their master without reference to their own wishes, though these are occasionally taken into consideration. As a rule, the owner marries his own male and female slaves to each other, but he also gives the female slaves as wives to third parties.

A female slave does not become free by marriage with a freeman, but the children of such a union are free (op. cit., p. 60).

§ 7. The Barea and Kunama, in northern Abyssinia, are living under conditions of pure democracy. There is no distinction of rank; wealth and poverty have no political significance; and there are no privileges, save those attaching to age. The only difference of status is that between employers and paid servants, and this is very slight. Few servants are required, since every one works. The servant, whether herdsman, cultivator, or maid, is called *kerai* (the Tigre word for 'wages'), and is paid by a few francs' worth of cloth. There are certain fixed days on which they can work for their own benefit, the cultivator or herdsman being allowed the use of his employer's oxen for ploughing on eight days during the season. A maidservant has half that time for work on her own account. An agreement is often made whereby the owner of the cattle ploughs for himself on two days and lets the man-servant use them on the third day. The manservant's term of service lasts, as a rule, from the rainy season until the harvest, but if there is a good understanding between master and man the latter often remains through the year without further payment. If the herdsman slaughters one of the herd the master has no right to demand compensation. The herdsman often leaves his herd in order to join in a raid. The booty belongs to him alone and the master receives nothing. It is only in exceptional cases that the Barea and Bazen possess slaves, obtained by plundering hostile tribes. Another source of supply for slavery is the sale of children (Munzinger ['83], pp. 481 et seq.).

XVI

SYMBOLS OF VALUE AND MONEY

§ 1. Various stages in the evolution of money. § 2. Tribal attitudes towards barter and monetary tokens. § 3. Specified objects as units of barter. § 4. Cowrie shells, copper ornaments, Aggri beads, &c. § 5. Silver in ancient Sumeria. § 6. Currency in ancient China. § 7. Estimating values of objects of barter. § 8. Factors to be taken into consideration. § 9. 'Internal' and 'External' money. § 10. Commercial transactions in present associations. § 11. Result of a fixed appraisal of values.

§ 1. In the evolution of money various stages must be distinguished. The point of departure is marked by favourite articles of barter, usually between communities of approximately equal standing, e.g. in New Guinea, the regular exchange of sago for pots, or of stone adzes for shells or fish, of arrows for tobacco, of arm-shells for pigs, and so on. This, as a rule, involves the exchange of traditional quantities or packages, as in the case of sago or tobacco, for corresponding quantities of the other articles.

Such favourite articles of barter are mostly found in trade between different communities or tribes. The Californian Hupa traded principally with the Yurok, from whom they obtained canoes, as their district produced no wood suitable for canoe building; they also obtained shells, beach fish, and seaweed. The Hupa took principally food-stuffs and skins in exchange. From the Pomo, in the south, mostly through the agency of the Huchnom, the Yuki obtained shells, sea-snails, and seaweed, giving skins in exchange. Among the Klamath and the Karok seaweed, salt, and baskets, as well as acorns and, most of all, canoes, were traded, for which the Klamath obtained obsidian, deerskins, and sweet pine kernels. The Maidu carried on a considerable trade with the Wintun. They received shells and pearls, which were considered as money. These pearls were counted by tens and strung on threads, and from this point made their way to the high Sierra. The hunting tribes gave bows and arrows, deerskins, sweet pine cones, and the like in exchange. In the north of the Pomo country there was a deposit of salt to which expeditions were made, but as the northern Pomo people demanded transit dues in the form of presents, conflicts were apt to occur (Kroeber ['25], pp. 132, 166 et seq., 236, 287, and 399).

§ 2. We must realize that the character of each human group and the specific geographical position of its settlement or district have a considerable share in determining the great difference of attitude towards barter and the development of monetary tokens between tribes living under generally similar climatic conditions. In New Guinea the sea-faring coast tribes are remarkable for stronger commercial habits than those shown by the Papuan hill-dwellers. The Mawatta had become a trading centre and acted as agents for dealings among other tribes, in particular those of the interior. They themselves were principally in need of sago, which they bought from the island of Kiwai. From places on the Torres Strait they imported shell armlets, crescents made of pearl shell, dugong spears, shell nose-pins, and other articles made from shells. They also traded in dogs' teeth, which were bartered for wooden drums, arrows, feathers, boars' tusks, and sometimes for sago. A moderate quantity of baskets, arm-shells, and coloured earth from the Wassi-Kussa district was mainly exported via the island of Bogu. Some of the tribes on the Fly River bartered pandanus mats and women's grass skirts for shells, at the rate of one mat and one skirt for a large melon shell and a tridacna shell. The former were used as containers and for other household purposes. Between Mawatta and Kiwai bows and arrows were bartered for prepared sago, a large package of sago being the price of a bamboo bow and twenty arrows. Cowries and the pearl shell crescents, already mentioned, were used by some tribes as charms to be placed on graves and for dancing rattles. The most important transaction, moreover, was the purchase of canoes from the boat-builders in Torres Strait, the boat-builders being under the necessity of giving long credit. A large canoe was bartered for two large arm-shells, and a small canoe for a melon shell, a dugong rib, and a string of dogs' teeth (Beaver ['20], pp. 75 et seq.). Cf. Malinowski ['21].

Among the mountain tribe of the Mafula, who live in the south of New Guinea, a pig was formerly always paid for in dogs' teeth; these are still the only payment accepted for some kinds of ornaments, such as are used for dances or ornamental nose-pieces. The dogs' teeth are strung in a chain equal in length to the body of the pig, measured from the nose to the base of the tail. A particular kind of ornament consisting of many small feathers fixed on a string can only be exchanged for a particular kind of shell necklace, both of which must be of equal length. Such exchanges only take place between members of different communities: the purchase of pigs at certain ceremonies within the community is only an apparent exception, such a purchase being in reality a matter of ceremony, not of ordinary barter. The exchange of goods does not take place in markets, as elsewhere in this region, but during visits to another community. The nearest approach to a market is the occasion of an important feast, when so large a supply of ornaments is required that they have to be procured from some other community which has recently held a feast and no longer requires the ornaments then used. Thus these ceremonial ornaments are constantly passing from village to village. A similar mode of barter obtains among the Toaripi, Lese, and Waima, who all export sago, areca-nuts, betel pepper, coco-nuts, and bananas, as well as bows and arrows, to the coast tribes, receiving in exchange arm-shells, strings of shell discs, and crescents of pearl shell (Seligman ['10], p. 93). The neighbouring islands of Tubetube and Teste follow a different fashion of trading; these sea-going races import almost everything they need for daily use, and as objects of barter they manufacture pots and shell ornaments: in addition they act as middlemen over a very considerable area along the coast. These shell ornaments consist of different kinds of bracelets, strings of shell discs (*sapisapi*), and lime spatulae of tortoise shell, &c. All these objects have reached the stage of bearing a definite money value among the Massim, that of least value being a certain narrow kind of belt decorated with *sapisapi*: a peculiar ornament consisting of a spirally-curved boar's tusk, and built up canoes must also be regarded as having attained the status of currency in some islands. The ornaments above enumerated are the equivalent of our jewellery and similarly ensure their owners (Seligman ['10], pp. 526 et seq.). In order to realize the importance of all this jewellery it is necessary to inquire how their particular value originally arose. This problem is largely solved when we ascertain what presents are given or exchanged in order to obtain a wife. On the actual possession of the woman the bridegroom presents her parents with ornaments, nets, or spears, a dog or a pig, and some vegetable food; during the following days they reciprocate with similar objects. The actual purchase price, in 1876, amounted to ten arm-shells; by 1909 it was from forty to forty-three (ibid., pp. 77

et seq.). We can gather from this that, in spite of the relative stability of customary values, time brings about a certain adjustment of price to circumstances. When the whites introduced iron and consequently facilitated the manufacture of arm-shells, these declined in value. Among the Roro the family of the bridegroom paid the bride's family three pearl-shell crescents, three conus arm-shells, ten fathoms of shell currency, feather headdresses, and other ornaments made of feathers, a neck pendant of dogs' teeth, and a pig (ibid., p. 267 note; cf. also pp. 710, 711).

§ 3. An example of the second stage in this evolution of values occurs when a particular coveted object has definitely come to be used as a unit of barter. Considered in historical sequence this second stage is not necessarily a development of the first stage.

The Bergdama women break up ostrich shells into small pieces, and pierce them carefully with the point of an arrow. These discs, laboriously polished, are strung on threads made from the sinews of animals and worn as necklaces. A sort of corselet is also made from these strings, but their principal use is as currency, for the purchase of axes, pots, salt, &c., from the Ovambo traders (Vedder, p. 59).

On the lower Shari, in the inner Sudan, pieces of iron formerly circulated as currency, corresponding with the money used by the Bongo, of which three types were recognized, *mahi*, which were plain lance-heads, from one to two feet long, *loggo-kulûti*, spade blades in the rough, and *loggo*, finished blades, which under the name of *melot* attained a wide distribution along the upper reaches of the Nile. The *loggo-kulûti* were circular, flat, iron discs, about the size of a plate, and from 0·25 to 0·3 metres in diameter, having on one side a short stem and on the other an anchor-shaped appendage. Great quantities of iron in this shape were stored up by rich people and along with lance-heads and spades formed part of the bride price which the wooer had to furnish. It was also used in various commercial transactions (Schweinfurth ['78], pp. 105 et seq.).

The most heterogeneous objects are used as currency in Africa, and often vary in value from district to district. In West Africa the most universally recognized medium of exchange, except for the well-known cowries, is salt, which among the Oual-Oualé is an important item of trade. In the last decade of the nineteenth century a kilo of salt was equivalent to about 1,300 cowries.

Another widely diffused article of exchange is the kola-nut, which is generally resold to the Mossi. A unit of 100 kola-nuts is worth 500 to 800 cowries in Oual-Oualé, and fetches from 1,500 to 2,000 from the Mossi and even, in times of shortage, up to 4,000 or 4,500. The Mossi manufacture cotton-stuffs (*taro* or *pende*) and sell them to the Dagomba at the rate of 1·7 metres for 100 cowries: the Dagomba, in the markets of Savelugu and Kompungu, give only 1·3 metres for 100 cowries. The Mossi also bring oxen, sheep, and donkeys for sale, oxen being rated at 25,000 to 30,000 cowries apiece, donkeys at 30,000 to 35,000, and sheep at 5,500 to 6,500. The caravans of the Mossi, about thirty men strong, enter the villages to the sound of stringed instruments, drums, with much shouting, each man bearing a bundle of cloth on his head. The senior member of the caravan immediately makes for the host whom he has chosen; but the real bargaining does not start until the second or third day, as the people of the Oual-Oualé are careful not to be in too great a hurry, or to show undue eagerness for the goods. The purchasers remove all the goods in one day, but give only large cowries in exchange, and as this currency would prove too burdensome to the Mossi they are obliged to exchange them for small ones at a loss of 10 per cent., 1,100 large cowries being worth only 1,000 small ones. The Mossi are badly treated by the Dagomba, especially in the dealings over cowries, as it takes a Mossi nearly a whole day to count a few thousand cowries. The cattle bought from the Mossi and slaves from the Gurunsi are re-sold in Salaga, Kintampo, and Daboya, slaves at a profit of nearly 100 per cent. As in most places where there is any approach to trade a small amount of silver appears, worn in the form of rings and bracelets. The Maria Theresa thaler, here called a real (face value 5·5 gold francs) is worth 4,000 cowries. Concerning the history of the Maria Theresa dollar, which, worn as a pendant, was actually regarded as possessing magical properties, we must refer to Fischel (pp. 1,076 et seq.). In connexion with this, attention must be drawn to the fact that it was not the intrinsic value of the coin which led to its being so highly appreciated, but the effect produced by its general appearance on the African's primitive mind, which caused it to be regarded as a powerful talisman. The conditions obtaining in the various districts of the Mossi mentioned above differ widely according to the elements composing the population and the local requirements.

Sea salt, for instance, has a large sale in the eastern part of Dagomba, and competes with the bars of salt from Taodéni, brought by way of Mossi, only in the northern part of Gambakka and Gurunsi. In the north salt is exchanged for butter and slaves, in the south for animals for slaughter, and in the west the sea salt comes into competition with that of the Daboya, who deliver theirs at an equal price in Oual-Oualé or South Gurunsi. A further important object of barter in these districts is gold dust, which is reckoned according to weight; it is principally brought in by the Wangara (Mandé) during the dry season, for the purpose of buying horses from the Hausa people (Binger, pp. 50 et seq., 100 et seq.).

§ 4. In the course of the seventeenth century large quantities of cowries were brought to the West Coast of Africa from the Maldive Islands by the Dutch and Portuguese, who used them as ballast and subsequently introduced them as money. At this period a slave fetched 100 lb. of cowries, which were then highly valued, a pound of cowries being equivalent to two Dutch gulden (Dapper [1671], p. 482).

The copper bracelets which, as well as the rough or polished bars of copper (Dapper, pp. 497, 499), are accepted as currency in various parts of West Africa, appear in part to have been brought there by the Dutch in the seventeenth century.

From the earliest ages glass beads have occupied a similar position, even in the East (Egypt and India), where they, like gold and real pearls, were valued as the possessors of magical life-giving properties. Perry (['23], pp. 43, 389, 393) draws attention to this association of ideas. A whole literature has grown up around the glass beads found in Africa and the East (see Price ['83]; Tischler ['87], pp. 5 et seq.; Rouffaer ['09]). Price draws attention to the fact that beads similar to the West-African ones occur in Anglo-Saxon burial mounds. As early as 1821 Hutton ([1821], p. 212) relates that the so-called Aggri beads were worth their weight or even sometimes twice their weight in gold among the Ashanti. They were found in the earth and their finder was looked on as a particularly lucky man. They were regarded as treasure trove, and were used for necklaces, leglets, and anklets, and other jewellery. It is remarkable that this commodity should be so widely distributed and so highly valued among communities of such diverse social development as those of West Africa, India, and

S

the Pelew Islands, of the North Pacific. They were not manufactured either in the west of Africa or in the South Seas, but
were dug out of the ground. Their peculiar value in the eyes of
all these peoples is almost certainly a result of their mysterious
origin. A detailed description of these beads is to be found in
Tischler's supplementary work to Andree (*Ztschr. f. Ethnologie*,
3 (1885); cf. also Mestorf ['oo]. For ancient times see Pliny
xxxvi. 66, 67; xxxvii, 21–23, 26). (For the 'bead-money' of Pelew
Islands cf. Kubary ['95] and Müller, p. 126 et seq.)

During the seventeenth century a brisk trade in slaves and
ivory was carried on by the Portuguese along the coast of Angola,
about the Congo Delta, and Loango. In the interior millet and
small stock were the chief media of exchange (Dapper [1671],
p. 557).

Among the Kpelle, women appear to have a certain economic
value, measured in terms of slave labour; if the king, for instance,
makes a demand for the labour of five persons, this can be commuted for a woman. Some of these women are set to work and
some are distributed among the king's retainers. Those not
disposed of in this way are sent to one of the king's farm settlements where, under the supervision of a house mother, they
undertake the cultivation of the fields (Westermann, pp. 115 et
seq.).

§ 5. In ancient Sumeria silver was already the common denomina-
tor to which the values of commodities were reduced. When a merchant (*damkar*) delivered ointment to a temple, and received wool
in exchange, the payment was not evaluated in terms of ointment
against wool, but the value in silver of both wares was first
calculated, although no payment in silver took place. The merchant first sold his ointment to the temple and subsequently bought
wool for further trade with the money credited to him; therefore
the goods were not paid for in silver, as was commonly the case in
other transactions, but were reckoned up against each other.
In the earliest times silver was generally paid for goods purchased,
though seldom used to pay rent for land, and then only as part
payment, and never for services rendered. In simple transactions
payment in silver became equivalent to payment in kind, but with
the passage of time, in consequence of the large demand, the
value of silver rose. When goods were purchased outright they
were generally paid for in silver. The part (percentage) of silver

in payment of rents, which continued to be paid principally in corn, also was increased, and systems of payment in silver and in kind began to exist side by side. Silver was increasingly substituted for the dues payable in kind to the town, the prince, and the king. Payment in corn, however, never quite went out of use, perhaps because of an insufficient internal supply of silver. It was principally the system of granaries, however, with their method of distributing rations, that helped to keep corn in circulation as a medium of exchange. One result of the rigid system of accountancy in use by the granaries was a fixed relation between the price of corn and that of silver, which was in use up to the time of Ur, one *gur* of barley equalling one *gin* of silver. Silver in all ages was reckoned according to weight, though there was no coined money. In order to estimate the comparative value of the food purchased by the Sumerians it must be mentioned that their daily portion of barley contained from one-half to one-third less calories than are required by the inhabitants of the temperate zones (Schneider, p. 91).

§ 6. A varied list of equivalents for currency is known to us as having existed in ancient China, from the time when gold, silver, copper, and tin first came into use; cowries and tortoise shell, for instance, were in circulation in the fourteenth century B.C. About 1200 B.C. bracelets and rings of gold, silver, and bronze were already being fashioned in accordance with the stable and unified Sumerio-Babylonian tariff of values (such bracelets and rings were subsequently also known in western Asia). In the thirteenth year of the reign of Ch'êng, the second king of the Chou dynasty, his minister Kiang Tai Kung created nine treasury posts in order to set up a table of values with regard to gold in cubes, bronze in rings, ingots, or discs according to weight, and silk according to measure. At the same time metal was in circulation in the form of hoes, spades, and sickles, which were unstamped, and were bartered according to weight. It was only during the course of the seventh century that large bronze knives of regular weight began to be stamped, recording the place of their origin. This did not prevent the salt trade, for instance, becoming of such importance in the state of Ts'i, that a salt standard was practically in existence. The cowries were later on replaced, about the sixth century, by metal imitations, stamped according to weight, as were also the bean-shaped metal ingots of this time. In the sixth century the large metal knife-blades, which were in existence in China almost up to the present day, were introduced. They were principally stamped and put into circulation in the city of Tsi-Moh, together with those of Au-Yang and Yug-Ling. Others followed their example. One of these stamped inscriptions is as follows: Returnable and negotiable currency current among the travelling merchants of Ts'i and Kwan Tchung. The spade-money played a similar part. In Honan, in the eastern duchy of Tchau, flat ring-tokens were issued about the fourth century. These are the origin of the Chinese cash, pierced with a hole in the centre. Three treasury offices were in existence at the same time, one for jewels, one for gold, and one for tokens and silk (Lacouperie, pp. 8 et seq.). The existence of these measures of value did not, of course, prevent the simultaneous circulation of other kinds in different parts of the country, as nearly always proves to be the case where the population is composed of ethnically diverse elements. When such various media of exchange are in circulation at the same period a balance will sooner or later be struck between two or more of them, as, for instance, in the archaic states, where so much metal equalled so much corn, or so many animals. In consequence the metals became symbolic of the produce for which they stood, such as cattle or corn. This is why the heads of cattle or ears of corn are so often seen stamped on ancient coins or bars of metal (cf. Laum, pp. 85 et seq.). In this connexion we may also mention the custom of offering substitutes in place of human or animal sacrifices.

§ 7. A special point to notice with regard to valuable objects is the fact that they become measures of value for estimating the quantity or the quality of the objects exchanged. In this case it is often quite unnecessary for the measures of value themselves to change hands; for they can serve as common denominators applied to other commodities exchanged. In any case such a proceeding presupposes a considerable increase of economic calculation.

In order to gauge the values obtaining among primitive peoples it is necessary to differentiate between their traditional point of view with regard to indigenous trade objects and to European goods. Where native objects of barter are concerned we must again draw attention to the fact that relatively stable values generally prevail. The situation as regards European goods is necessarily quite different, as the natives are not yet in a position to estimate the value of even our common objects according to their own traditional standards. It is, therefore, not surprising that, as we learn from the early writers, the natives of St. Domingo were ready to exchange their gold for pencils, nails, broken needles, glass beads, pins, laces, broken plates, &c. Hence the inconsequence of their demands, an Indian one day wanting an axe and the next a fish-hook, or, perhaps, a couple of glass beads, or a comb, in exchange for precisely the same item of native goods. I had the same kind of experience with tribes in the interior of New Guinea, where the natives had never been in communication with any white men. Naturally these people estimate the value of all goods according to their own standards, without reference to costs of production in Europe. In course of time each tribe among the South-American Indians had become known for its own particular manufacture, which grew to be its chief object of inter-tribal trade (Roth ['24], pp. 632 et seq.).

§ 8. To theoreticians who only take into consideration the practical use of an object, it may seem superfluous to differentiate between objects of value according to their destination; but it is of the utmost importance to know whether an object is treated as a treasure and hoarded as such, as, for instance, a neck pendant or a mat, or if it is an article destined for daily use, to be exchanged against others when necessary, as, for example, fruit against meat; or, finally, whether the object is regarded as capital capable of yielding profit, and to what degree, and also whether the object is the potential source of others of its own kind. All these factors must be taken into consideration before we can properly realize their effect on the economic life of the people. It must be confessed though that nowadays, giving due weight to the differentiation of the above-mentioned categories, it is not particularly important to distinguish between various objects belonging to the same category, whether a treasure is a bracelet, a feather ornament, or a more or less elaborately treated shell. An exception, however, must be made in favour of metal, due to its malleability and its divisibility; since it can be made into articles of almost any shape, such as lance-heads, rings, knife-blades, &c., it has attained a peculiar symbolic significance, which has certainly influenced its transition from the status of a medium for local payments in kind to that of universal currency. These premises, however, are obviously based on the assumption that the art of smelting is understood, which is not the case with a few isolated primitive tribes in Africa, who can hardly be credited with this knowledge even at the present day.

§ 9. Schurtz ['98] emphasizes the difference between internal and external money. We must not, however, accept this differentiation without examining it more closely. In the unstratified communities of hunters and collectors and hunters, and digging-stick cultivators, 'money' is principally used within the community in order to make friendly presents on the occasion of marriages. Generally, however, the gifts are repaid with return presents to approximately the same amount. For this purpose, it is mainly a question of ornaments and food-stuffs. If the woman has been bought the economic return consists in the services which the bridegroom has to render to his father-in-law. Real purchase of women usually necessitates the giving of useful articles, such as pots (e.g. among the Bànaro, on the upper Augusta River [Sepik]). Apart from this, it is a question whether we are always justified in speaking of 'internal money' in this case, for in exogamous communities the women marry into another sept and thus into another economic unit. The same applies to blood money, which serves to settle the blood feud, and thus always passes from one blood-feud community, the ultimate political unit, to another. It is known that blood-guiltiness cannot be atoned for within the same political community. We must further clearly understand that in small homogeneous communities difference of race, culture, and speech is of slight importance as regards relations with the neighbouring community, unless the latter is cut off by the sea or a mountain range or, perhaps, by a large river. For this reason the value attached to treasures occasionally spreads, as has been hinted above, into communities with a different culture. Thus the pieces of so-called internal money which are current within narrower limits gain in importance as external money, as is the case with shells and pieces of shell to which a special connexion with the female sex was assigned. But the most important commodities for external trade are, above all, articles for practical use and consumption, such as canoes, baskets, salt, &c. Yet an exchange of these goods also takes place among communities of the same tribe to an extent which is not to be underrated.

§ 10. In graded communities the chief function of commodities is to serve as a medium of contributions and of payments; these are mostly made in kind, eatables and manufactured articles, paid by the lower grades to the higher, who retain a certain portion for their own use, while prepared to distribute the remainder according to the needs of the people. These conditions do not exclusively affect such practical objects, but also concern those regarded as possessing peculiar symbolical significance or magical properties, as, for instance, the Pelewan beads or the Samoan mats. In such districts where the high chiefs, or princes, and their nobles are the connecting links between a number of different communities, that which is generally known as internal money and that which is called inter-tribal money take on a less vague character. Such communities are not held together by a common law or edict, as is the case with our modern nations, but every community lives according to its own customs, nor is the relationship marked by the erection of comprehensive boundary-posts or landmarks, but shows itself in a series of commercial transactions. An interchange of purchase and sale pervades such an example of a 'pre-state' association. A correlative result of the principle of common distribution in vogue among hunter and collector tribes is that richer persons and those of higher rank are expected to contribute more generously than the lower and poorer. An example of this system can be observed as affecting cattle, in Africa, or yams, as in the Trobriands, or again objects treated as treasures, as on Pelew. An association between the higher classes of different communities can also manifest itself in an interchange of give and take, as, for instance, in the *kula* exchange already mentioned in the section dealing with commerce. The more important commodities so exchanged acquire a status peculiar to them alone, and play a large part in the daily life of the people.

All the same, a distinction is often made between sacred and profane objects, the customs affecting yams in the Trobriands being an example of the latter, and the significance of the various kinds of beads on Pelew (cf. Kubary ['95]), or the *kula* objects, of the former (cf. Laum, pp. 39, 43, with regard to ancient Greece).

§ 11. We can thus see that in these examples of pre-state conditions the evaluation of objects of value results from the amount of the customary contributions, from the position held by the leading personages, and from the concrete relationship in which they stand to the commoners of their several communities.

The primitive objects of value are distinguished by their unique-
ness, i.e. by the difficulty of replacing or copying them.   The
simple exchange of two commodities, as among the Mafula, which
has been described by Williamson ['12], or among others, the exchange of meat for grain, may be regarded, more or less, as the
original form of barter. A higher stage is represented by the
traditions governing Pelew money, where the purchasing power
extends to particular groups of objects, commonly resulting in the
creation of a stable scale of values.

With the creation of a working connexion between two objects
which results in a fixed appraisal of their respective qualities as
interchangeable units, we see how the values of primitive existence
tend to become stereotyped; services rendered or work accom-
plished begin to acquire a stable value. However, we must not
over-estimate this stability; we have already seen that varying
conditions not only affect the price of European goods, but that
the evaluation of the principal commodities, mostly home products,
has been found to vary in different parts of the world, such as
New Guinea, West Africa, and South America, at least, after the
lapse of a sufficient period.

The coming into existence of an established authority creates
a fixed traditional scale of values for various objects. Interchange
tends to develop one-sidedly, especially by the system of re-
partition and taxes, and we note, for instance, the introduction
of a fixed tariff regulating the payment of fines in kind. It is
under such conditions that internal money and inter-tribal
money first begin to be sharply differentiated from each other.
It is only where a larger association of communities exists that
general objects of trade attain the status of common denominators to which the values of other objects are reduced, thus
becoming units of calculation for the evaluation of services
rendered or payments to be made. This state of affairs, which
tends to place certain objects in a pivotal position with regard to
all kinds of transactions, naturally presupposes a strong government, such as we see in the ancient East, in Sumeria for example.
The proportional values of corn, silver, and cattle become fixed,
and, consequently, these come to represent basic units in the
economic system. These conditions obtaining with regard to the
association of objects, which the connexion of symbolic ideas with
particular things helped to strengthen, and also the faculty of

reproducing themselves possessed by corn and cattle, kept the sense of individual property rights latent. These objects attained a status equivalent to real money, partly as a result of the aforementioned factors and partly owing to the numbers of people they affected.

XVII

PARTNERSHIP AND COLLECTIVISM

§ 1. Theory and fact. § 2. Collectivism among hunters and trappers.
§ 3. Among pastoral people. § 4. Among hoe-agriculturists. § 5. In stratified communities (sept collectivism). § 6. Wife collectivism. § 7. Partial
collectivism (fellowship). § 8. The importance of collectivism.

§ 1. Collectivism plays a peculiar part in the scientific theory of
national economy. Constructive thinkers of the romantic-rational-
istic period regarded collectivism as an original condition of the
human race. Where it existed it was believed that original or
natural conditions were to be found, and the return to nature
and to such natural conditions appeared an ideal to be aimed at.
Political idealists, who are apt to disregard actual facts, past
or present, and try to induce men to believe what they want to
be, not what really was or is, have made use of this romantic-
rationalistic trend of constructive thought for their own purposes.
Objective science, however, is charged with the task of pursuing
the actual facts. This is by no means so simple as would appear
from superficial and hasty generalizations.

We must recognize various distinctions. We find certain
tendencies towards collectivism in all the most important forms
of life and culture which have been influenced by economic
considerations. Yet already there are considerable distinctions,
arising from the extent and the character of the associations
within which a communal economic system is in action; i.e.
whether the economic unit is represented by the clan, the family,
the village community, the extended family owning slaves, the
manorial estate, or the tribe. Collectivism, therefore, is always
connected with such associations, and usually only extends to
certain parts of their economic system, by no means necessarily
excluding private ownership or inheritance.

In many cases collectivism only applies to the soil. Among
primitive tribes the land is often the common property of the
entire community. It is the domain from which the members of
the settlement who are related to each other gain their livelihood
in a traditional fashion, the district defended against enemies by
the common action of the group. From a legal point of view this
common ownership of the soil is of the nature of public law, since

the group exercises sovereign rights over the district. Hunters and trappers have no landed property as individuals, because the individual has no interest in any particular piece of land. Value is attached to the animals of the chase, to fruits and herbs which can be gathered, or to certain kinds of earth and stone. The idea that the right to use them should be restricted to certain individuals never arises, because it is felt that all these things exist in comparative plenty, and it is open to any individual to procure them. But as soon as the individual has obtained possession of such things his claim to them as a rule becomes paramount. That he should share his possessions with others, or that others share with him probably results from more complicated conditions.

The appearance of powerful leaders and chiefs who carried out a division of the spoil, seems to have been of special importance for the development of collectivism. Among hoe-cultivators the economic chief, who arranges not only the co-operative cultivation of the soil produce but also the harvesting and in many cases the division of the crops, makes his appearance. Within the political community certain septs or even families frequently laid claim, on traditional grounds, to certain pieces of land, but this does not imply the existence of private property.

Ownership among primitive peoples is by no means so simple a matter as is often supposed by legal experts who have grown up among the terminology of Roman law. Where the requirements of ownership taken from the later Roman law are absent, it is easy to go to extremes and speak of 'collectivism'. For instance, among the inhabitants of the Trobriand Islands the building of canoes is a very complicated matter (Malinowski ['22], pp. 112 et seq.) in which the leading chief and the magician, the builder and the various assistants all play a part, in return for which these persons have a corresponding share in the catch or in the profits of the trading expedition. While, on the othe other hand, the whole tribal life of the Trobriand Islands is permeated by continual giving and taking (p. 167) this process is based, not so much on the exchange of property as on the building-up of social ties, e.g. of obligations of relationship, in which the giving often indicates the superiority of the giver, and is only occasionally a token of subordination to a chief (p. 175).

§ 2. Forbes reports that the Kubus, a nomadic hunter tribe in the interior of Sumatra, admit merely a common claim of each horde to its own hunting-ground. However, even in this case personal claims are sometimes asserted: if a man finds in the forest a tree containing a bees' nest or one bearing resin (*damar*), he clears the ground round the tree and strikes it several times while repeating certain magical formulas in order to enforce his traditional claim. This symbolic action is respected by others. Among the hordes which are constantly on the move there exists no right of ownership to the hastily erected huts, which are inhabited for a month at most. A hut of this kind is abandoned if the owner moves to another place, but he never moves beyond the traditional boundaries of the district (Hagen, p. 156).

Knabenhans (['17] pp. 89 et seq.) rightly rejects the two extreme views formerly accepted with regard to ownership, especially among the Australian aborigines, i.e. the conception that they practised unrestricted collectivism (Letourneau, pp. 25, 527), as well as the other theory that hunters and collectors are purely individualistic (Karl Bücher, chap. 'Der wirtschaftliche Urzustand', pp. 1–38). The actual facts, unfortunately, do not square with the theories inspired by the need of systematization. As regards the Australians, Knabenhans arrived at something like the following conclusion, based on a comparison of the literature dealing with the subject: in the first instance a clear distinction must be made between the hunting and trapping done by the men, and the collecting activity of the women. The results of hunting, trapping, fishing, and collecting are gained in the district over which the political group exercises sovereign rights. There is no question of tilling the soil or of accumulating stores, since they live from hand to mouth. When the possibilities of obtaining food in the neighbourhood of a water-hole are exhausted, they move on and search for a new area within the limits of the traditional district. In these circumstances it is natural that personal ownership of the ground should not develop. Man and wife put together what they have separately obtained but keep separate stores. There is, however, this difference, that roots, small animals, &c., collected by the woman are destined for the use of the whole family, while the meat provided by the man is often regarded as his exclusive personal property. At the same time, this does not apply when the spoils of the hunt are larger, for custom and considerations of utility then demand that the surplus over and above what the individual can consume should be shared with the other members.

Moreover, these peoples usually have no arrangements for preserving meat. Besides, the fortunate hunter would be exposed to the ill-will of his companions, if he failed to share with them. The regulations for division of the spoil are frequently of the minutest character: certain persons receive particular pieces, or everything in excess of a certain amount must be divided in accordance with fixed rules (Eylmann, p. 173; Howitt, pp. 756 et seq.). This division is sometimes made by the fortunate hunter himself and sometimes by the chief or some other man possessed of authority, preference often being given to certain senior relatives. Many totemistic food prohibitions are doubtless due to a manifest favouring of the old men as regards the provision of food. Children, women, and young men are generally less favoured in this respect. In some places sons-in-law are obliged to make certain contributions to their fathers-in-law (Spencer and Gillen ['99], p. 469), which usually means that the younger members have to provide food for the leading old men. The most important economic advantage enjoyed by the old men in this connexion is that, owing to polygamy, they have every facility for making use of the women's work. The term collectivism is even less applicable when speaking of the products of handicraft (weapons, ornaments, utensils, &c.)

§ 3. The Yakut herdsmen (Turcoman tribes) of Siberia possess herds of horses which are the collective property of the clan. When these tribes took to keeping cattle the clan broke up into families, and the collective property thereupon passed from the clan to the families (Czaplicka, p. 57). Among pastoral peoples we frequently find, side by side with the common property in cattle some cases of individual ownership, mostly also in cattle. The grazing land, on the other hand, is as a rule common property. This is the case, for example, among the Masai (Merker ['04], p. 204). Among the African pastoral peoples in general private property principally takes the form of cattle.

§ 4. Among certain Papuan tribes of western Dutch New Guinea hunting and fishing are practically of no importance. The principal food-stuffs are the sweet potato, taro, and a few vegetables. They distinguish between (1) private plantations, (2) plantations belonging to a family, and (3) plantations belonging to the settlement, in many cases even to an association of settlements. As a rule, all the villagers take part in clearing the land, sometimes assisted by friends from other settlements who are recompensed with a share in the common evening meal. Weeks and months are often devoted to the work. While the clearing is in progress some of the people are busy with the fatiguing and monotonous work of making a hedge to keep pigs from breaking into the gardens. The actual work of planting is undertaken exclusively by the women. All the female villagers assist in the case of a large family or village plantation. The men make sure of a certain precedence as regards the distribution of food (Wirz ['24], pp. 84 et seq.).

§ 5. A peculiar combination of property claims with something resembling inheritance appears in the sept property of the Hindus. Khandekar and Vaidya ['06] (Appendix) give the following description: The right of a Hindu to inheritance begins at his birth and ends with his death. At the same time there is nothing in a Hindu sept resembling a right of succession. The whole family with its male and female members forms a kind of corporation. There are persons in it who may be regarded as co-owners, namely those who have a right to a share when a partition is made, while others can only claim maintenance. In cases where partition is not allowed there arises no idea of right of succession on the part of any member of the sept. Each individual has simply the right to live in the family house and to be supported there. From this he derives his income, while sharing in the respect paid to the sept according to the amount of its wealth. The claims of the individual are based on membership of the sept, not on any kind of individual qualities or services. However, should a partition be made, the position of the individual as son, grandson, &c., is of great importance in determining the share he is to receive. Except on such occasions no one ever has a special right to any particular part of the sept property. When the common ancestor dies all the surviving sons, grandsons, and great-grandsons form a community, which thus extends for three generations in the male line. No others can obtain any part of the estate. The persons to whom possession was transferred are those who lived together in the same house, or were under the leadership of one head (cf. Mayne, ch. 16).

This sept community recalls the old Irish one (*derbfine*), but with the difference that in the latter case four generations were considered, and there were even cases in which it was extended to the fifth. MacNeill (p. 164) recalls the fact that the Roman *patria potestas* was apparently a more primitive form of social connexion that the Irish or the Hindu sept. It appears, in fact, that the large sept communities mentioned represent one-sided developments.

Family communism is expressed in the Roman Laws of the Twelve Tables by the fact that the son cannot own property independently, and that the father can only release him from his tutelage by a complicated procedure (namely by selling him three times to the *pater fiduciarius*).

We know that the southern Slav house-community was also a comparatively late and artificial development (F. S. Krauss ['85], pp. 64 et seq., and Zoričič). Cf. also Lewinski.

In the Inca empire also the land was evidently the property of the sept (Trimborn ['25], p. 583), yet the tribute lands belonged to the central authority which had secured the ownership of the koka plantations (p. 584). The use of the common lands, which belonged to the village as a whole, was determined by a periodical drawing of lots by the individuals (p. 585). As among the Germanic tribes at the time of Tacitus, and in ancient Mexico, the house and its dependencies were privately owned. Arable land could also be made private property by a special order of the Inca (p. 588). This special right of ownership was heritable. Thus we see that there were different kinds of property in land: (1) land belonging to the king, with a special claim on his part to certain plantations, pastures, cattle, and mines; (2) communal land with pasture and cattle; (3) special private land. The so-called 'communism' consisted substantially in a patriarchal supervision of the people's activities with the object of raising contributions. It appears that, in the earliest times, the Peruvians lived in small independent communities ruled by the heads of families or septs; but in war they were commanded by some distinguished warrior. Joyce is perhaps not wrong in assuming that the later Inca state represents nothing more than the overlaying of one tribe by another. The basis of the Peruvian social structure was the family. In this case also the peculiar system of a twofold division makes its appearance. A class of officials supervised the work done by the people, and saw that the products of labour were fairly distributed. It is evident in this case that the whole of this 'state communism' really represented nothing more than an enormously extended manor. And it is for this reason only, that the populace credited the ruling class with supernatural powers and, having a religious dread of them, allowed them to exercise minute supervision over their doings. The Peruvian 'communism' is nothing more than a vast system of tribute which provided for the maintenance of the officials of the upper stratum, but also led to an exchange of goods regulated by the will of that ruling stratum (Joyce ['12], pp. 99 et seq.). For other state collectivism in America, see Wissler, p. 184.

The common property of the sept or family is transferred to the patriarchs after some system of government has been evolved. This applies both to the personal claims of the paterfamilias and to the chief's political right of disposal. This is clearly evident, for instance, among the Somali in East Africa, who are strongly influenced by Muhammadan ideas. The father of the family (*abba-maná*) considers himself the sole owner of his farm from which he cannot be dislodged by the tribe. He tills the fields, and makes use of the pasture and forests with the aid of his children and other relatives, to whom he distributes individual portions according to their number and strength. The total yield, however, belongs to him, and the tribe, as such, has no claim to any part of it. Animals, on the other hand, usually belong to individuals. The right to immovable property in the Muhammadan part of North-East Africa is based on the assumption that every piece of land in the tribe belongs to the chief and that he alone has the right of disposal over landed property. The spoils of war, having been won by common action, constitute an exception to the general rule. The captured mules, horses, and cattle for slaughter are collected together in one place, horses and mules being assigned to the leaders of the army, while the cattle are shared among all the members of the tribe (Paulitschke, ii. 144 et seq.).

§ 6. There is or was formerly a certain common right to women among the Bakitara of East Africa; the wife of a member of the clan is also the wife of his fellow-clansmen, that is, of the man who are called 'brothers' by her husband. At the same time a man can at least use his influence to persuade his wife to refrain from relations with one of his clan brothers with whom he is not on good terms; but he could not accuse her of unfaithfulness if she refused (Roscoe ['23/b], p. 265).

§ 7. We must leave as an open question whether the partial collectivism, exhibited in individual institutions, festivals, and the like, is to be regarded as surviving from an earlier and more extensive economic system, as the older theorists would have us believe. For instance, facts reported from the north-west of Madagascar (*Tsimihety*) regarding a feast preceded by elaborate ceremonies, in which the food was both cooked and eaten in common (Decary, p. 343), cannot be interpreted as a sign of collectivism.

The possession of land by families or septs is very general, but the participation of the individual in this respect varies greatly. In stratified societies where economics have assumed considerable importance, as, for example, among the Ewe tribes of Togo, West Africa, the special private possession of family land is granted to individuals (Asmis, p. 139). We meet with a special kind of communal property, for instance, in the district of Lome. While land usually belongs to families, movable property is individualized. Hunting and fishing are usually free, but individual families living near the most productive swamps have developed special rights to set basket traps and defend these rights against rival claims occasioned by increased population. Twelve or more members of these families unite to form fishing societies and elect a foreman and two assistants. Each member receives the result of one day's catch as his share, while the foreman claims six days' and the assistants two, or three, days' catch. The catch is not, however, divided according to any abstract calculation of the average daily takings, but the individual's share in the concrete result of an actual day's work is necessarily subject to chance (Asmis, pp. 105 et seq.).

§ 8. Family and sept communism has its parallel in the collective responsibility of the members of the family or sept, such as we encounter in the case of blood feuds or surety. We find it further in the structure of extended families possessing slaves. The political organization of archaic governmental systems was based, in the ancient East, but also in Peru, on the legal fiction that the ruler was the father or *paterfamilias* of a community embracing all his subjects, as, for example, all the Chinese (Sternberg, p. 148).

The influence of traditional peculiarities on the mode of life and on economics in general, more especially under ancient and primitive conditions, was probably active (as has recently been pointed out) in the ancient English village communities. Peake ['22] assumes that the Alpine race was distinguished by comparatively large village settlements (built on piles) where property was held in common (op. cit., pp. 61, 65 seq.). The motive for this, in his opinion, was the husbandry principally practised by these tribes. A certain communism of wives seems to have gone hand in hand with this (op. cit., p. 31). The interests of these unwarlike people were usually confined to their own communes to which they clung persistently, and there was no tendency towards the union of larger areas (op. cit., pp. 54 et seq., 65). Conquests by various northern tribes led to the communes being attached to the manor and becoming dependent on it (op. cit., pp. 77 et seq., 97 et seq., 125, 146 et seq., 181).

XVIII

PRINCIPLES OF PRIMITIVE ECONOMICS

§ 1. Stability and reluctance to change. § 2. Limitations in communal system. § 3. 'Consumers' and 'producers'. § 4. The beginnings of work. § 5. The stimulus of needs and desires. § 6. Directness of primitive economic process. § 7. Developments of individualism. § 8. Disintegrating processes. § 9. Lines of development. § 10. A summary.

§ 1. Let us now inquire how far the various economic forms of primitive society have anything in common with the economics of the present day. We can, in the first place, point to the great stability characteristic of every primitive form of culture, naturally including economics. The reason for this is, as has already been explained, the simplicity and uniformity of technique. The fewer innovations that are introduced into a culture, the more uniform does it remain. In this connexion it is irrelevant to inquire whether the innovations have their origin in the same culture or are imported from outside. Where either is the case a special process of adoption into the community is necessary. It is not sufficient that discoveries should be made by individuals, but such discoveries must be raised by the community to the rank of cultural traditions in order to take effect. The same applies to the adoption or imitation of alien culture, arts, knowledge, customs, or institutions. Attention has already been drawn in the earlier chapters to the difficulties attending the adoption of alien arts. In order that such a novelty can penetrate successfully, the influence of authoritative personalities in the community must be exercised in its favour. But this obviously involved special difficulties, especially in the groups ruled by a gerontocracy. Not only did they allege magical reasons (which, indeed, really existed), but doubtless they had a genuine dread of novelties, and the changes caused by them encountered internal checks. Progress in primitive societies was more especially influenced by slowness of thought, suspicion, and fear of everything new and strange. But it was this very fact which led to the achievement of that internal harmonization of culture so characteristic of the economic life of every tribe. This is the only thing which makes it possible for men to appear so intimately connected with the way in which they conduct their lives that one cannot picture them in any other economic surroundings. This is most completely true of the artisan castes.

§ 2. In primitive economics, more or less strongly developed features of communal economics occur everywhere. But this communal system is only applied to the obtaining of food, while articles of daily use, tools, and ornaments are generally left to the ownership of individuals or families. As we have seen, the line to be drawn between private or family economics and collective economics in the political group varies greatly in individual tribes and cultures.

It may also be said that the result of the work belongs to the individual who has done the work, in so far as the community does not lay claim to it. This even applies to the more primitive forms of slavery. The systematically conducted economic system of slavery, however, does not belong to the real primitive state but, where it occurs, as in Africa or in the Sunda Islands, would seem to have been imported from higher, or at least archaic, forms of culture.

Expansion in primitive economics is governed by similar conditions. Conquest, as understood in higher cultures, is unknown, owing to the comparatively large space available for living, and subjection, in our sense of the word, is equally unknown. While hunting tribes are on the whole comparatively peaceable, such combats as we observed among the hoe cultivating tribes and less advanced herdsmen, are principally connected with the prosecution of blood and other feuds, but do not involve any idea of economic or political expansion. For this reason, earlier super-stratifications can hardly be attributed to conquest, as supposed by the earlier theory.

Nomad tribes must, indeed, have been compelled, up to a point, to adapt themselves to their new surroundings, but they doubtless did so no more than was absolutely necessary. They would live, at first, side by side or intermingled with the earlier settled population with whom they were allied in a loose form of symbiosis requiring time to develop into a state of mutual dependence. An organized super-stratification can only be regarded as a later result from this state of things.

§ 3. The hunter and collector tribes, and the traders, have been described as consumers and contrasted with the productive agriculturists and cattle-breeding pastoral peoples, who are the producers. Aristocratic strata, such as are found among robber herdsmen (Tuareg) and fighting herdsmen (Manchus), have also been called 'consumers'. This kind of terminology can only result from a superficial view, which classes together things essentially different, for the small community where the women are the cultivators usually only 'produces' for its own use, not for that of others or for a market or for outside customers. The products of handicraft, on the other hand, are much more frequently made for outsiders. The hunters (Congo pygmies, Kubu) who bring forest produce, such as resin, honey, or meat, for sale to the agriculturists produce these commodities for the use of others. The trader in primitive society is almost always still, to a considerable extent, a producer, and lives on the food-stuffs which he has himself produced, as described in the case of the Mailu, or in that of the trading journey (*hiri*) of the Motu. The same applies to aristocracies and to robber and fighting tribes. So far, these conditions have usually been too much regarded from the modern European standpoint of one-sided specialization.

§ 4. On the other hand, it is probably more important to invite attention to the beginnings of labour, which is a stage in evolution, since it is labour which first suggests the possibility of replacing a man's own strength by that of others and devolving the exertion of working on others by the invention of slavery and serfdom. Hunting and pastoral tribes are not workers. Robbery and war arose from the resistance encountered by these people when they recognized the benefits of agriculture but were unwilling to acquire them by their own work. The forcible carrying-off of women cultivators as wives and the exaction of tribute brought about decisive changes in economics and in political and social development. The more frequent change of place and the greater mobility of pastoral, seafaring, and fishing tribes, who were led into bartering and litigation by the endeavour to increase their food supplies, resulted in their greater activity by a sifting and selecting process, that in the end made them able to impose their power of organization on other people.

§ 5. In a survey of long periods of time and many people we perceive an extraordinary variability in needs. The only things which remain constant are a few powerful impulses which demand continual and unconditional satisfaction, but even these are quite definitely limited. We have seen that, for the satisfaction of the first necessity of life, food, communal methods are adopted as a rule. Sexual laws and marriage ordinances regulate love. The house, too, is provided, if not by co-operation (as in the case of the sept houses in Borneo, see Hose ['26]), then by solicited work, as we have seen. It is only the personal desire for position, which makes itself felt even in the lowest communities, that opens up the economic possibilities of the power of distribution and the accumulation of treasures and wealth.

The way in which these interacting impulses are usually satisfied in any particular culture is shown by the needs of the community in question. The needs of hunters are different from those of agriculturists, while these, again, differ from those of pastoral peoples or those engaged in agriculture combined with handicraft. Homogeneous small communities have different needs from those experienced by the graded society of pre-state and state associations. These needs determine various non-economic phenomena, e.g. arts, morality, &c.

§ 6. The primitive economic process is characterized by the fact that, primarily, it is direct, especially in the three main types of homogeneous societies—predatory tribes, digging-stick agriculturists, and simple herdsmen.

This directness is due to the autarchic character of each community, i.e. to the fact that each small community mainly lives on its own resources, and its existence does not depend on the acquisition of a considerable number of foreign goods, by barter, —the latter being restricted to luxuries. There is consequently no temptation for making gains or profits.

But it would be a wrong construction to think, as the romanticists did, that each individual cares for himself. Neither is the extreme opposite true, suggesting a kind of primeval collective paradise. If we are ready to regard the fundamentals of primitive economics with a balanced and realistic mind we are struck by the fact that we see the same emotional powers at work as with us, only sometimes in different proportions.

§ 7. Individualism is more accentuated among herdsmen, especially cattle people and horsemen, and is intensified because they excel as leaders and rulers of other tribes, especially agriculturists. The pastoral man is an organizer and thinker, a man of imagination and enterprise, aggressive and active, sometimes violent, sometimes cunning. The agriculturist sticks more to collective principles, is meditative, more passive, has an inclination to luxury, revels in feasts, is a builder and painter, enjoys life.

The hunting and collecting races, however, are a good-natured, friendly set, but shy and intimidated before their more aggressive or boisterous cousins. They keep their traditional hardships of life, prefer liberty to luxury, are particularly adapted to their country, hate and despise the intruders.

§ 8. The directness and simplicity of the small autarchic (self-sufficing) communities is shattered by contact with the various types sketched. Various processes ensue. Some of them have been depicted in several instances in this book. Two main types may be introduced here.

(a) One is the primary blending of herdsmen with agriculturists or hunters from whom they take their wives. In each of these cases new economic conditions are started and with a particular division of labour between the sexes. Other conditions are often involved. For instance, the taking of the wives from the lower clans leads to deterioration of the former position of the women. A great variety of conditions follows: as a rule no aristocracy arises, but influential chiefs can be found.

(b) The second possibility is an ethnic aggregation without blending of races, at least in the beginning. The process that follows has been already sketched. It leads sooner or later to a breaking-up of the leading clans, the association with all kinds of other people, on account of the struggle for power and influence, of the awakened and cherished individualism of the leading personalities. This implies differentiation in the real possibilities and the symbols for acquiring power. From them the estimation of values is derived. The economic and other values are means for obtaining social and political influence, whereby followers in rival conflicts may be acquired. This individualism introduced by the pastoral people infected also the others, and the bastards of the various clans. The strife for power is disintegrating also for the other strata of society, which eventually are individualized, or at least dissolved into families with their dependent serfs and slaves.

§ 9. Two main lines of development may be traced. (1) Either transformation into more or less autocratic, patriarchal, and self-sustaining 'manors', without any central power or a relatively weak one, results. Or (2) a strong centralization of power with a system of taxes and distributions, worked by the help of servants (officials) from all clans and even of foreigners. The central factor of the associated commonwealth, in fact, becomes its despot. But in this function he is considered as a kind of transcendent embodiment of the whole commonwealth, as a living symbol of superhuman power, of a power which is in no way limited by rationalistic considerations. Consequently he is made responsible for everything that happens, whether he is able to influence it (war preparations), or not (the weather, the crops, diseases of cattle, &c.). This development comes mostly as a later stage, not always reached, and its continuity is rather uncertain.

Economic life has considerably changed under the new conditions described. Money and wealth have become means for power and also means for subsistence of all the persons who function in the complicated mechanism of state. In this manner a new individualistic method of economy comes into being.

§ 10. To summarize, it may be said that (1) communal economics in the small homogeneous communities are confined to the obtaining of food; (2) where several communities have become connected by permanent commercial relations, the economic system begins to be based on the family instead of upon clan or sept, particularly when trade is to some extent the means of gaining a livelihood; (3) when a strong government combines a considerable number of communities into an ethnically stratified society, the economics of distribution gain the upper hand, and (4) social grading according to property and economic values helps the development of self-sufficing households and the transformation of clans or septs into castes or guilds even when the government is less powerful.

XIX

THE SPIRIT OF PRIMITIVE ECONOMICS

§ 1. The attitude of primitive societies in economic matters unlike our own. § 2. Modern machine *v.* primitive tool. § 3. Different forms of activity and behaviour. § 4. Illustration: form of ancient Chinese economic system. § 5. Cannot be dismissed as magic or sorcery. § 6. Behaviour determined by different sphere of ideas. § 7. Sympathetic understanding required. § 8. General conclusion.

§ 1. As communal economics provide for the most essential need, which is food, and there is no general currency, the attitude of primitive societies in economic matters does not correspond to our own. The importance of blood-relationship has not been forced into the background, as is the case among us, and the family has not been broken up into individuals, as in modern society, where this results in associations formed partly on a vocational and partly or an ideal basis. The result in the various primitive types of economics is an attitude from which we must conclude the existence of a different economic spirit. The directness of primitive economics further entails a different economic distribution consequent on the lack of a universal currency. In a society in which values have only a limited purchasing power, the earning of money has not the importance which it has in our present economic system, all the more since commercial intercourse is only conducted between one place and the next and does not affect the economic organization. Above all, failure to earn money does not lead to personal ruin, however great the importance attached to wealth in stratified societies. Communal economics, even if only partial, protect the individual from starvation. The individual is not abandoned to his fate, unless he has been expressly excluded from the community or is purposely allowed to die because he is old or sick.

§ 2. However technique may differ in individual cultures, no primitive societies are dominated by the modern machine, which reduces man to dependence. The primitive tool is much more at the service of man than man is dependent on it. Combined machines, such as the tread-wheel, the potter's wheel, and the like, are absent, as they first make their appearance in the archaic states. The man of primitive culture, therefore, works without the

compulsion of the tool or the stimulus of gain; on the other hand,
however, he is subject to the powers of nature, to the weather, to
the flora and fauna, to hill, forest, and water.

The Bushmen with their wretched tools, their sticks, dig graves
for the dead and bury all their personal property with them, even
the laboriously carved arrows, for this property all belongs to the
deceased (Passarge, pp. 109 et seq.). From this soil, in which the
dead have been laid to rest, the roots are dug up in the following
year and the father of the family smokes a little hemp, thus transporting himself into a world of dreams, the other world of the dead,
and invokes his father in the grave who made the roots grow. It is
only when his permission has been given that the roots can be
eaten without fear (Meinhof, p. 49). These two facts demonstrate
the conditioning of economics by religious notions, the way in
which rational economy is constantly interrupted by irrational considerations. But can we really call such considerations 'irrational'?
If so, then only from our point of view, and not from that of the
Bushman. For a whole sequence of reasoning has caused him to
bury the valuable possessions with the corpse; while other objec-
tions arise to eating the first-fruits of the harvest without further
ado, which ought to happen according to the distorted picture of
the 'unchecked savage' imagined by many a theorist.

§ 3. The different conditions of life and economics are also the
cause of different considerations guiding the choice of leaders for
the community and also the choice of mates. There is no need of
the pursuit of gain in order to achieve one's purpose in these communities; quite other forms of activity and behaviour lead in them
to recognition and distinction, success, and respect. These naturally vary according to the individual economic types discussed
above. If, therefore, we speak of the different economic spirit of
these strange and distant societies as compared with our own, we
are really comparing things that do not admit of comparison. A
different style of living naturally allows another economic spirit to
make its appearance.

§ 4. In attempting to ascertain the reasons for difference between
economic conditions in ancient China and those in western Europe,
Grosse (pp. 114 et seq.) arrives at the conclusion that the difference
is to be sought not so much in the degree as in the form of the
Chinese economic system. He lays particular emphasis on the
different philosophical view of life, which is, in any case, a synthetic

term which we must analyse into its sociological and psychological factors. In this connexion he speaks of the completeness in itself and the internal balance of Chinese civilization. The spirit permeating the structure of Chinese society is also applicable to more primitive communities where society is stratified. The relation of master, employer, and business manager to apprentice, journeyman, employee, and workman is of a family character with moral ties, apart from the payment of wages. The association, guild, or other agency holds the employers and merchants together in such a way that the individual finds, on the one hand, his support and, on the other, his limitation, in the association. The man who is favoured by fortune, or who has risen by his own ability and has become rich or powerful, finds himself in China under obligations to his association which became more stringent the higher he rises. Not only the whole household, including the servants, and not only the whole of his relatives, near and distant, live on him as a matter of course, but even the various associations of his town or village, the guilds and the clubs of fellow-provincials and every conceivable kind of association make the most exorbitant claims on him. For this reason, at the present day, Chinese who have become rich prefer to retire to the foreign colonies where it is easier to escape from such obligations. On this patriarchal basis there is but limited room for strong individualism, which is thus prevented from making immediate use of technical improvement; the association acts as a check in this direction.

On the other hand, such a state of affairs has the advantage of a tendency towards social equality, and for this reason we never hear of social cleavage, class hatred, or class envy in ancient China. Economic crises were almost exclusively due to nature, or to political events. It was precisely this harmony in all domains of human activity which was the support of a complete and many sided civilization, but, at the same time, it led to that state of affairs which we describe as 'stagnation' in China. But we must not forget the position, described above, of the individual in his association, or the connexion between economic life and social institutions, on the one hand, and the other sides of cultural life, on the other, which are of extraordinary importance for the state of affairs described. Chinese family law, in constrast to Roman or German law, recognized no coming of age for individual members of the family. In every respect, even in economic matters, the individual remained a minor and the *paterfamilias* had full right to dispose, not only of the family fortune but also of the wages earned by individual members of the family. These institutions are, however, connected with great economic efficiency. In the whole of China, markets are held every five days at places not very distant from each other, to which the Chinese merchants bring their wares from distances of hundreds, even thousands of kilometres. The products of the well-developed industry are excellent, even if produced with primitive tools and by primitive methods. These products of local trading establishments and of a manifold home industry are marketed in all directions in spite of primitive means of communication, by means of much-frequented roads, inland waterways, and coastal navigation. Nor is this all, for a well-organized system of credit and transfer payments is in use by numerous banks. All these factors, though interlinked in quite a different way from that of the modern European economic structure, make the success of the Chinese merchant possible, more particularly as against his neighbours in the north, the south, and the west. The Chinese people have effected silent conquests and settlements, as by penetrating into Manchuria and across their north-western frontier. They are the upholders of a vast economic expansion by peaceful means.

§ 5. Within the several economic types great fluctuations occur which, when compared with each other, show that under similar conditions a commercial spirit may be alive in one tribe (e.g. southern New Guinea) and absent in another. But we have recognized the reasons for and the internal connexions between such variations.

It would, however, be a mistake to think that economic factors have had no effect on the life of primitive peoples. It is a complete misunderstanding of the actual facts if primitive economics are dismissed at the present time as magic or sorcery. This is as grossly to misunderstand the actual circumstances as is done by ascribing to the natural man considerations only applicable to the *homo oeconomicus*, a procedure at variance with all the principles of psychology. It may not be out of place to glance for a moment at the economic life of a hunter and collector tribe as it appears under the changed conditions of life at the present day, as this will enable us to see how they have rearranged their economic system. The Kamtchadals of northern Siberia live principally by catching migratory salmon and by hunting sable and bartering their skins to traders, principally of Chinese origin, for tobacco, spirits, sugar, in fact, even for pocket-mirrors and gramophones. These hunters and trappers have become so specialized that they no longer live directly on the result of the chase but principally hunt those animals of which they can trade the skins in order to make their lives more pleasant and comfortable. Owing to the fact that the sable skins are the articles most desired by the foreign traders, they become values and units of exchange even among the Kamtchadals themselves. For example, one of them bought a boat with a sable skin, receiving a fox skin in addition to the boat (Bergmann, pp. 71 et seq.).

§ 6. As a matter of fact, the natural man conducts his economics according to his own judgement of what is right and prudent. Granted that this may lead him into errors and miscalculations in technique and organization, and that fear of the failure of his undertakings may give rise to beliefs and practices stigmatized by us as superstitious, it has, after all, to be admitted that his behaviour is due to a sphere of ideas determined by entirely different conditions. The methods he adopts may often appear muddled, from our point of view, so that we call his way of thinking and acting 'magical', yet, from his point of view, he is acting correctly and rationally. It cannot be claimed that our present-day rationalistic point of view and our modern economic way of thinking can be applied to primitive culture.

§ 7. Saving is of minor importance in the less advanced economic systems, since the accumulation of symbols of value is of importance only for the chiefs—patriarchs of the upper stratum of society. The more numerous the values and the more complicated the economic and social system, the greater importance is attached to saving. In the ancient Persian moral maxims it is strictly forbidden to waste things possessing any value. Even something weighing no more than a thread, or what a maiden lets fall when spinning, must not be wasted (Darmesteter, i. 79).

We must not attempt to master the economic spirit with the aid of terms taken from our modern life and ways of thinking, but we can only estimate it by means of a sympathetic understanding of thought and behaviour which are based on quite other requirements in technique and knowledge, skill and organization.

§ 8. Economic systems depend a good deal on the degree of skill and the accomplishments of a given people at a certain time.

The achievements in skill and knowledge, and a greater efficiency in any society, presupposes a more primitive condition of an earlier time. The plough requires as antecedent the use of a hoe, the hoe the use of a stick or a stone. But the plough drawn by an ox means also previous domestication of cattle, and this in turn arises from the discipline and caution of the old methods of the hunting communities sticking to one particular herd. The same applies to modern scientific progress: the aeroplane is inconceivable before the improvements of the automobile motor, &c.

Comparing the periods in time we are able to construct an objective connexion between the outstanding accomplishments of each society. The more efficient and more complex ones, relying on the more primitive ones, seem to proceed in a straight line from the former. This indicates an accumulation of knowledge and skill. We cannot imagine a reversal of it. Therefore we term this process 'accumulative and irreversible'. On it depends the development of civilization. This process, however, does not move on one line only. Bringing the outstanding achievements into direct connexion with each other we abstract from their connexion with a community. This process of irreversible accumulation of skill and knowledge moving through different communities and many societies, passes through various stages of decay or diversion, which we ignore when looking backward, but which we cannot foretell for the future. In each society internal processes constantly are at work which may take advantage of inventions, new accomplishments of neighbours, and so forth. They are assimilated to the society which accepts them; sometimes there is a slight or more important change, another time the innovations may be accepted wholesale or rejected altogether.

Therefore the economic application of a certain ability varies according to time, place, and people. The cultural constitution is a decisive factor in this adaptation. By this process the interdependence between the accumulative process and the social life of man is established. This refers especially to economic organization connected with the use of any tool or device. The same instrument or ability may serve different economic functions in various societies. Among the different tribes of the Pacific Islands almost the same technical methods for acquiring food-stuffs prevail, but varying social systems imply considerable differences in the form of the economic organization of the tribes.

The accumulative process influences the economic structure not only directly by providing new means of production, but perhaps sometimes still more by various indirect ways. The transition from hunter life to that of a herdsman involves considerable changes of the economic system directly conditioned by the accumulative process. If the intensive specialization of potters or blacksmiths induces them to neglect their gardens and they fall into dependence on an agricultural or peasant community, it may also lead to political dependence which may in time lead to taxation and economic subordination, &c. Or a caste of artisans may produce for a market and therefore rely on an income in money for their other needs (such as food): this economic dependence then leads under certain social conditions to political dependence, &c.

These changes in political and economic life, however, are reflected in other spheres of human existence, such as in the forms of marriage. In an indirect way they may lead to alterations of the social pattern of mental attitude towards any institution. Alterations of this kind do not consist in accumulation. In human relations there is no increase. The possibilities of alteration are rather limited. There are always the same principles applied in matrimonial relations as well as in political institutions. This process of change is reversible. At one time a certain people may choose one way while another people choose the opposite. A matrilineal people may become patrilineal, and later return to some matrilineal institutions or vice versa. A democratic people may by stratification become aristocratic and plutocratic, and at a later time revert to democratic institutions. Within a very limited number of possibilities in principle different constitutions are built up.

Any alteration brought about, very often by the influence of the accumulative process, is accompanied by high emotions. The change from one principle to the other is felt as progress by the defenders of the innovation. In fact it is the result of emotional valuation. This progress, however, has nothing to do with the process of accumulation described above.

In economic institutions we have to distinguish between the repercussions of the accumulative process and the changes within the realm of limited possibilities, particularly in the case of collectivistic or more individualistic structures, such as those which are self-sufficient and those which rely on exchange.

Consequently in all discussions of evolution we have to bear in mind that there is no unilinear process, and no straight line. What we may call evolution is this accumulative process operating in societies of different levels and aggregations, each one having its own life.

Any ideas, technical procedures, inventions, knowledge, &c., are accepted by a community both from neighbouring peoples and from members of their own group. Some of these new acquisitions are integrated within their culture. In this process of integration certain old cultural institutions, ideas, crafts, &c., are eliminated, and the new acquisition substituted. The grinding of stone axes is not necessary and is soon forgotten when iron blades are introduced; the spinning wheel is not needed after products of modern manufacture are used. Sometimes the old and new may exist side by side. The horse wagon can be seen side by side with the automobile. Still another possibility is the fusion into a new configuration. The contact between agriculturists and herdsmen ended in a fusion of their principal means of subsistence and in the invention of the plough as described already. This process of accepting new things and rejecting used ones may be compared to the digestive system of an organism by which external matter entering the body is converted into a part of it or eliminated.

The cultural function of a community or a society is a systematizing one, i.e. it brings the achievements of the accumulative process in contact with human reactions. Economics therefore must be considered in this connexion. Primitive economics as studied in the preceding pages is not distinguished from any other form of economics, as far as human relations are concerned, and rests on the same general principles of social life. But in primitive economics, we are observing earlier levels of the accumulative process, which continues, as it seems, indefinitely, and grows beyond man's ability to direct it.

DIAGRAMS

ILLUSTRATING THE DEVELOPMENT OF ECONOMIC
METHODS AND SIMPLE TECHNICAL SKILL

(Note the division of labour between the sexes)

DIAGRAM I

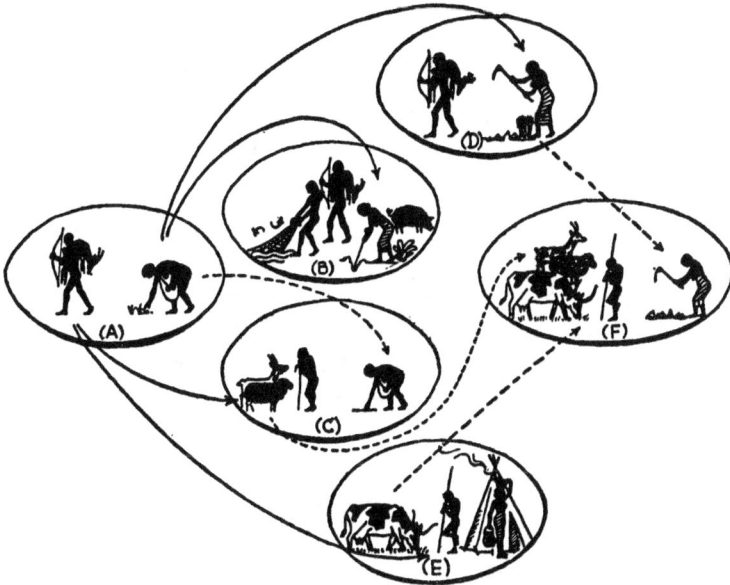

See Part II, Chapters I, II, and III

DIAGRAM I. (A) Men as hunters and trappers. Women as collectors. (Type—Bergdama of S.W. Africa.) (B) Men still hunting, trapping, fishing. Women using digging-stick. Pig associated at early date. (Melanesian type.) (C) Women remain collectors. Men keep sheep and goats. (Type—W. Sahara.) (D) Hoe cultivation mainly by women, cereals being grown. Men still hunting and trapping. (Type—Pangwe, &c.) (E) Men keep cattle. Women make and care for milk vessels. Work hides for tents and clothing. (Type—Masai.) (F) Marriage one alternative result of contact between herdsmen and female agriculturists. Meat, milk, cereals, produced in same family. (Type—Wanyamwezi.)

Technical progress is shown by solid lines; continuance of similar methods by dotted lines.

DIAGRAM II A

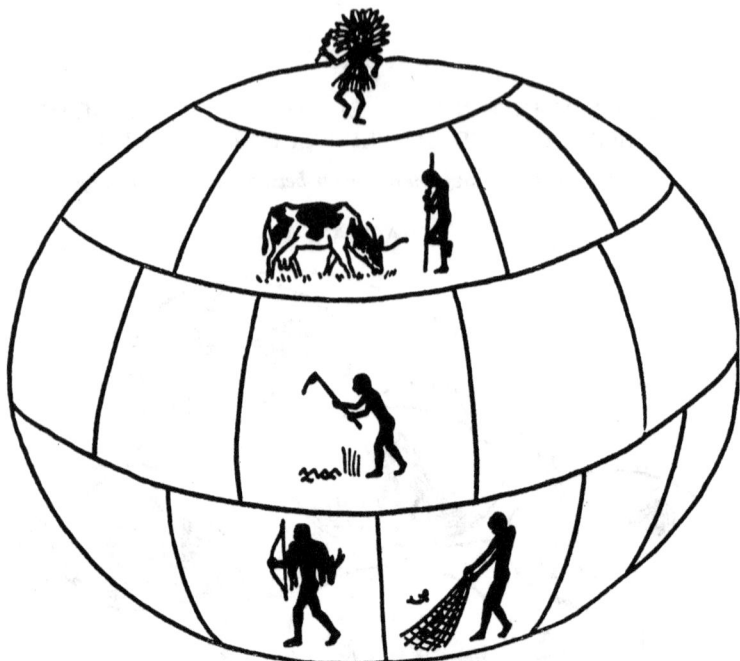

See Part II, Chapters IV and V

DIAGRAMS II A and II B illustrate other alternative developments resulting from contact between herdsmen and agriculturists, cf. Diagram I (F). (Horizontal lines show social strata; vertical lines, divisions into clans or septs.)

In II A pastoral and agricultural people are associated in a stratified commonwealth. Marriages are made within the same stratum of clans or septs. The leading place is accorded to the pastoral stratum of clans. In such a loose mutually dependent group a sorcerer or rain-maker becomes the influential personality. (Type—Bakitara.)

DIAGRAM II B   291

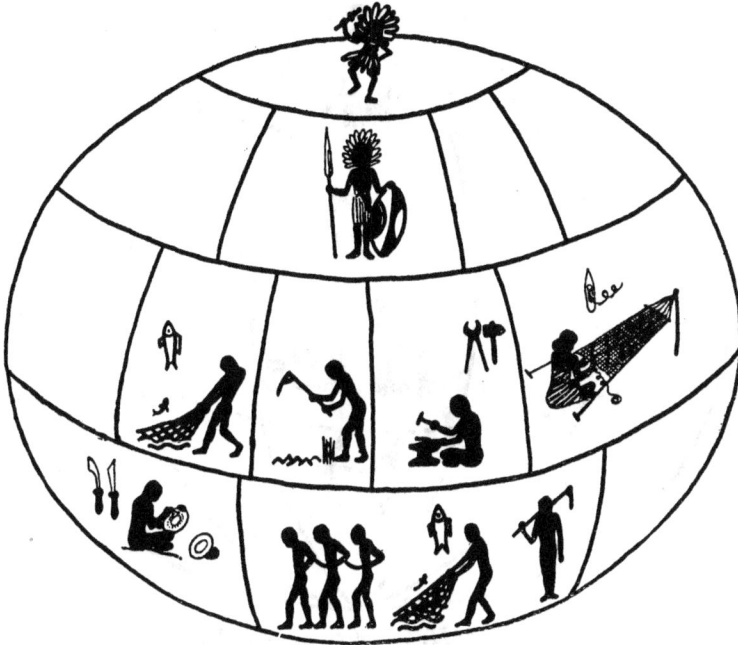

See Part II, Chapter VI

In II B an ethnically stratified association of agriculturist-artisans and fishermen-hunters is shown. No difference exists in the methods of gaining a livelihood among these strata. There is a complicated system of rank and grades. The clans and septs mostly lead their own lives on a democratic basis. Handicrafts are often traditional. Power is exercised on religious and magical lines. Prisoners of war are made and in small numbers used as slaves. (Type—Borneo, Micronesian and Polynesian Islands, &c.)

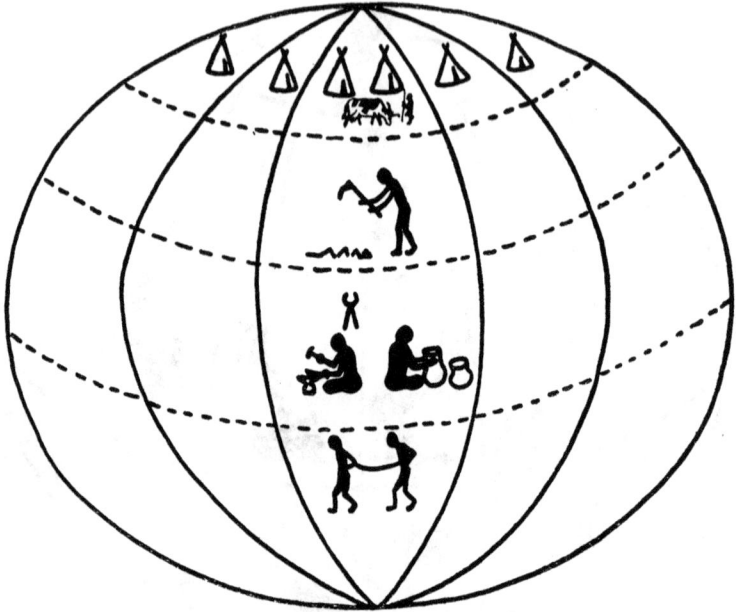

See Part II, Chapters VII and IX.

DIAGRAMS III A and III B show how the aggregations of II A may lead along two differing lines of development.

In III A the ethnically and socially stratified society establishes 'manors' under the leadership of herdsmen. The clans of the herdsmen became divided up into families which are more or less in rivalry. Each draws together agriculturists, artisans, and 'detribalized' prisoners of war and slaves The vertical organization—the family with serfs and slaves and tenants—predominates, the horizontal stratification indicating only the parallel constitution of other 'familiae'. (Cf. Diagram VI.) (Type— Kasbahs of Morocco.)

DIAGRAM III B   293

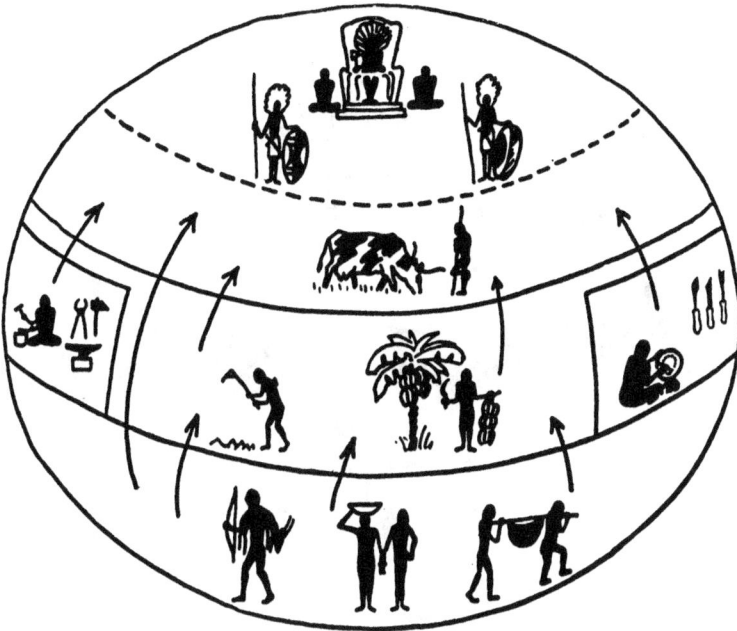

See Part II, Chapter VIII.

III B shows how the commonwealth of herdsmen-agriculturists and hunters may come under a despotic organization. Starting from the conditions of II A the rival 'manors' (III B) have either been destroyed or united under a single dynasty ('familia'). The ruling family, supported by other aristocratic families (often functioning as priests or heads of secret associations) are seen at the top. The dotted line shows the gradation of relations between the supreme ruler and the wealthy class. Clan bonds still survive in the middle ranks of agriculturists and artisans. In the lower stratum detribalized slaves are seen. A great part of the people is maintained by the taxes paid by others. This is indicated by arrow-headed lines. This system means the beginning of an individualization in society in the upper and lower strata. (Type—Banyankole.)

See Part II, Chapter VIII; Part III, Chapter XIV.

DIAGRAM IV shows that under certain conditions the types presented in Diagrams II and III may lead to the establishment of a 'tyranny'. The herdsmen-agriculturists-hunters may be organized under the rule of a man not belonging by origin to their traditional aristocracy. Such a man is bound to protect himself by a guard of warriors. He generally has to compromise with the born leaders of the group by taking some of them as councillors and respecting their priestly organization. Wealth and property count for more than descent. Artisans begin to play an important part beside the agriculturists. There are many serfs and slaves. (Type— Baganda, Ashanti, ancient Oriental states, &c.)

DIAGRAM V   295

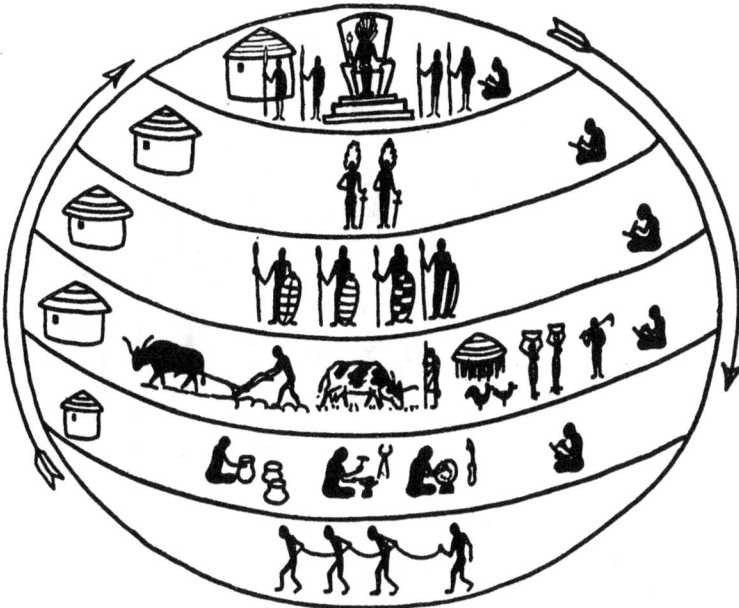

See Part III, Chapter XI

DIAGRAM V shows a despotic archaic state, administered by officials. The society is graded according to descent, wealth, and official rank. A blending of herdsmen and agriculturists has resulted in a farming population which breeds herds and flocks and tills the soil. The hoe is transformed into a plough, drawn by oxen or mules. Technical progress is evident. Storehouses (see left) are ready for the reception of taxes in kind. Arrowheaded lines indicate the circulation of taxes. They are partly paid by each grade to the grade above. They are disbursed from the centre as salaries in kind to the officials shown sitting at the right. Peasants, hunters, fishermen, artisans, and also herdsmen are bound to pay dues. Slaves give large service to the state in administrative and private work. (Type—Abyssinia, old Egypt, ancient Peru.)

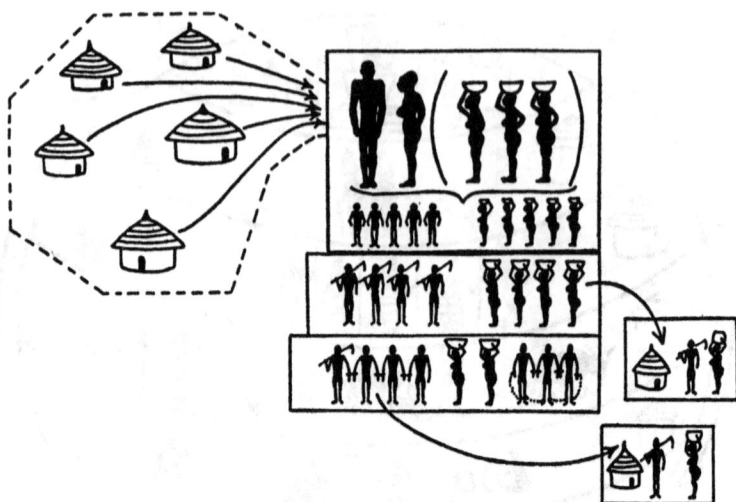

See Part III, Chapters XIV and XV

DIAGRAM VI represents a typical 'familia' in a 'manor'. In the upper rectangle the father with his principal wife are shown. Beyond her, in brackets, the subordinate wives are seen. Each one generally leads a household of her own. Beneath are the children, boys and girls. In the second rectangle the houseborn serfs and maids appear. Underneath them are shown the male and female slaves, some bought, some captured in warfare. On the left upper corner the various settlements of taxpaying peasants (*metoikoi*) are symbolized. They all owe duty to the father of the family. The small rectangles on the right lower corner indicate that a male or female serf or slave may be endowed with a *peculium*, a personal farm. (Type—Morocco, W. Africa, ancient Greece and Rome.)

DIAGRAM VII   297

See Part III, Chapter IX.

DIAGRAM VII illustrates the functioning of the collective system of taxation and redistribution in kind.

Two left rectangles. Upper.—The male hunter brings his prey home to
the 'men at the holy fire under the sacred tree'; the female collector
carries her onions in her skin bag to the chief and the food-master that he
may taste the spoil. Lower.—The chief of the small sept is seen re-distri-
buting the meals prepared from the prey and the spoils. (Drawn from the
Bergdama, S.W. Africa.)

Two centre rectangles. Upper.—Breeders of flocks of sheep and goats,
agriculturists, hunters, potters, &c., bring their taxes to a chief. Lower.—
At certain festivals a ceremonial re-distribution takes place, not only of
meat and crops, but also of skins, mats, pots, spades, &c. (Drawn from
graded hunter-agricultural society in Africa, &c.)

Two right rectangles. Upper.—People of an ethnically or socially stratified commonwealth bring their taxes in kind to the treasury of the ruler,
whether aristocrat or supreme king. Officials receive the fee of the herds
and flocks, game, grains, objects manufactured by the artisans, &c. The
storehouses in which these are kept are shown. These taxes in kind are
used partly for the payment of salaries and are partly passed on to rulers
of higher grade. Lower.—The payment of salaries in kind to officials,
warriors, and servants is symbolized. The stairs indicate the system of
rank.

The right corners of the three lower rectangles each show seated figures
exchanging goods. They indicate that the continuance of direct barter
between the people whether privately or in markets, is unaffected by the
collective exchange.

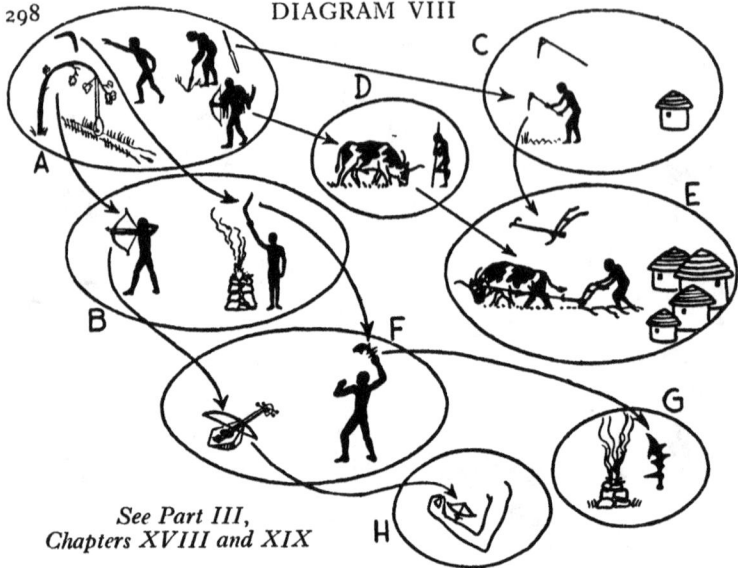

DIAGRAM VIII

*See Part III,
Chapters XVIII and XIX*

DIAGRAM VIII illustrates progress in culture and civilization. An oval indicates a cultural unit: progress is traced by lines with arrow-heads. Four lines of progress start from oval A.

1. The trap made with a bent sapling shows the discovery of the elasticity of wood. It preceded the invention and discovery of the bow as a weapon, to which a line leads in oval B. Thence a further line leads to oval F where we find the musical bow. Once again in oval H we find the bow becomes a surgical instrument, for bleeding.

2. In oval A the boomerang is a weapon thrown by a hunter. The progress line leads to B, where, as in the Solomon Islands and the New Hebrides, it is a ceremonial instrument. The invention of iron-smelting changed the material, and the boomerang became the 'throwing iron' of oval F (the Sudan peoples, &c.). Among the Bantu of W. Africa it became a ceremonial object again (oval G). Elsewhere it is found as a household instrument.

3. To the right in oval A a woman is busy with a digging-stick. In oval C it has become a hoe, having a handle fixed to it. Later, by pulling this instrument, firstly by man's power and then by that of oxen or mules, the plough was evolved (oval E).

4. In oval A, the hunter is the forerunner of the men who bred and tamed oxen (oval D), and so made possible the use of them shown in oval E.

Looking backward, these improvements appear like an accumulation of knowledge and ability in the lapse of time, one linked on to the other. This can be termed technical and scientific progress. Looking forward, those who worked their way from A to G were never absolutely sure of the real importance of one contrivance or idea. Things at first considered improvements sometimes ran into blind alleys. What is known as 'culture' is developed in a particular society. Men interacting on each other on intellectual and emotional planes combine the knowledge, experience, and attitudes of all into a unified whole called 'culture.'

BIBLIOGRAPHY

AMUNDSEN. Short Cut to the W. Mandarin. 1910.

ARMSTRONG, W. E. Rossel Island. 1928.

ASMIS. Die Stammesrechte der Bezirke Misahöhe, Anecho und Lome-Land. Z. f. vgl. Rechtswiss., 26. 1911.

BACON. The Song of Roland. 1914.

BARTON, F. R. Ifugao Economics. University of California Publications in Archaeology, Anthropology, and Ethnology, 15. 1922.

BEAVER, Wilfred N. Unexplored New Guinea. 1920.

BEECH, M. W. H. Kikuyu System of Land Tenure. Journal African Society, 17. 1917/18.

BELL. Tibet, Past and Present. 1924.

BERGMAN, Sten. Vulkane, Bären und Nomaden. Reisen und Erlebnisse im Wilden Kamtschatka. 1926.

BEST, Elsdon. Art of the 'Whare Pora'; Notes on Clothing of the Ancient Maori, &c. Transactions of the New Zealand Institute, 31. 1898.

—— Maori Agriculture. New Zealand Dominion Museum Bulletin, 9. 1925.

BIEBER, J. Kaffa. Anthropos Bibliothek, 2/2. 1920.

BINGER. Du Niger au Golfe de Guinée. 1892.

BOAS, Franz. America and the Old World. Congrès internat. des Américanistes, 21. 1924.

BOLLIG. Die Bewohner der Truk-Inseln. Anthropos Bibliothek, 3/1. 1927.

BORN. Einige Beobachtungen ethnographischer Natur über die Oleai-Inseln. Mitteilungen aus den deutschen Schutzgebieten, 17. 1904.

BOWDICH, T. E. Mission from Cape Coast Castle to Ashantee. 1819.

BRAUNGART, Richard. Die Nordgermanen. 1925.

BREITKOPF. Wucher und Schuldsklaverei in Kpando (Togo). Anthropos, 14–15. 1919–20.

BROWN, George. Melanesians and Polynesians. 1910.

BROWN, A. Radcliffe. Notes on the Social Organization of Australian Tribes. Journ. R. Anthrop. Inst., 48. 1918.

—— — The Andaman Islanders. 1922.

—— — The Social Organization of Australian Tribes. 'Oceania', i. 1–4. 1930–1.

BÜCHER, Karl. Die Entstehung über Volkswirtschaft. 1919.

—— Arbeit und Rhythmus. 1924.

BUCK, P. H. The Evolution of Maori Clothing; by the Rangi-Hiroa. Journ. Polynesian Soc., 34, pp. 61, 91, 223, 321. 1925.

CHAMBERLAIN, R. V. Place and Personal Names of the Gosiute Indians of Utah. Proceed. Americ. Philos. Soc., 59. 1913.

COOK, O. F. Foot Plough Agriculture in Peru. Annual Report, Board of Regents, Smithsonian Institution, Washington, for 1918. 1920.

CRÉVAUX. Voyage dans l'Amérique du Sud. 1883.

CZAPLICKA, M. A. Aboriginal Siberia. 1914.

CZEKANOWSKI, Jan. Forschungen im Nil-Kongo-Zwischengebiet. 1917.

DAPPER, O. Nauwkeurige beschrijving der Afrikaansche Gewesten van Egypten Barbaryen, Libyen, Bildugered, Negroslant, Guinea, Etheopien en Abyssinien. Amsterdam. 2 ed. 1668/1676.

— — Eigentliche Beschreibung der Inseln in Afrika. 1671.

— — Afrika, &c. 1685.

DARMESTETTER, James. The Zend Avesta (Part II) in 'Sacred Books of the East'. 1883.

DECARY. Notes ethnographiques sur les populations du district de Maromandia. Revue d'Ethnographie et des Traditions Populaires. Paris. 1924.

DENNET, R. E. Nigerian Studies, or the Religion and Political System of the Yoruba. 1910.

DESCAMPS, Paul. Comment les conditions de vie des sauvages influencent leur natalité. Revue de l'Institut Solvay, 3/I. 1922-3.

— — La natalité et la mortalité chez les demi-sauvages. Revue de l'Institut Solvay, 3/II. 1922-3.

— — La propriété chez les sauvages. Revue de l'Institut Solvay, 3/I. 1923.

— — L'atelier chez les sauvages. Revue de l'Institut Solvay, 4/I. 1923-4.

DOPSCH, Alfons. Wirtschaftliche und Soziale Grundlagen der europäischen Kulturentwicklung aus der Zeit von Caesar bis auf Karl den Grossen. I. 1918; II. 1920.

— — Die Wirtschaftsentwicklung der Karolingerzeit. 1921.

— — Der Kulturzusammenhang zwischen der spätrömischen und frühgermanischen Zeit in Südwestdeutschland. (Kbl. Go. dt. G. A. V. 75). 1927.

DRIBERG, J. H. The Lango. 1923.

ERDLAND, P. A. Die Marshall-Insulaner (Anthrop.-Bibl. 2/1). 1914.

ERKES. China. 1919.

EYLMANN, E. Die Eingeborenen der Kolonie Süd-Australien. 1908.

FEWKES, J. W. The Cave Dwellings of the Old and New Worlds Ann. Rep. Smithsonian Inst. for 1910 (1912). 1910.

FEWKES, J. W. Casa Grande, Arizona, and Antiquities of . . . Arizona. 28th Ann. Rep. Bur. Am. Ethn. 1912.

FIRTH, R. W. The Maori Carver. Journ. Polynesian Soc., 34. 1925/b.

— — — Economic Psychology of the Maori. Journ. R. Anthrop. Inst., 55. 1925/a.

— — — Some Features of Primitive Industry. Economic Journ. Supplement: The Ec. History, Series 1. 1926.

— — — Maori Hill Forts. Antiquity, I/1. 1927.

FISCHEL. Le Thaler de Marie-Thérèse. Archives Sociologiques, 28. 1913.

FRAZER, J. G. The Magic Art. (The Golden Bough, II.) 1911.

— — — The Dying God. (The Golden Bough, III.) 1911.

FRIEDERICI, Georg. Die Schiffahrt der Indianer. Stud. u. Forsch. zur Menschen- und Völkerkunde. H. 1. 1905.

— — In den vorkolumbischen Verbindungen der Südseevölker mit Amerika. Anthropos, 24. 1929.

FROMM, P. Ufipa Land und Ufipa-Leute. Mitteilungen aus den deutschen Schutzgebieten, 25. 1912.

FÜLLEBORN. Das deutsche Nyassa- und Ruwuma-Gebiet. 1906.

GLOTZ, Gustave. Le travail dans la Grèce ancienne. 1920.

GOGITSCHAYSCHWILI. Gewerbe in Georgien. Ergänzungsheft 1 der Zeitschrift für die gesamten Staatswissenschaften. 1901.

GROSSE. Wirtschaftsverhältnisse im alten China, &c. Ostasiatische Rundschau, 9/5. 1928.

GUTMANN, Bruno. Das Recht der Dschagga. 1926.

HADDON, &c. Cambridge Anthropological Expedition to Torres Straits Report, 5. 1901.

HAGEN, B. Die Orang-Kubu auf Sumatra. (Veröffentl. a. d. städt. Völker-Museum, Frankfurt a. M., 2.) 1908.

HAHL, A. Rechtsverhältnisse und Rechtsanschauungen der Einge-borenen. Nachrichten über Kais. Wilh. Land u. d. Bismarck Archipel, 13. 1897.

HAHN, Eduard. Von der Hacke zum Pflug. 1914.

— — Die Haustiere und ihre Beziehungen zum Menschen. Leipzig. 1896.

— — Das Alter der wirtschaftlichen Kultur der Menschheit. Heidel-berg. 1905.

— — Die Entstehung der wirtschaftlichen Arbeit. Heidelberg. 1908.

— — Die Entstehung der Pflugkultur. Heidelberg. 1909.

HAHN, Ida. Dauernahrung und Frauenarbeit. (Z.E., 51.) 1919.

HARRISON. Evolution of Domestic Arts. Handbook Horniman Museum. 1924.

HATT. Notes on Reindeer. Nomadism. Memoirs American Anthro-
    pological Association, 6/2. 1920.
HEEPE, M. Weitere Yaundetexte. Zeitschr. f. eingeborenen Sprachen,
    10. 1920.
HERSKOVITS. The Cattle Complex. American Anthropologist, 28.
    1926.
HINTZE, Otto. Wesen und Verbreitung des Feudalismus. Sitzungs-
    berichte der preussischen Akademie der Wissenschaften, Phil.-
    hist. Klasse, 20. 1929.
HOBHOUSE, L. T. Morals in Evolution. 1923.
HOSE, Charles. Natural Man, a Record from Borneo. 1926.
HOSE, Charles, and MCDOUGALL, William. The Pagan Tribes of
    Borneo. 1912.
HOWITT, A. W. Native Tribes of South-East Australia. 1904.
HÜBNER, Rudolf. Grundzüge des deutschen Privatrechts. 1913.
HUTTON, J. H. A Voyage to Africa. 1821.

JOHNSON, R. S. The History of the Yoruba. 1921.
JOYCE, P. W. A Social History of Ancient Ireland. 1903.
JOYCE, T. A. South-American Archaeology. 1912.
— — — Mexican Archaeology. 1914.
— — — South-American Archaeology. 1916.
— — — Central-American and West-Indian Archaeology. 1926.

KAHRSTEDT. Die spartanische Agrarwirtschaft. Hermes, 54. 1919.
KANDT, Richard. Gewerbe in Ruamda. (Z.E., 36.) 1904.
KARSTEN, Rafael. Contributions to the Sociology of the Indian Tribes
    of Ecuador. Acta Academiae Aboensis, Humaniora 1/3. 1920.
KEYSSER, Ch. Aus dem Leben der Kaileute, in Neuhauss: Deutsch-
    Neu-Guinea III. 1911.
KHANDEKAR AND VAIDYA. The Bombay Hereditary Office Act (Appen-
    dix). Poona. 1906.
KNABENHANS, A. Arbeitsteilung und Kommunismus im australischen
    Nahrungserwerb. (Festschrift für Ed. Hahn.) 1917.
— — Die politische Organisation bei den australischen Eingeborenen.
    1919.
KOPPERS, Wilh. Unter Feuerland-Indianern. 1924.
KORNEMANN, Ernst. Die Stellung der Frau in der vorgriechischen
    Mittelmeerkultur. (Orient und Antike, 4.) 1927.
KRAFFT, Max. Die Rechtsverhältnisse der Ovaknanjama und Ovan-
    donga. Mitteilungen aus den deutschen Schutzgebieten, 27. 1914.
KRAUSS, F. S. Sitte und Brauch der Südslaven. 1885.
KROEBER, A. L. Anthropology. 1923.

KROEBER, A. L. Handbook of the Indians of California. Smithson Inst. Bur. American Ethnology, Bulletin 78. 1925.

KROPF, A. Das Volk der Xosa-Kaffern im östlichen Südafrika. Ein Beitrag zur afrikanischen Völkerkunde. (Berliner Afrikan. Missions-Gesellschaft.) 1889.

KUBARY, J. S. Die sozialen Einrichtungen der Palauer. 1885.

— — — Ethnographische Beiträge zur Kenntnis des Karolinen Archipels. 1895.

KUIPER, J. F. Japan en de Buitenwereld in de 18 Eeuw. 1921.

LACOUPERIE, Terrien de. Catalogue of Chinese Coins from the VIIth Century B.C. to A.D. 621, including the Series in the British Museum; ed. by R. St. Poole. 1892.

LAMBERT, Le Père. Mœurs et Superstitions des Néo-Calédoniens. 1901.

LANGE. Die Lehensfürsten nach der Schlacht von Sekigahara 1600. Mitteilungen des Seminars für orientalische Sprachen, 15. 1912.

LAUM, Bernhard. Heiliges Geld; eine historische Untersuchung über den sakralen Ursprung des Geldes. 1924.

LEITNER, G. W. v. Kafiristan, a Sketch of the Bagashgeli Kafirs and their Language (Kalasha). Journal of the United Service Institution of India. 1881.

LENOIR, Raymond. Sur l'institution du Potlach. (Revue philosophique.) 1924-5.

— — Les conditions de la fabrication en Mélanésie occidentale. Revue de l'Institut Solvay, 5/II. 1924-5.

LETOURNEAU, Ch. L'évolution du Commerce dans les diverses races humaines. Bibliothèque Anthropologique, Tome XVIII. 1897.

LEWIŃSKI, Jan. S. The Origin of Property and the Formation of the Village Community. (Lectures, London School of Economics and Political Science, 30.) 1913.

LIEBERMANN, F. Die Gesetze der Angelsachsen, II. 1906/12.

LINNÉ. The technique of South-American Ceramics. Göteborga Kungl. Vetenskaps och Vitterhets-Samhälles. Handlingar 4. Följden Bd., 29/5. 1925.

LOEWENTHAL, J. Irokesische Wirtschaftsaltertümer (eine Untersuchung zur ersten Entdeckung Amerikas um 1000 n. Chr.). Ztschr. f. Ethnologie, 52-3. 1920-1.

MAASS, Alfred. Sterne und Sternbilder im malayischen Archipel. Zeitschr. f. Ethnologie, 52-3. 1920-1.

MACLEOD. The Family Hunting Territory and the Lenape Political Organization. Amer. Anthrop., 24. 1922.

304 BIBLIOGRAPHY

MacNEILL. Celtic Ireland. 1921.

MALINOWSKI, B. The Natives of Mailu. Trans. R. Soc. South Australia, 39. 1915.

— — The Primitive Economics of the Trobriand Islanders. Economic Journal, 31. 1921.

— — Argonauts of the Western Pacific. 1922.

MANGIN. Les Mossi (Soudan occidental). Anthropos, 9. 1914.

MAURIZIO, A. Pflanzen, die vor jedem Anbau zur Nahrung dienten Ber. d. deutschen botanischen Gesellschaft, 44/3. 1926.

— — Der Aehrenschnitt, die Sichel und das Aehrenlesen. (Journal für Landwirtschaft.) 1927/a.

— — Die Geschichte unserer Pflanzennahrung von den Urzeiten bis zur Gegenwart. 1927/b.

MAXWELL. Irish History from Contemporary Sources. 1923.

MAYER, Ernst. Germanische Geschlechtsverbände und das Problem der Feldgemeinschaft. Zeitschr. Savigny-Stiftung für Rechtsgeschichte (Germ. Abt.) 44. 1924.

— — Zur Lehre vom germanischen Uradel. Anthropol. Papers Amer. Museum of Natural History, 37. 1916.

— — Der germanische Uradel. Zeitschr. Savigny-Stiftung für Rechtsgeschichte (Germ. Abt.), 32. 1911.

MAYNE, John D. Hindu Law and Usage. 1914.

MEANS, Philip Ainsworth. Some Comments on the Inedited Manuscript of Poma de Ayala. American Anthropologist 25/1. 1923.

MEINHOF, Carl. Die Religionen der Afrikaner in ihrem Zusammenhang mit dem Wirtschaftsleben. Institut f. Sammenlignende Kulturforskning, Ser. A7. Oslo. 1926.

MEISSNER, Bruno. Babylonien und Assyrien I. 1920.

— — Schafschur in Babylonien. Oriental. Literatur-Zeitung, 14. 1911.

MERKER, M. Die Masai. Ethnographische Monographie eines ostafrikanischen Semitenvolkes. 1904.

MESTORF. Glasperlen aus Frauengräbern der Bronzezeit. (Mitt. Anthrop. Vereins in Schleswig-Holstein, 13.) 1900.

MEYER, Ed. Kleine Schriften. 1910.

MEYER, Felix. Wirtschaft und Recht der Herero. 1905.

MIELKE. Die Entstehung und Ausbreitung des Strassendorfes. Zeitschr. f. Ethnologie, 58. 1926.

MONTELIUS. Kulturgeschichte Schwedens. 1916.

MOOKERJI. Men and Thought in Ancient India. 1924.

MORGAN, de. Feudalism in Persia, its Origin and Development and Present Condition. Annual Report Board of Regents, Smithsonian Institution, Washington. 1913.

MÜLLER-WISMAR, W. Yap. 1917.

MUNZINGER, W. Über die Sitte und das Recht der Bogos. 1859.
— — Ostafrikanische Studien. 1883.
MURIE. Pawnee Indian Societies. Anthropological Papers of the American Museum of Natural History, 11/7. 1914.

NANSEN, Fridtjoff. Eskimoleben. 1891.
NEGELEIN, v. Die Stellung des Pferdes in der Kulturgeschichte. Globus, 84/22. 1903.
NEURATH. Antike Wirtschaftsgeschichte. 1918.
NIEBOER, H. I. Slavery as an Industrial System. 1900.
NORDENSKIÖLD, Frh. Erland. Eine geographische und ethnographische Analyse der materiellen Kultur zweier Indianerstämme in El Gran Chaco (South America). Vergl. Ethnogr. Forsch., I. 1918.
— — — The Ethnography of South America seen from Mojos in Bolivia. Comparative Ethnographical Studies, III. 1924.

PAASONEN, H. Sur quelques mots relatifs à l'agriculture empruntés par les langues finno-ougriennes au proto-aryen ou à l'aryen ancien. Journal de la Société finno-ougrienne, 34. 1917.
PALLAS, P. S. Reisen durch verschiedene Prov. des russischen Reichs, I–III. 1771–3.
PASSARGE, S. Die Buschmänner der Kalahari. 1907.
PAULITSCHKE, Philipp. Ethnographie Nordost-Afrikas. I. 1893; II. 1896.
PEAKE, Harold. The English Village. 1926.
— — The English Village, the Origin and Decay of its Community. 1922.
— — The Beginning of Civilization. Journ. R. Anthrop. Institute, 57. 1927.
PECHUËL-LÖSCHE, E. Volkskunde von Loango. 1907.
PERRY, W. T. The Children of the Sun. 1923.
PFEIFFER. Die steinzeitliche Technik und ihre Beziehungen zur Gegenwart. 1912.
PHILIPPS, G. B. The Composition of some Ancient Bronze in the Dawn of the Art of Metallurgy. American Anthropologist, 24. 1922.
— — — The Primitive Copper Industry of America. American Anthropologist, 27. 1925.
— — — The Metal Industry of the Aztecs. American Anthropologist, 27. 1925.
PREUSS, K. Th. Religion und Mythologie der Uitoto. 1921.
PRICE. On Aggri Beads. Journal Anthrop. Inst., 12. 1883.

RADIN, Paul. Maya, Nahuatl and Tarascan Kinship Terms, American Anthropologist, 27. 1925.

RATTRAY, R. S. The Iron Workers of Akpafu. (J.R.A.T., 46.) 1916.

— — — Ashanti. Oxford. 1923.

REHSE. Kiziba. 1910.

REUTERSKIÖLD. Die Entstehung der Speisesakramente (translated from the Swedish). 1912.

RIVERS, W. H. R. The Todas. 1906.

— — — — History of Melanesian Society. 2 vols. 1914.

— — — — The Boomerang in the New Hebrides. Man, 15. 1915.

RIVET, Paul. L'Orfèvrerie colombienne (Technique, aire de dispersion, origine). XXIᵉ Congrès internat. des Américanistes. 1924.

RODD, F. R. People of the Veil. 1926.

ROSCOE, John. Twenty-five Years in East Africa. 1921.

— — The Banyankole. 1923/a.

— — The Bakitara. 1923/b.

ROSTOVTZEFF. The Social and Economic History of the Roman Empire. 1926.

ROTH, Ling. The Aborigines of Tasmania. 1890.

ROTH, Walter Edmund. Ethnological Studies of North-West-Central Queensland Aborigines. 1897.

— — — An Introduction to the Study of the Arts, Crafts, and Customs of the Guiana Indians. Thirty-third Report American Bureau of Ethnology. 1924.

ROUFFAER. Waar kwamen de radselachtig Moetisalah's (Aggri-Kralen) in de Timorgroep oorsprongelijk van daan? (Whence came the mysterious Aggri-beads in the Timor-Archipelago and what is their origin? Bijdragen tot de taal- land- en volkenkunde van Nederlandsch Indie, 6/6. 1909.

ROUTLEDGE, W. S. With a Prehistoric People (Akikuyu). 1910.

SAHAGUN. Histoire générale des choses de la Nouvelle Espagne. 1680.

SANDERSON, Meredith. Some Marriage Customs of the Wahengas, Nyassaland. Journal African Society, 22. 1922/23.

SARFERT, E. Kusae. Ergebn. der Südsee Exped. 1908–10 der Hamburger Wissensch. Stftg. 2 vols. 1919–20.

SARGENT, R. Louisa. The Size of the Slave Population at Athens during the fifth and fourth centuries before Christ. Univ. Illinois Studies in Social Sciences, 12/3. 1924.

SCHENK, A. La Suisse préhistorique. 1912.

SCHMIDT, Max. Zur Rechtsgeschichte Afrikas. I. Aus altholländischen Berichten. Zeitschrift für vergleichende Rechtswissenschaft, 30. 1913.

SCHNEIDER, Anna. Die sumerische Tempelstadt. (Staatswissenschaftliche Beiträge, 4.) 1920.

SCHNEIDER, O. Muschelgeld-Studien, bearb. v. Ribbe. 1905.

SCHUMACHER. Kultur- und Handelsbeziehungen des Mittelrheingebiets und insbes. Hessens während der Bronzezeit. Westdeutsche Zeitschrift für Vorgeschichte, 20. 1901.

SCHURTZ, Heinrich. Grundriss einer Entstehungsgeschichte des Geldes. 1898.

SCHWEINFURTH, G. Im Herzen von Africa. 2nd ed. (1st ed. 1878). 1918.

— — Über wild gesammelte Arten von Reis in Afrika. (Ber. d. dtsch. botan. Ges., 44/3.) 1926.

SCHWENZNER, W. Zum altbabylonischen Wirtschaftsleben. Mitteilungen der vorderasiatischen Gesellschaft, 19. 1915.

— — Das geschäftliche Leben im alten Babylonien nach den Verträgen und Briefen dargestellt. (Der alte Orient, 16.) 1917.

SELIGMAN, C. G. The Melanesians of British New Guinea. 1910.

— — — The Veddas. 1911.

SHIROKOGOROFF, S. M. Social Organization of the Manchus. Journ. Asiatic Society, North-China Branch, 3rd Extra. 1924.

SIRELIUS, U. T. Über die Art und die Zeit der Zähmung des Rentiers. Journal de la Société Finno-Ougrienne, 35. 1916–20.

SMITH, Edwin W., & DALE. The Ila-Speaking Peoples of Northern Rhodesia. 1920.

SOERGEL, W. Die Jagd der Vorzeit. 1922.

SPEISER, Felix. Ethnographische Materialien aus den Neuen Hebriden und den Banks-Inseln. 1923.

SPENCER, B., and GILLEN, F. J. The Native Tribes of Central Australia. 1899.

— — The Northern Tribes of Central Australia. 1904.

— — Across Australia. 1912.

— — The Arunta; A Study of a Stone Age People. 2 vols. 1927.

SPIEGELBERG, Wilhelm. Arbeiter und Arbeiterbewegung im Pharaonenreich unter den Ramessiden. (ca. 1400–1100 v. C.) 1895.

SPIESS, Carl. Blicke in das Zauber- und Götterwesen der Anilõer Westafrikas. Mitteilungen des Seminars für Orientalische Sprachen, 8. 1905.

SPIETH. Die Ewe-Stämme. 1906.

STASCHEWSKI, F. Die Banjangi. Baessler Archiv, Beiheft, 8. 1917.

STEINMETZ, S. R. Rechtsverhältnisse von eingeborenen Völkern in Afrika und Ozeanien. 1903.

STERNBERG, Th. Der Geist des chinesischen Vermögensrechtes. Zeitschrift für vergleichende Rechtswissenschaft, 26. 1911.

STREHLOW, C. Die Aranda u. Loritja-Stämme in Zentral-Australien, bearb. v. Frh. v. Leonhardi (Veröffentl. des Völker-Museums, Frankfurt a. M.). 1907–20.

STUDER. Die praehistorischen Hunde. Abhandlungen der schweizer paläontologischen Gesellschaft, 28. 1901.

STUHLMANN, Franz. Handwerk und Industrie in Ostafrika. 1910.

— — Mit Emin Pascha ins Herz von Afrika. 1894.

TESSMANN, Günter. Die Pangwe, 1913.

— — Die Urkulturen der Menschheit. Zeitschrift für Ethnologie, 50. 1918.

THURNWALD, R. Staat und Wirtschaft im alten Aegypten. Zeitschrift für Sozialwissenschaft, 4. 1901.

— — Staat und Wirtschaft in Babylon zu Hammurabis Zeit. Jahrbücher für Nationalökonomie und Statistik, 26/27. 1903/4.

— — Forschungen auf den Salomo-Inseln und dem Bismarck-Archipel. I. Lieder und Sagen; III. Volk, Staat und Wirtschaft. 1912.

— — Ethno-psychologische Studien an Südseevölkern. Beiheft 6 der Zeitschrift für angewandte Psychologie. 1913.

— — Entstehung von Staat und Familie. Blätter für vergleichende Rechtswissenschaft und Volkswirtschaft, 16. 1921.

— — Die Gestaltung der Wirtschaftsentwicklung aus ihren Aufängen heraus. Erinnerungsgabe für Max Weber. Die Hauptprobleme der Soziologie. 1923.

— — Eingeborenenrecht des papuanischen und melanesischen Gebiets. in 'Eingeborenenrechte d. ehemal. dtsch. Schutzgebiete'. 1930.

TISCHLER, Über Aggry-Perlen und über die Herstellung farbiger Gläser im Altertume. Schriften der physik.-ökonom. Ges. Königsberg, 27. 1887.

TÖNJES, Hermann. Ovamboland. 1911.

TORDAY, Emil. On the Trail of the Bushongo. 1925.

TREGEAR, Edward. The Maori Race. 1904.

TRIMBORN, H. Der Kollektivismus der Inkas in Peru. Anthropos, 20. 1925.

— — Die Gliederung der Stände im Inka-Reich. Journal de la Société des Américanistes, 19. 1927.

VARGES. Der deutsche Handel von der Urzeit bis zur Entstehung des Frankenreichs. Programm des Realgymnasiums Ruhrort. 1903.

VEDDER, H. Die Bergdama S.-W. Afrikas. Veröffentl. d. Hamburger Universität. 1923.

VELTEN, C. Sitten und Bräuche der Suaheli. 1903.

VINOGRADOFF, Paul. Outlines of Historical Jurisprudence, I. 1920.

WEBER. Indische Streifen. 1868–79.

WEEKS, John H. Among Congo Cannibals (references to the German translation: 'Dreissig Jahre am Kongo'). 1914.

WEST, E. W. Pahlavi Texts, II. The Dâdistâni-Dînîk, &c. (Sacred Books of the East, 18.) 1882.

WESTERMANN, Diedrich. Die Kpelle. 1921.

WESTERMANN, W. L. The Development of the Irrigation System of Egypt. (Classical Philology, 14.) 1919.

WHEELER, Gerald C. The Tribe and Intertribal Relations in Australia. 1910.

WILLIAMSON, R. W. The Mafulu, Mountain Tribe of New Guinea. 1912.

— — — The Social and Political Systems of Central Polynesia. 1924.

WILSON. Ancient Drains, Maori Drains, North Auckland. Journal Polynesian Society, 31. 1922.

WIRZ, Paul. Anthropologische und ethnologische Ergebnisse der Zentral Neu-Guinea Expedition 1921–2. Nova-Guinea, 16, Heft 1. 1924.

— — Die Marind-anim von Holländisch-Süd-Neu-Guinea, II/3. 1925.

WISSLER, Clark. The American Indian. 1922.

WISSMANN. Im Innern Afrikas. 1888.

ZECH, Graf. Land und Leute an der Nordwestgrenze von Togo. Mitteilungen aus den deutschen Schutzgebieten, 17. 1904.

ZINTGRAFF, E. Nord-Kamerun. 1895.

ZORIČIĆ, Milovan. Die bäuerlichen Hauskommunionen in den Königreichen Kroatien und Slavonien. Arbeiten des 8. Internat. Kongresses für Hygiene und Demographie in Budapest, 1894. 1897.

INDEX

(Names of Authors referred to are in italic).

For Product Safety Concerns and Information please contact our EU
representative GPSR@taylorandfrancis.com
Taylor & Francis Verlag GmbH, Kaufingerstraße 24, 80331 München, Germany